MY EARLY TIMES

By

CHARLES DICKENS

Compiled and Edited by
PETER ROWLAND

AURUM PRESS

The editor and publisher acknowledge the kind assistance of the
Dickens House Museum and the Guildhall Museum in locating the
illustrations.

First published in Great Britain 1988
by The Folio Society Limited
This slightly revised and expanded edition published 1997 by
Aurum Press Ltd, 25 Bedford Avenue, London WC1B 3AT

A catalogue record for this book is available from the British Library.

ISBN 1 85410 518 3

Typeset by Action Typesetting Ltd, Gloucester
Printed and bound in Great Britain by
Butler & Tanner Ltd, Frome

MY EARLY TIMES

CONTENTS

'Last night ... I found my mind curiously disturbed, and wandering away through so many years to such early times of my life ... I could not help considering what strange stuff all our little stories are made of.'
– letter to Maria Winter (née Beadnell), 10 February 1855

INTRODUCTION

CHARLES John Huffam Dickens, the greatest English novelist of the nineteenth century and arguably the greatest novelist of all time, was born on 7 February 1812 and died on 9 June 1870. During the fifty-eight years and four months which elapsed between those two dates he wrote fourteen novels, plus part of a fifteenth left unfinished by his death, five 'Christmas Books' which can be classified as novelettes, fifty short stories, six plays, *A Child's History of England*, *The Life of Our Lord*, two travel books and two hundred and fifty essays and articles on virtually every subject under the sun, not to mention countless editorial contributions to articles published in *Household Words* and *All the Year Round*.

Merely to itemise this massive output, bearing in mind that the average Victorian novel was about six times as long as its twentieth-century counterpart, leaves one momentarily exhausted, yet it was, even so, not simply as a writer that Dickens made his impact on nineteenth-century England: his energy knew no bounds, and it was as a reformer, publicist, campaigner and exuberant dynamic force that, for almost thirty-five years, he dominated the literary scene in a way which was, and remains, unparalleled. There had been nobody quite like the Inimitable before, and – with the possible exception of Chaplin – there has been nobody quite like him since, albeit a score of conscious imitators.

The stream of characters that he conjured into existence – from Mr Pickwick, Sam Weller, Jingle, Wackford Squeers, Newman Noggs, Bill Sikes, Fagin, Little Nell, Quilp, Dick Swiveller, Mrs Gamp, Captain Cuttle, Mr Toots, Betsey Trotwood, Mr Micawber and Uriah Heep, at one end of the spectrum, to Joe Gargery, Mr Pumblechook, Miss Havisham, Magwitch, Bradley Headstone, Eugene Wrayburn, Mr Boffin, Durdles and Mr Sapsea at the other – are among the great immortals of English literature. Mrs Bardell fainting into Mr Pickwick's arms, Oliver Twist asking for more, Nicholas Nickleby thrashing the proprietor of Dotheboys Hall with that respected gentleman's very own cane, Paul Dombey asking his sister what it was that the waves were always saying, Betsey Prig giving vent to her profound conviction, after years of cogitation, that there was no sich a person as Mrs Harris, Scrooge confronted by Marley's ghost, Mr Micawber delivering his words of wisdom on the subject of annual income and annual expenditure, Sydney Carton philosophically moving up the line to his doom, Pip encountering the convict in the graveyard, Mr Wopsle's portrayal of Hamlet, the dolls' dressmaker admonishing her bad child, Mr Podsnap holding forth to the foreign gentleman on the wonders of the English constitution, John Jasper and Edwin Drood cracking nuts as they exchange confidences, are among the unforgettable scenes which all of us know by heart. The sanctimonious abode of Mr Pecksniff, Peggoty's boat on the Yarmouth sands (although upended by Phiz rather than Boz), the Dedlocks' place in Lincolnshire, the vast gloomy mansion inhabited by Mrs Clennam, Wemmick's castle, are just a few of the places that are rather more familiar to us than our own homes. Dickens created characters, plots, scenes and atmospheres with a wave of the wand and his books were deliberately designed to appeal to all ages and all classes. He was the Universal Home Entertainer, in an age which knew not television or radio, and millions of readers throughout the world awaited, with mounting excitement and impatience, the latest instalment of the latest blockbuster. He could make them laugh and he could make them cry. He also took an impish delight, like his own fat boy (the prototype of Alfred Hitchcock), in making their flesh creep. Dickens was larger than life. He was a public institution. He was also the public's faithful servant, constantly being called upon to perform – and perform he did, until the very last day of his life.

But Dickens was something more than a storyteller *par excellence*. He could also bring home to his readers, with devastating clarity, the injustices of Victorian England, and could make them aware of the need for better educational facilities, for the replacement of overcrowded slums by decent homes with proper sanitary arrangements, for the reform of the Poor Law and the abolition of the workhouse, for better treatment of the sick, especially the mentally ill, for the reform of the legal system in general and the Court of Chancery in particular, for the reform of both central government (as exemplified by the Barnacles and the Circumlocution Office) and of local government (as represented by Mr Bumble), and for a greater degree of tolerance and humanity among mankind at large. He preached the sanctity of marriage and extolled the delights of family life. In a sense, indeed, he invented Christmas, for the Christmas we know today, streamlined and vulgarised though it is, is essentially the Victorian Christmas which Dickens did so much to create and publicise. (Though it is Prince Albert, admittedly, who introduced the Christmas tree into Britain.) The great majority of our Christmas cards, with the stage coaches rattling through the snow to some cheerful destination, bearing ladies with muffs and gentlemen with top hats, are relentlessly 'Dickensian' in character: the festivities at Dingley Dell are remembered still.

Yet Dickens, whatever else he may have been, was no saint. He found it impossible to practise what he preached. His own domestic life was in turmoil largely, it seems, because marriage bored him. He resented the constant arrival of yet another mouth to feed, a regular event for which he held himself in no way responsible, and felt himself hard done by at having to support not only his own immediate dependants but also his parents and brothers and sundry poor relations. He was continually in need of fresh sensations, fresh sights and fresh acquaintances, a restless soul searching for a satisfaction which invariably eluded him. He was arrogant and conceited, albeit having much to be conceited about, and opposition of any kind to his wishes could drive him into a positive frenzy of rage. His high spirits bordered, at times, on acute eccentricity, to put it no more strongly, and his family and friends sometimes went in fear of him. Fundamentally a good man, impatience was his besetting sin and he did not suffer fools gladly; the avowed opponent of hypocrisy, he was capable of adopting lofty moral attitudes which had rather more in common with those of Mr Pecksniff than he would have cared to admit; a sensitive, creative soul, he could nevertheless drive a hard bargain and was quite capable, when the occasion demanded it, of riding roughshod over his publishers while indignantly complaining, at the same time, that he was being treated with a greater degree of harshness than any other mortal man had ever had to endure. He was, in short, as much a mixture of inconsistencies as the rest of us, but his contemporaries had placed him on a pedestal and were consequently disconcerted to discover, from time to time, that their idol was not infallible.

* * *

ALTHOUGH born in Portsmouth, Dickens spent the formative years of his boyhood (1817-22) in Chatham. His father was employed as a navy pay clerk by the Admiralty and his work periodically necessitated the Dickens family (consisting, for the greater part of the time, of half-a-dozen children, with Charles as the eldest son) uprooting itself in search of a fresh residence. Brought up in a household whose standards were basically lower middle-class, as evidenced by the presence of two nurse-maids, with pretensions (and distant connections) to an even higher order of things, young Charles – after attending school in Chatham – experienced a rude awakening in 1824; the family, newly installed in London, found itself acutely short of money and instead of being sent to a new school, as he had confidently expected, Charles found himself working in a blacking warehouse, where his job was to paste labels on bottles. Worse was to follow: his father was arrested for debt and sent to the Marshalsea prison. Charles was obliged to fend for himself to a large extent, but his father was released after three months, the warehouse job eventually came to an end and his schooling was resumed until 1827. On leaving school he worked for a time in a solicitor's office before learning shorthand and becoming a newspaper reporter in 1831. In the spring of 1830 he had fallen head over heels in love with Maria Beadnell, but her family did their best to discourage his courtship and Maria herself, initially delighted by his attentions, tired of them at last and brought their relationship to an end in 1833.

From this point onwards Dickens flung himself into his reporting activities with a redoubled zest and had very soon made a reputation for himself as one of the speediest shorthand reporters that the Press gallery at the House of Commons had ever known. After being momentarily attracted by the idea of a career on the boards he tried his hand at writing a few 'sketches' and stories, which were seized upon eagerly by newspaper and magazine editors and eventually published in two volumes as *Sketches by Boz*. It was, however, the appearance of *The Pickwick Papers* (1836-37) that electrified the nation and really made his name. Thereafter, it seemed, he could do nothing wrong. His marriage to Catherine Hogarth followed close upon the heels of the triumph of *Pickwick*, although the death of her young sister Mary, who had been living with them, plunged Dickens into a paroxysm of grief and temporarily brought him to a halt. But the bandwagon soon resumed its progress: *Oliver Twist* (1837-39), *Nicholas Nickleby* (1838-39), *The Old Curiosity Shop* (1840-41), *Barnaby Rudge* (1841) poured out during the four years which followed *Pickwick* and the money poured in at a fantastic pace (although precious little, Dickens claimed, found its way to his own pocket, and there began the first of his interminable wrangles with publishers). It seemed, for a time, that success would be his for ever and ever. The Dickens family, with birth following birth almost as rapidly as book followed book, moved from one splendid house to another. Society flung open its doors to him. Trips to Europe were followed by a tour of the United States – which proved, in the event, to be somewhat controversial in character.

Reaction did, admittedly, set in. There was talk of the 'remarkable rocket'; sales of some of his books decreased; reviewers became hostile and complained that there was nothing very fresh in the latest production, whatever it might be. John Forster, Dickens's close friend and adviser at this time, felt obliged to take his protégé in hand and urged him to be more sparing in his output, with a view to making the public wax impatient for more. *Martin Chuzzlewit* (1843-44), perhaps his funniest book, was regarded, for a time, as a comparative failure, although sales of the monthly parts gradually picked up, and it was *Dombey and Son* (1846-48) which restored him to full public favour and adoration. In the meantime, however, *A Christmas Carol* (1843) proved as much of a sensational success as ever *Pickwick* had been, although the series of little books which followed it as seasonal offerings, with the notable exception of *The Cricket on the Hearth*, never quite hit the literary jackpot to the same fantastic extent.

Each of the major novels to date, although packed with a mass of fascinating characters and episodes, characterised by irrepressible high spirits and supremely enjoyable to read, was essentially the work of a young man who still had much to learn about the world and human nature. *Dombey and Son* had shown a greater degree of care and thoughtfulness in its construction, although a certain amount of melodrama had featured in the plot, but it was the work which followed – *David Copperfield* (1849-50) – which marked the true flowering of his genius and the drawing together of his skills in a wonderfully controlled, mature production which Dickens himself, looking back a few years later, confessed was his own favourite among his works. As we shall see, it owed much of its character – especially in its earliest chapters – to an account of his own life which Dickens had begun to write a short time before.

The two major works which followed *David Copperfield* – *Bleak House* (1852-53) and *Little Dorrit* (1855-57) – are tremendous volumes, reflecting the highest skills of the novelist's craft, in which Dickens reviewed, in effect, the structure of society in contemporary England and expressed, in unforgettable terms, his disquiet at what he saw. The title originally intended for the second of these two volumes, *Nobody's Fault* – a phrase frequently employed by Government spokesmen to excuse the ghastly maladministration of the Crimean War – indicates the bitterness and sardonic frame of mind in which he couched his indictment of the governing class. Sandwiched between these two masterpieces was *Hard Times*, a much shorter volume but one which carried, nevertheless, an impact of its own in depicting an industrial society governed by the doctrines of Utilitarian economy – or, as Dickens saw it, by the Gradgrinds and Bounderbys of capitalist England.

From this point onwards, Dickens was no longer writing novels as a full-time occupation. Amateur theatricals gradually took up more and more of his energy, but another project dear to his heart was securing a magazine that was all his very own and *Household Words*, from 1850 onwards, was just that. Each issue carried a miscellany of anonymous articles, at least one of them by Dickens himself, and most of them reflected his editorial control to a marked extent – many of them, indeed, carrying substantial interpolations by himself. More and more he took upon himself the role of leader of a team, whether it be the producer (and leading actor) in a play or editor (and part proprietor) of a monthly journal. He disliked being alone, but he found himself acutely bored and depressed by his marriage to Catherine: *'primus inter pares'* was the role which appealed to him most, and he derived more pleasure from the companionship of Wilkie Collins than he did from that of his wife.

The collapse of his marriage in 1858, an event which attracted massive publicity (not least because Dickens himself highlighted the event in *Household Words*), ushered in the last weary decade of his life. Georgina Hogarth, another of Catherine's sisters, remained with him to look after the children and manage his household, but his emotional needs were now satisfied from two separate sources: the first being Ellen Ternan, a young actress who eventually (it seems) became his mistress, and the second being the series of public readings from his own works, bringing him into greater direct contact with his hysterical public than ever before. He toured the country and he toured the United States, almost killing himself in the process and deriving a wild satisfaction from recounting, in particular, the murder of Nancy by Bill Sikes. It was only by the combined pressure of his doctor and his closest friends that he was eventually prevailed upon, early in 1870, to bring the readings to an end.

In a sense, Dickens had exhausted himself, both physically and creatively, by the production of *Bleak House* and *Little Dorrit*: he would never surpass these two masterpieces and, indeed, never really made the attempt. His next book, *A Tale of Two Cities* (1859), finely written though it is, was, by comparison, a lightweight affair, amounting to little more than an adventure story, and *Great Expectations* (1860-61) is related in a similarly spare, concise fashion: as a story in its own right it is superb, but in comparison with what had gone before there is an undeniable falling off in momentum and power. The cast of thousands, as it were, is replaced by a comparatively modest repertory company. It must be acknowledged, however, that the diminished scale of these books resulted, in part at least, from the fact that they were published in *All the Year Round*, the journal which had replaced *Household Words* in the wake of Dickens's matrimonial crisis.

In his last completed novel, *Our Mutual Friend* (1864-65), Dickens endeavoured to revert to the standard of his immediate post-*Copperfield* creations and came honourably close to succeeding, but it is the work of a tired man (while writing it he was involved in a horrendous train crash at Stapleford, five years to the very day before he died, which left him severely shaken). The straining after effect is, at times, rather too apparent: we are aware of the backstage machinery clanking away, with the producer puffing and panting as he turns the handles to manipulate the scenery and a fresh tableau trundles into view: what had been effortless when Dickens was in his prime had now become rather too much like hard work.

Paradoxically, however, as his energy declined, and the ability to keep a dozen balls in the air at once gradually left him, so the actual standard of his writing improved: quantity went down, but quality went up. Where he had used fifty or even five hundred words to describe a setting in his earlier works, he now made do with five – but those concentrated five would go straight to the heart of the matter with an equal if not greater effectiveness than his earlier, more verbose description. Conserving his energies in this fashion, learning new techniques, paring himself down to what was absolutely crucial, were not the least of his achievements. His later essays are, similarly, finely honed when compared to the exuberant outpourings in *Sketches by Boz* and do, for precisely that reason, give greater satisfaction to the reader.

Nowhere is his mastery of these new, sophisticated techniques of story-telling more effectively deployed than in the twenty-three chapters of *Edwin Drood* (1870) in which, with the minimum use of words, a beautifully-wrought masterpiece of suspense gradually unfolds itself: the pace is deceptively leisurely, but the deft manipulation and the sparkling imagery are superb. Writing in his chalet at Gads Hill Place and preoccupied, once again, with the old cathedral town of Rochester, thinly disguised as Cloisterham, the master magician weaves one last, lingering spell over his readers.

TOWARDS the end of his life, according to Georgina Hogarth,* Dickens was toying with the idea of writing his autobiography. Fourteen years earlier, when declining to actively assist a potential biographer, he had added that he would probably 'leave my own record of my life for the satisfaction of my children.'** In fact, the idea went back a long way. Since his mid-thirties, indeed, he had been intermittently persuaded that a personal record of some kind was needed, for it seems to have been in the summer of 1847 that he began to write an account of his boyhood. Precisely what purpose he had in mind in undertaking this exercise is not altogether clear and it may be that it was not even clear, in the first instance, to Dickens himself. Confession is good for the soul and it could be argued that the very act of setting something down on paper was catharsis enough in itself to relieve him of a burden of guilt that he had been carrying for a quarter of a century. Yet confession implies

* See Nina Burgis's Introduction to the Clarendon edition of *David Copperfield* (1981), p. xxi.
** Letter to Edward Walford dated 4 Oct. 1856, *The Letters of Charles Dickens*, Pilgrim edition, Volume Eight [1856-1858], edited by Graham Storey and Kathleen Tillotson (1995), p. 200.

that, at that some stage in one's life, one has done something wrong, and this was not at all what Dickens believed: he was convinced, instead, that a very great wrong had been done to him, a child of exceptional talents whose abilities (in marked contrast to those of his sister) had been ignored by his complacent, uncaring parents, and that it was only by God's good grace, and his own determination and dedication, that the situation had been redressed. Dickens had been aware, from his earliest youth, that he was someone special and he was astonished that others had apparently overlooked what was, to him, blindingly obvious. That he, Charles Dickens, now generally considered the greatest writer in the land, should ever have been obliged to work in a blacking warehouse, in the company of such common associates as Bob Fagin and Poll Green, was humiliating beyond belief. For many years he had brooded over this episode and his bitterness appears, if anything, to have intensified rather than diminished with the passage of time.

In the twentieth century aspiring young novelists have been only too keen to proclaim their working-class origins and to reveal the deprivations they had to endure in their childhood; in the nineteenth century, however, it was, so far as Dickens was concerned, a matter for profound shame rather than rejoicing: a disgrace, a humiliation, a repellent, grisly episode that needed to be concealed so thoroughly that his friends and associates, the public at large and even his own family would not know, until after his death, that it had ever taken place. It needed to be expunged from the record, to be treated as a non-event. On the other hand, Dickens had a passionate desire to communicate the fact that, virtually alone and unaided, he had hauled himself out of the gutter and climbed to the highest pinnacle that the world of letters had to offer. It was galling that nobody, apart from himself, was in a position to appreciate the sheer magnitude of his achievement. While hesitating to tell his contemporaries that he had once known abject poverty, therefore, he thought that posterity ought to be made aware of the fact.

Committing to paper an account of his youth was evidently something that he had had in mind for some time. 'I hope you will like Mrs Pipchin's establishment,' he wrote to Forster on 4 November 1846, à propos *Dombey and Son*. 'It is from the life and I was there – I don't suppose I was eight years old; but I remember it all as well, and certainly understood it as well, as

I do now. We should be devilish sharp in what we do to children. I thought of that passage in my small life, at Geneva. Shall I leave you my life in MS when I die? There are some things in it that would touch you very much, and that might go on the same shelf with the first volume of Holcroft's.'* Thomas Holcroft, it must be explained at this point, was an eighteenth-century playwright and novelist whose father (a shoemaker initially) had fallen upon hard times and taken on a variety of itinerant jobs. Holcroft's colourful childhood experiences had constituted the first volume of his memoirs, published in 1816, seven years after the author's death; subsequent volumes had been written by Hazlitt.

Forster, a leading literary and theatrical critic, the editor of *The Examiner* and the author of several biographies and historical works, was only two months younger than his friend but Dickens, half in fun and half seriously, affected to believe that Forster would survive him and write his own biography – which is, indeed, precisely what happened. On this occasion, at any rate, Forster did not rise to the bait, but a few months later, in March or April 1847, he himself brought up the subject of Dickens's early life by asking him whether he remembered having seen, in his boyhood, Charles Wentworth Dilke, the friend of Keats and 'his father's acquaintance and contemporary, who had been a clerk in the same office in Somerset House to which Mr John Dickens belonged. Yes, he said, he recollected seeing him at a house in Gerrard Street, where his uncle Barrow lodged during an illness, and Mr Dilke had visited him; never at any other time. Upon which I told him that someone else had been intended in the mention made to me, for the reference implied not merely his being met accidentally, but his having had some juvenile employment in a warehouse near the Strand; at which place Mr Dilke, being with the elder Dickens one day, had noticed him, and received, in return for the gift of a half-crown, a very low bow. He was silent for several minutes; I felt that I had unintentionally touched a painful place in his memory; and to Mr Dilke I never spoke of the subject again. It was not however then, but some weeks later, that Dickens made further allusion to my thus having struck unconsciously upon a time of which he never could lose the

* John Forster, *The Life of Charles Dickens*, edited, annotated and introduced by J.W.T. Ley (1928), p. 479.

remembrance while he remembered anything, and the recollection of which at intervals haunted him and made him miserable even to that hour.'*

'Very shortly afterwards', so Forster records, Dickens told him the full story of his unhappy childhood, partly in conversation and partly by letting him see some written reminiscences which he now began to produce. The composition of these recollections continued throughout 1847 and 1848. 'I hardly know why I write this,' ran a covering letter dated 7 May 1848 to one of the instalments, 'but the more than friendship which has grown between us seems to force it on me in my present mood. We shall speak of it all, you and I, Heaven grant, wisely and wonderingly many and many a time in after years. In the meanwhile I am more at rest for having opened all my heart and mind to you.'**

The death of his sister Fanny on 2 September 1848, following a prolonged and harrowing illness, would presumably have brought back some more childhood memories, and 'The Child's Dream of a Star' (written eighteen months later) is certainly a very prettified version of their relationship, but it was the composition of his last Christmas book, *The Haunted Man*, written in October and November 1848, which provided him with an opportunity of proclaiming his grievances to those who were astute enough to read between the lines. Its hero, Redlaw, is Dickens himself – or, at any rate, the gloomy side of Dickens, masquerading as a complete person. He is, we are told, a great chemist 'and teacher on whose lips and hands a crowd of aspiring ears and eyes hung daily', but we find him sunk in depression, reviewing the events of his early life with a spectre who is a darker version of himself.

'Look upon me!' exclaims the spectre. 'I am he, neglected in my youth, and miserably poor, who strove and suffered, and still strove and suffered, until I hewed out knowledge from the mine where it was buried, and made rugged steps thereof, for my worn feet to rest and rise on.... No mother's self-denying love, no father's counsel, aided *me*.... My parents, at the best, were of that sort whose care soon ends and whose duty is soon done; who cast their offspring loose, early, as birds do theirs; and, if they do well, claim the merit; and, if ill, the pity.... I had a sister.... Such glimpses of the light of home as I had ever

* Forster, *op. cit.*, p. 23.
***Ibid.*, p. 521

known, had streamed from her. How young she was, how fair, how loving!' The sister's loving heart, it transpires, had led her into an unhappy marriage while Redlaw himself, prevented from speaking out because of his poverty, had been smitten by a corresponding passion of his own. 'I was too poor', he declares, 'to bind its object to my future then, by any thread of promise or entreaty. I loved her far too well, to seek to do it. But, more than ever I had striven in my life, I strove to climb! Only an inch gained, brought me somewhat nearer to the height. I toiled up!' His sister, 'doubly dear, doubly devoted, doubly cheerful in my home, lived on to see me famous, and my old ambition so rewarded when its spring was broken,' and had then died, 'gentle as ever, happy, and with no concern but for her brother.'

'Memory is my curse,' cried our hero, 'and, if I could forget my sorrow and my wrong, I would!'

His wish is granted, but Redlaw is soon brought to realise that, spiritually, one is all the poorer for having cast one's memories into oblivion, and Milly Swidger (the humble heroine of this rather tedious book) timidly points out to him that 'it is a good thing for us to remember wrong that has been done us' since this enables us to exercise forgiveness. 'Pardon me, great Heaven!' exclaims Redlaw, lifting up his eyes, 'for having thrown away thine own high attribute!' His memories are restored to him, thanks to Milly's intercession, and they all live happily ever afterwards. 'Of course,' wrote Dickens to Forster on 21 November, 'my point is that good and bad are inextricably linked in remembrance, and that you could not choose the enjoyment of recollecting only the good. To have all the best of it you must remember the worst also.'*

Dickens had commenced writing *The Haunted Man* on 5 October and he completed it on 30 November. He then, it seems, looked again at the various reminiscences which he had written during the preceding eighteen months, perhaps retrieving them from Forster for this purpose, and worked them up into a continuous narrative which he showed his friend for the first time on 20 January 1849. 'The description', runs a tantalising entry in Forster's diary for that date, 'may make none of the impression on others that the reality made on him.... Highly probable that it may never see the light. No wish. Left to J.F. or

* *Ibid.*, p. 508.

others. No blotting, as when writing fiction, but straight on, as when writing ordinary letter.'*

'We must always forgive those who have done us any harm', wrote Dickens in 1849, 'when they come to us and say they are truly sorry for it. Even if they do not come and say so, we must still forgive them.'** Whether Dickens exercised much forgiveness so far as his parents are concerned is a moot point. He certainly retained a considerable amount of affection for his father. 'The longer I live,' he once told Forster, 'the better man I think him'† and he recalled him, in a letter to M. de Cerjat written on 13 November 1865, as 'my poor father ... the jolliest of men'.†† But towards his mother, his feelings remained what can best be described as equivocal.‡

The wrong that had been done Dickens, looked at dispassionately, amounted simply to the fact that his parents (having problems of their own) were at one time somewhat neglectful of his welfare and that he was, so he described himself in a letter to Washington Irving dated 21 April 1841, 'a very small and not over-particularly-taken-care-of-boy'. Almost equally humiliating, however, was the fact that some ten years after the blacking warehouse episode he, Charles Dickens, should have been rejected as a suitor by Maria Beadnell, for whom he had conceived a passion so intense that the passions of more ordinary mortals paled into insignificance in comparison. He had thus been wronged twice over. He blamed his own parents for the first great wrong; he blamed Maria's parents – and, of course, Maria herself – for the second.

Rejected, so he believed, because his worldly prospects had not been good enough, he hardened his heart and resolved that no woman would ever again be granted the opportunity to play havoc with his feelings: in his courtship of Catherine Hogarth, indeed, he adopted a 'take it or leave it', domineering attitude from the very start. He also set out to conquer the world, flinging himself heart and soul into his chosen career, as a means of demonstrating to the Beadnell family just how mistaken they had been in their judgment of him. Success followed success

* *Ibid.*, pp. 11 – 12f.
** *The Life of Our Lord* (1934), p. 45.
† Forster, *op. cit.*, p.552.
†† *The Letters of Charles Dickens*, vol. II, edited by his sister-in-law and his eldest daughter (1980), p. 240.
‡ See Dr Michael Slater, *Dickens and Women* (1983), pp. 3 – 24.

but he feared, privately, that his character had deteriorated as a result. 'I have never been so good a man since,' he wrote to Maria (now Mrs Winter) in 1855, when they resumed their acquaintance after a lapse of more than twenty years, 'as I was when you made me wretchedly happy. I shall never be half so good a fellow any more.'*

Dickens undoubtedly felt all the better for having written an account of his childhood and for having had Forster peruse it: misfortunes shared are misfortunes halved, and henceforth there would be at least one person who would understand what he had felt, would appreciate the traumas that he had undergone and who would marvel at the extent to which, primarily by his own efforts, he had made a name for himself in the world. Forster, all being well, would pass the information on to posterity, and posterity would first of all sympathise with him, in the guise of a miniature Mrs Gummidge, for having been a lone lorn creetur, and then applaud him, in the guise of a massive Mr Bounderby, as one who had known rough times but who had nevertheless pulled himself through solely by the strength of his own exertions.

Having dealt with his early childhood, and the episode in the blacking warehouse, Dickens continued his autobiography towards the point of his unrequited passion for Maria Beadnell – and found that he was unable to go on. The wounds inflicted on his pride and confidence at that time were still too raw to bear much probing. 'A few years ago (just before *Copperfield*)', he told Maria in 1855, 'I began to write my life, intending the manuscript to be found among my papers when its subject should be concluded. But as I began to approach within sight of that part of it, I lost courage and burned the rest.'**

This could not have been, however, a case of spontaneous combustion, for while work on the autobiography evidently came to an end the manuscript as such was not consigned to the flames in the first instance. At Forster's suggestion, Dickens began writing his next book, *David Copperfield*, in the first person and soon found, much to his delight, that he was able to absorb into it – word for word in many places – substantial portions of his autobiography. 'I really think I have done it

---

* *The Letters of Charles Dickens*, vol. II, edited by Walter Dexter (1938), p. 629.
** *Ibid.*, p. 633.

ingeniously,' he reported to Forster on 10 July 1849, 'and with a very complicated interweaving of truth and fiction.'* The personal history, adventures, experience, and observation of Charles Dickens, which he never meant to be published on any account, were transformed into the memoirs of David Copperfield the Younger of Blunderstone Rookery. Warren's blacking warehouse became Murdstone and Grinby's wine and spirits warehouse; Mr and Mrs John Dickens (and family) became Mr and Mrs Wilkins Micawber (and family) and Maria Beadnell became Dora Spenlow. In this version, admittedly, Dora marries the narrator instead of rejecting him, but it is soon made painfully clear to the reader that, while she is undoubtedly an attractive, endearing little thing, Dora is nothing more than a 'child wife', unable to provide the intellectual companionship he craves and patently unworthy of his great love. Her speedy demise, from that point onwards, becomes inevitable. Her husband, in the meantime, has mastered the art of shorthand and after reporting the debates in Parliament is well on the way to becoming a great novelist. His ultimate reward awaits him in the person of Agnes Wickfield, Dickens's ideal woman and one whom, in real life, it is most improbable that he ever encountered.

THE manuscript of the autobiography was presumably destroyed as soon as it had served its purpose in relation to *David Copperfield*. And yet, in another sense, we haven't lost it at all. In addition to the substantial portions salvaged by Forster (taken, perhaps, from the original 'instalments'), and to certain key passages which can be retrieved (or 'clawed back', to use a Treasury phrase) from *Copperfield*, Dickens himself, from 1850 onwards, constantly drew upon his childhood reminiscences for papers which he contributed to *Household Words* and (later) to *All the Year Round*. They also feature in some of his speeches. Not only, therefore, do we have his own account of his father's imprisonment in the Marshalsea and the blacking warehouse episode, but he tells us, in graphic detail, about his earliest impressions, his toys, his books, the stories his nurse told him, the children he played with, the pantomimes and plays he was taken to see and the schools he

* Forster, *op. cit.*, p. 497

attended. We see Chatham, Rochester and London through the eyes of a child. He recalls, time and time again, episodes from his earliest years, including – in particular – the time when he 'went astray' in the City of London – before moving on to the tale of growing up, of falling in love and coming to man's estate. We even have his own account of the anguish he suffered in his passion for Maria Beadnell, for the words which he was unable to write in 1848 came flooding out in a torrent seven years later in letters to Maria herself, at the time when they first renewed their acquaintance. We have equally vivid accounts of what it was like to be a reporter in the early 1830s, tearing about the countryside in all weathers on behalf of the *Morning Chronicle* or sitting in cramped conditions of extreme discomfort in the tiny space reserved for the gentlemen of the Press at Westminster, and we hear, at first hand, of the origins of *Sketches by Boz*, *The Pickwick Papers* and *Nicholas Nickleby*. Letters written at the time tell us of the traumatic effect that the death of Mary Hogarth had upon him and how, as a result of several intense dreams, he was able to regain comfort and reassurance from the conviction that her spirit was somehow watching over him.

Opinions may vary as to the manner in which Dickens would have terminated his autobiography, but since he was chiefly concerned, in the late 1840s, with the period of his early life it has been assumed that the year 1839, marked by the conclusion of *Nicholas Nickleby*, is a not unreasonable point at which to bring the narrative to an end. We thus have, in the text which follows, an account of his life, from the time of his birth to his twenty-seventh year, told in what are, for 99% of the time, his own words. Editorial emendations have been limited, in the main, to the odd linking sentence or the insertion of a few explanatory words. Occasionally, when there is a need for one version of a particular episode to be merged with another, the outcome is a 'concocted' passage. These deviations from the authentic words of the master are pinpointed in the Notes which follow the text. The royal 'we', used on many occasions by the essayist purporting to reflect on universal experiences, has been pared down to the first person singular, as seems more appropriate for the recollections of one particular individual. Other than this, what follows is pure Dickens.

It would be foolish to pretend, however, that the compilation recreates in its entirety the text which was consigned to the flames in 1849 or 1850. It is clear, for example, from those passages of the original autobiography that have come down to us via Forster that Dickens referred at some point in the destroyed version to the mysterious illness which he suffered from intermittently as a child ('my old disorder'). By utilising some remarks which Dickens made to George Dolby, however, it has proved possible to insert a passing reference to these spasms (see pages 15 and 181), and we should bear in mind his report to Catherine in 1835 that he had passed the whole night 'in a state of exquisite torture from the spasm in my side', the severity of which exceeded anything he had felt since childhood.* Another portion of the destroyed manuscript evidently described how, standing on a table, he performed comic songs and monologues ('the old readings') for the amusement of his father and his friends.

We would also, presumably, have been told rather more about his parents and his brothers and his sisters – although not so much as all that because, with the possible exception of his sister Fanny (of whom he was, so he tells us perhaps rather too emphatically, in no way whatsoever jealous), he was essentially uninterested in his siblings. The one person in whom he *was* interested, above all others, was himself, and we scarcely needed, in confirmation of this, his confession in 1869 that he was 'accustomed to observe myself as curiously as if I were another man'.** For we are aware not only that the child Dickens has a very high opinion of his own importance and feels very sorry for himself but that the adult Dickens is watching his earlier self (as well as his current self) with an eagle eye and trying to gauge the effect that his appearance and activities would have had upon other people. He is constantly wondering what they could have made of 'a little chap like me'. (The heretical notion that they might not have been greatly interested in 'a little chap like him' simply does not occur to Dickens.) To the end of his days, indeed, he continued to ruminate over the short period of distress through which he had passed during the blacking warehouse episode. 'The never-to-be-forgotten misery of that old time', he wrote to Forster in June 1862, almost forty years after the events in question, 'bred a certain shrinking

* *Mr & Mrs Charles Dickens*, edited by Walter Dexter (1935), p. 40.
** In a 'Household Words' essay reprinted in *The Uncommerical Traveller* ('A Fly-leaf in a Life').

sensitiveness in a certain ill-clad, ill-fed child.'* The omissions in the text that follows, in short, may not be too significant.

There is, finally, the question of veracity. Some of the tales which Dickens relates of his younger days, especially of his prowess in the classroom, cast him in a very good light – in far too good a light, according to some of his childhood contemporaries, who waxed indignant after reading the first edition of Forster's biography. Some of the incidents in 'I go astray' verge on the preposterous. Just how much is pure unadulterated fact and how much has been fictionalised must be left for the reader to determine. At the end of 'I go astray' Dickens solemnly assures us that 'this is literally and exactly' what happened (just as his nurse used to swear that the horrendous ghost stories that she told him at bedtime had all involved her own relatives) and who are we to quarrel with this assertion? The autobiography that is absolutely truthful in every crucial respect has, after all, still to be written. Judged by the standards of the twentieth century, as well as by those of the nineteenth, Dickens is, on the whole, as honest as we have any right to expect – and the pleasure that he gives to the reader, in the glorious abundance of his recollections, is beyond comparison.

Peter Rowland

* Forster, *op. cit.*, p. 39.

MY EARLY TIMES

CHATHAM REVISITED

(AND ROCHESTER TOO)

*'I received my earliest and most enduring impressions
among barracks and soldiers, and ships and sailors'
– 'Where We Stopped Growing', January 1853*

IT lately happened that I found myself rambling about the
scenes among which my earliest days were passed: scenes from
which I departed when I was a child, and which I did not revisit
until I was a man. This is no uncommon chance, but one that
befalls some of us any day; perhaps it may not be quite unin-
teresting to compare notes with the reader respecting an
experience so familiar and a journey so uncommercial.

I left Chatham in a stage-coach and was cavalierly shunted
back into it by train. My ticket had been previously collected,
like my taxes, and my shining new portmanteau had had a great
plaster stuck upon it, and I had been defied by Act of
Parliament to offer an objection to anything that was done to
it, or me, under a penalty of not less than forty shillings or
more than five pounds, compoundable for a term of imprisonment. When I had sent my disfigured property on to the hotel,
I began to look about me; and the first discovery I made, was,
that the Station had swallowed up the playing-field.

It was gone. The two beautiful hawthorn-trees, the hedge,
the turf, and all those buttercups and daisies, had given place
to the stoniest of jolting roads: while, beyond the Station, an
ugly dark monster of a tunnel kept its jaws open, as if it had
swallowed them and were ravenous for more destruction. The
coach that had carried me away, was melodiously called

Simpson's Blue-Eyed Maid, and belonged to Simpson, at the coach-office up-street; the locomotive engine that had brought me back, was called severely No. 97 and belonged to the S.E.R., and was spitting ashes and hot water over the blighted ground.

When I had been let out at the platform-door, like a prisoner whom the turnkey grudgingly released, I looked in again over the low wall, at the scene of departed glories. Here, in the haymaking time, had I been delivered from the dungeons of Seringapatam, an immense pile (of haycock), by my own countrymen, the victorious British (boy next door and his two cousins), and had been recognised with ecstasy by my affianced one (Miss Green), who had come all the way from England (second house in the terrace) to ransom me, and marry me. Here, had I first heard in confidence, from one whose father was greatly connected, being under Government, of the existence of a terrible banditti, called 'The Radicals', whose principles were, that the Prince Regent wore stays, and that nobody had a right to any salary, and that the army and navy ought to be put down – horrors at which I trembled in my bed, after supplicating that the Radicals might be speedily taken and hanged. Here, too, had we, the small boys of Boles, had that cricket match against the small boys of Coles, when Boles and Coles had actually met upon the ground, and when, instead of instantly hitting out at one another with the utmost fury, as we had all hoped and expected, those sneaks had said respectively, 'I hope Mrs Boles is well', and 'I hope Mrs Coles and the baby are doing charmingly.' Could it be that, after all this, and much more, the Playing-field was a Station, and No. 97 expectorated boiling water and redhot cinders on it, and the whole belonged by Act of Parliament to S.E.R.?

As it could be, and was, I left the place with a heavy heart for a walk all over the town. And first of Simpson's up-street. When I departed from Chatham in the strawy arms of Simpson's Blue-Eyed Maid, Simpson's was a moderate-sized coach office (in fact, a little coach-office), with an oval transparency in the window, which looked beautiful by night, representing one of Simpson's coaches in the act of passing a milestone on the London Road with great velocity, completely full inside and out, and all the passengers dressed in the first style of fashion, and enjoying themselves tremendously. I found no such place as Simpson's now – no such bricks and rafters, not to mention the name – no such edifice on the teeming earth. Pickford had come and knocked Simpson's down. Pickford had not only knocked Simpson's down, but had knocked two or three houses down on each side of Simpson's and then had knocked the whole into one great establishment with a pair of big gates, in and out of which, his (Pickford's) waggons are, in these days, always rattling with their drivers sitting up so high, that they look in at the second-floor windows of the old-fashioned houses in the High Street as they shake the town. I have not the honour of Pickford's acquaintance, but I felt that he had done me an injury, not to say committed an act of boyslaughter, in running over my childhood in this rough manner; and if I ever meet Pickford driving one of his own monsters, and smoking a pipe the while (which is the custom of his men), he shall know by the expression of my eye, if it catches his, that there is something wrong between us.

Moreover, I felt that Pickford had no right to come rushing into Chatham and deprive the town of a public picture. He is not Napoleon Bonaparte. When he took down the transparent stage-coach, he ought to have given the town a transparent van. With a gloomy conviction that Pickford is wholly utilitarian and unimaginative, I proceeded on my way.

Of what use on earth is a single man? I mean – of how small an amount of practical labour is an individual capable, when he compares his powers, not only with the entire magnitude of great public works, but with one of the countless number of subordinate parts, nay, one of mere temporary details and preliminaries? I often have this feeling in gazing at large edifices and almost everything I looked at in Chatham and Rochester engendered it in an unusual degree.

There was Rochester Castle to begin with. I surveyed that massive ruin from the Bridge, and thought what a brief little practical joke I seemed to be, in comparison with its solidity, stature, strength and length of life. I went inside; and, standing in the solemn shadow of its walls, looking up at the blue sky, its only remaining roof (to the disturbance of crows and jackdaws, who garrison the venerable fortress now), calculated how much wall of that thickness I, or any other mere man, could build in his whole life – say from eight years old, to eighty – and what a ridiculous result would be produced. I climbed the rugged staircase, stopping now and then to peep at great holes where the rafters of floors were once – bare as toothless gums now – or to enjoy glimpses of the Medway through dreary apertures like eye-sockets without eyes; and, looking down from the Castle ramparts on the old Cathedral, and on the crumbling remains of the old Priory, and on the row of staid old red brick houses where the Cathedral dignitaries live, and on the shrunken fragments of one of the old City gates, and on the old trees with their high tops below me, felt quite apologetic to the scene in general for my own juvenility and insignificance. One of the river-boatmen had told me, on the Bridge (as country folk usually do tell of such places) that in the old times when those buildings were in progress a labourer's wages were 'a penny a day, and enough too'. Even as a solitary penny was to their whole cost, it appeared to me was the utmost strength and exertion of one man towards the labour of their erection.

It must be acknowledged that there are few things in this beautiful country of England, more picturesque to the eye, and agreeable to the fancy, than an old Cathedral town. Seen in the distance, rising from among corn-fields, pastures, orchards, gardens, woods, the river, the bridge, the roofs of ancient houses, and haply the ruins of a castle or abbey, the venerable Cathedral spires, opposed for many hundred years to the winter wind and summer sun, tower, like a solemn historical presence, above the city, conveying to the rudest mind associations of interest with the dusky Past. On a nearer approach, this interest is heightened. Within the building, by the long perspectives of pillars and arches; by the earthy smell, preaching more eloquently than deans and chapters, of the common doom; by the praying figures of knights and ladies on the tombs, with little headless generations of sons and daughters kneeling around them; by the stained glass windows, softening and mellowing the light; by the oaken carvings of the stalls, where the shorn monks told their beads; by the battered effigies of archbishops and bishops, found built up in the walls, when all the world had been unconscious, for centuries, of their blunt stone noses; by the mouldering chapter-room; by the crypt, with its barred loopholes, letting in long gleams of slanting light from the Cloisters where the dead lie, and where the ivy, bred among the broken arches, twines about their graves; by the sound of the bells, high up in the massive tower; by the universal gravity, mystery, decay and silence. Without, by the old environing Cathedral close, with its red-brick houses and staid gardens; by the same stained glass, so dark on that side though so bright within; by the pavement of half-obliterated

Rochester from Star Hill.

tombstones; by the long echoes of the visitors' footsteps; by the wicket gate, that seems to shut the moving world out of that retirement; by the grave rooks and jackdaws that have built their nests in steeple crevices, where the after-hum of the chimes reminds them, perhaps, of the wind among the boughs of lofty trees; by the ancient scraps of palace and gateway; by the ivy again, that has grown to be so thick and strong; by the oak, famous in all that part, which has struck its mighty root through the Bishop's wall; by the Cathedral organ, whose sound fills all that space, and all the space it opens in the charmed imagination.

There may be flaws in this whole, if it be examined too closely. It may not be improved by the contemplation of the shivering choristers on a winter morning, huddling on their gowns as they drowsily go to scamper through their works; by the drawling voice, without a heart, that drearily pursues the dull routine; by the avaricious functionary who lays aside the silver mace to take the silver pieces, and who races through the Show as if he were the hero of a sporting wager. Some uncomfortable doubts may, under special circumstances, obtrude themselves, of the practical Christianity of the head of some particular Foundation. He may be a brawler, or a proud man, or a sleek or an artful. He may be usually silent, in the House of

Lords when a Christian minister should speak, and may make a point of speaking when he should be silent. He may even be oblivious of the truth; a stickler by the letter, not the spirit, for his own purposes; a pettifogger in the supreme court of God's high law, as there are pettifoggers in the lower courts administering the laws of mortal man. Disturbing recollections may arise, of a few isolated cases here and there, where country curates with small incomes and large families, poor gentlemen and scholars, are condemned to work, like blind horses in a mill, while others who do not work get their rightful pay; or of the inconsistency and indecorum of the Church being made a Robe and Candlestick question, while so many shining lights are hidden under bushels, and so many black-cloth coats are threadbare. The question may present itself, by remote chance, whether some shovel-hats be not made too much on the model of the banker's shovel with which the gold is gathered on the counter, and too little in remembrance of that other kind of shovel that renders ashes unto ashes, and dust to dust. But, on the whole, the visitor will probably be content to say, 'the time was, and this old Cathedral saw it, when these things were infinitely worse; they will be better; I will do all honour to the good that is in them (which is much) and I will do what in me lies for the speedier amendment of the bad'. In this conclusion, I think the visitor of the old Cathedral would be right.

As I sauntered along the old High Street on my way back towards Chatham, I seemed to dwindle more and more. Here, was another old gate; here, were very old houses, with the strangest gables; here, was a queer, queer, little old house, founded by Richard Watts, Esquire, for the nightly shelter of so many poor travellers, 'not being rogues or proctors', who were to be dismissed in the morning with a Godspeed and fourpence each.

Coming into Chatham, it appeared to me as if the feeble absurdity of an individual were made more and more manifest at every step I took. Men were only noticeable here by scores, by hundreds, by thousands, rank and file, companies, regiments, detachments, vessels full for exportation. They walked about the streets in rows or bodies, carrying their heads in exactly the same way, and doing exactly the same thing with their limbs. Nothing in the shape of clothing was made for an individual; everything was contracted for, by the million. The children of Israel were established in Chatham, as salesmen, outfitters, tailors, old clothesmen, army and navy accoutrement makers, bill discounters, and families. The cannon, and pyramidal piles of cannon-balls, renounced the insignificance of individuality, and combined by the score. In the town-barracks, if I saw one soldier pipe-claying a belt, I was sure to see twenty: nineteen of whom might have been compound reflections of the first one in a combination of looking-glasses. No man cooked his dinner in a saucepan; the whole regiment's dinner came out of a copper. The muskets stood in racks, and even the drums were gregarious. Up in the airy Artillery Barracks, Private Jones or Brown lived in a mansion labelled '120 men', or '160 men' – that was his door-plate – he had no separate existence. The only fact that made the least approach to the recognition of an individual was a sentry-box; but that, after all, was for the accommodation of all the rank and file in the barracks, as their turns came.

I took a walk upon the Lines, and mused among the fortifications; grassy and innocent enough on the surface, at present, but tough subjects at the core. Here I saw the artfullest pits and drawbridges, the slyest batteries, the most unexpected angles and turnings; the loneliest, deep-set, beetle-browed little windows, down among the stinging-nettles at the bottom of trenches, indicative of subterranean passages and bomb-proof rooms. Here, I saw forts, and citadels, and great guns hiding their muzzles deceitfully behind mounds of earth; and the low flat tops of inner buildings crouching out of the range of telescopes and aim of shells; and mysterious gateways and archways, honey-combed with loopholes for small arms; and tokens of undermined communication between place and place; and narrow passages beset by dark vaults with gratings to fire through, that one would like to see the inside of, they are so mysterious, and smell so chill and earthy. Steeped in these mysteries, I wandered round the trenches of Fort Pitt, and away to Fort Clarence – a dismal military prison now, like an old Giant's Castle 'new-hatched to the woeful time' – and looking down upon the river from the sloping bank, I saw even there, upon the shore, a strained little fort, with its blank, weather-beaten brick face staring at the mud; which fort, I settled in my own mind, somehow communicated with all the other forts, and had unknown means of blowing them up in the air if need should be. Then, I went back to the Lines, and strolled away to the low stagnant level of the river in that direction, by other solitary trenches, forts, drawbridges, and posts of guard.

Everywhere, I found some fragments of a comprehensive engineering scheme for cutting off, cutting down, blowing up, alluring on to his own destruction, or driving back to his defeat, 'the enemy' – all these contrivances having reference to men by the hundred, and the thousand, and the ten thousand, without the least offence to any individual.

It is a mercy I have not a red and green lamp and a night-bell at my door for in my very young days I was taken to so many lyings-in that I wonder I escaped becoming a professional martyr to them in after-life. I suppose I had a very sympathetic nurse, with a large circle of married acquaintances. However that was, as I continued my walk through Chatham, I found many houses to be solely associated in my mind with this particular interest. At one little greengrocer's shop, down certain steps from the street, I remember to have waited on a lady who had four children (I am afraid to write five, though I fully believe it was five) at a birth. This meritorious woman held quite a reception in her room on the morning when I was introduced there, and the sight of the house brought vividly to my mind how the four (five) deceased young people lay, side by side, on a clean cloth on a chest of drawers; reminding me by a homely association, which I suspect their complexion to have assisted, of pigs' feet as they are usually displayed at a neat tripe-shop. Hot caudle was handed round on the occasion, and I further remembered as I stood contemplating the greengrocer's, that a subscription was entered into among the company, which became extremely alarming to my consciousness of having pocket-money on my person. This fact being known to my conductress, whoever she was, I was earnestly exhorted to contribute, but resolutely declined; therein disgusting the company, who gave me to understand that I must dismiss all expectations of going to Heaven.

How does it happen that when all else is change wherever one goes, there yet seem, in every place, to be some few people who never alter? As the sight of the greengrocer's house recalled these trivial incidents of long ago, the identical greengrocer appeared on the steps, with his hands in his pockets, and leaning his shoulder against the door-post, as my childish eyes had seen him many a time; indeed, there was his old mark on the door-post yet, as if his shadow had become a fixture there. It was he himself; he might formerly have been an old-looking young man, or he might now be a young-looking old man, but there he was.

In walking along the street, I had as yet looked in vain for a familiar face, or even a transmitted face; here was the very greengrocer who had been weighing and handling baskets on the morning of the reception. As he brought with him a dawning remembrance that he had had no proprietary interest in those babies, I crossed the road, and accosted him on the subject. He was not in the least excited or gratified, or in any way roused, by the accuracy of my recollection, but said, Yes, summat out of the common – he didn't remember how many it was (as if half-a-dozen babies either way made no difference) – had happened to a Mrs What's-her-name, as once lodged there – but he didn't call it to mind, particular. Nettled by this phlegmatic conduct, I informed him that I had left the town when a child. He slowly returned, quite unsoftened, and not without a sarcastic kind of complacency, *Had* I? Ah! And did I find it had got on tolerably well without me? Such is the difference (I thought when I had left him a few hundred yards behind, and was by so much in a better temper) between going away from a place and remaining in it. I had no right, I reflected, to be angry with the greengrocer for his want of interest, I was nothing to him: whereas he was the town, the Cathedral, the bridge, the river, my childhood, and a large slice of my life, to me. (By 'town', incidentally, it must be understood that I refer to both Chatham and Rochester, because if anybody knows to a nicety where one ends and the other begins, it is more than I do.)

Of course the town had shrunk fearfully since I was a child there. I had entertained the impression that the High Street was at least as wide as Regent Street, London, or the Italian Boulevard at Paris. I found it little better than a lane. There was a public clock in it, which I had supposed to be the finest clock in the world: whereas it now turned out to be as inexpressive, moon-faced, and weak a clock as ever I saw. It belonged to a Town Hall, where I had seen an Indian (who I now suppose wasn't an Indian) swallow a sword (which I now suppose he didn't). The edifice had appeared to me in those days so glorious a structure, that I had set it up in my mind as the model on which the Genie of the Lamp built the palace of Aladdin. A mean little brick heap, like a demented chapel, with a few yawning persons in leather gaiters, and in the last extremity for something to do, lounging at the door with their hands in their pockets, and calling themselves a Corn Exchange!

The Theatre was in existence, I found, on asking the fish-

11

monger, who had a compact show of stock in his window, consisting of a sole and a quart of shrimps. To the Theatre, therefore, I repaired for consolation. But I found very little, for it was in a bad and declining way. A dealer in wine and bottled beer had already squeezed his trade into the box-office, and the theatrical money was taken – when it came – in a kind of meat-safe in the passage. The dealer in wine and bottled beer must have insinuated himself under the stage too; for he announced that he had various descriptions of alcoholic drinks 'in the wood', and there was no possible stowage for the wood anywhere else. Evidently, he was by degrees eating the estab-lishment away to the core, and would soon have sole possession of it. It was To Let, and hopelessly so, for its old purposes; and there had been no entertainment within its walls for a long time except a Panorama; and even that had been announced as 'pleasingly instructive', and I know too well the fatal meaning and the leaden import of those terrible expressions. No, there was no comfort in the Theatre. It was mysteriously gone, like my own youth. Unlike my own youth, it might be coming back some day; but there was little promise of it.

The clock that had so degenerated since I last saw it admon-ished me that I had stayed here long enough; and I resumed my walk.

I had not gone fifty paces along the street when I was suddenly brought up by the sight of a man who got out of a little phaeton at the doctor's door, and went into the doctor's house. Immediately, the air was filled with the scent of trodden glass, and the perspective of years opened, and at the end of it was a little likeness of this man keeping a wicket, and I said, 'God bless my soul! Joe Specks!'

Through many changes and much work, I had preserved a tenderness for the memory of Joe, forasmuch as we had made the acquaintance of Roderick Random together, and I had believed him to be no ruffian, but an ingenuous and engaging hero. Scorning to ask the boy left in the phaeton whether it was really Joe, and scorning even to read the brass plate on the door – so sure was I – I rang the bell and informed the servant maid that a stranger sought audience of Mr Specks. Into a room, half surgery, half study, I was shown to await his coming, and I found it, by a series of elaborate accidents, bestrewn with testi-monies to Joe. Portrait of Mr Specks, bust of Mr Specks, silver cup from grateful patient to Mr Specks, presentation sermon from local clergyman, dedication poem from local poet, dinner-card from local nobleman, tract on balance of power from local refugee, inscribed *Homage de l'auteur à Specks*.

When my old schoolfellow came in, and I informed him with a smile that I was not a patient, he seemed rather at a loss to perceive any reason for smiling in connection with that fact, and inquired to what was he to attribute the honour? I asked him, with another smile, could he remember me at all? He had not (he said) that pleasure. I was beginning to have but a poor opinion of Mr Specks, when he said reflectively, 'And yet there's something too.' Upon that, I saw a boyish light in his eyes that looked well, and I asked him if he could inform me, as a stranger who desired to know and had not the means of reference at hand, what the name of the young lady was, who married Mr Random? Upon that, he said 'Narcissa', and after staring for a moment, called me by my name, shook me by the hand, and melted into a roar of laughter. 'Why, of course, you'll remember Lucy Green,' he said, after we had talked a little. 'Of course,' said I. 'Whom do you think she married?' said he. 'You?' I hazarded. 'Me,' said Specks, 'and you shall see her.'

So I saw her, and she was fat, and if all the hay in the world had been heaped upon her, it could scarcely have altered her face more than Time had altered it from my remembrance of the face that had once looked down upon me into the fragrant dungeons of Seringapatam. But when her youngest child came in after dinner (for I dined with them, and we had no other company than Specks, Junior, Barrister-at-law, who went away as soon as the cloth was removed, to look after the young lady to whom he was going to be married next week), I saw again, in that little daughter, the little face of the hayfield, unchanged, and it quite touched my foolish heart. We talked immensely, Specks and Mrs Specks, and I, and we spoke of our old selves as though our old selves were dead and gone, and indeed they were – dead and gone as the playing-field that had become a wilderness of rusty iron and the property of S.E.R.

Specks, however, illuminated Chatham with the rays of interest that I wanted and should otherwise have missed in it, and linked its present to its past, with a highly agreeable chain. And in Specks's society I had new occasion to observe what I had before noticed in similar communications among other men. All the schoolfellows and others of old, whom I enquired about, had either done superlatively well or superlatively ill – had either become uncertified bankrupts, or been felonious and got themselves transported; or had made great hits in life, and done wonders. And this is so commonly the case, that I never can imagine what becomes of all the mediocre people of people's youth – especially considering that we find no lack of the species in our maturity. But, I did not propound this difficulty to Specks, for no pause in the conversation gave me an occasion. Nor, could I discover one single flaw in the good doctor – when he reads this, he will receive in a friendly spirit the pleasantly meant record – except that he had forgotten his Roderick Random, and that he confounded Strap with Lieutenant Hatchway; who never knew Random, howsoever intimate with Pickle.

When I went alone to the Railway to catch my train at night (Specks had meant to go with me, but was inopportunely called out), I was in a more charitable mood with Chatham than I had been all day; and yet in my heart I had loved it all day too. Ah! who was I that I should quarrel with the town for being changed to me, when I myself had come back, so changed to it! All my early readings and early imaginations dated from this place, and I took them away so full of innocent construction and guileless belief, and I brought them back so worn and torn, so much the wiser and so much the worse!

PART ONE

CHILDHOOD

'As to my means of observation,
they have been pretty extensive. I have been
abroad in the world from a mere child.'
– *letter to J.H. Keunzel, July (?) 1838*

My birth and early life

I was born on a Friday, and it is a most astonishing coincidence
that I have never in my life – whatever projects I may have deter-
mined on otherwise – never begun a book, or begun anything of
importance to me, but it has been on a Friday.

I was born at Portsmouth, an English seaport town principally remarkable for mud, Jews and sailors, on 7 February 1812.
My father holding in those days a situation under Government
in the Navy Pay Office, which called him in the discharge of his
duties to different places, I came to London, a child of two
years' old, left it again at six, and then left it again for another
seaport town – Chatham, in the county of Kent. I have many
happy memories connected with Kent and am scarcely less
interested in it than if I had been a Kentish man bred and born,
and had resided in that county all my life.

But neither Portsmouth nor Chatham contributed much to
my physical strength, for I was always a puny, weak youngster
and never used to join in games with the same zest that other
boys seemed to have. I never was remarkable, during my
younger days, for anything but violent, spasmodic attacks,
which used to utterly prostrate me, and for indomitable
energy in reading. Cricket, 'chevy', top, marbles, 'peg in the
ring', 'tor', 'three holes', or any of the thousand and one boys'
games, had no charm for me, save such as lay in watching
others play.

I remained at Chatham some six or seven years and then
came back to London with my parents and half-a-dozen brothers and sisters, whereof I was second in seniority.

John Dickens.

Earliest recollections

The first objects that assume a distinct presence before me, as I look far back, into the blank of my infancy, are my mother with her pretty hair and youthful shape, and my nurse, with no shape at all, and eyes so dark that they seemed to darken their whole neighbourhood in her face.

I believe I can remember these two at a little distance

apart, dwarfed to my sight by stooping down or kneeling on the floor, and I going unsteadily from the one to the other. I have an impression on my mind which I cannot distinguish from actual remembrance, of the touch of my nurse's forefinger as she used to hold it out to me, and of its being roughened by needlework, like a pocket nutmeg-grater.

This may be fancy, though I think the memory of most of us can go farther back into such times than many of us suppose; just as I believe the power of observation in numbers of very young children to be quite wonderful for its closeness and accuracy. Indeed, I think that most grown men who are remarkable in this respect, may with greater propriety be said not to have lost the faculty, than to have acquired it; the rather, as I generally observe such men to retain a certain freshness, and gentleness, and capacity of being pleased, which are also an inheritance they have preserved from their childhood.

I might have a misgiving that I am 'meandering' in stopping to say this, but that it brings me to remark that I build these conclusions, in part upon my own experience of myself; and if it should appear from anything I may set down in this narrative that I was a child of close observation, or that as a man I have a strong memory of my childhood, I undoubtedly lay claim to both these characteristics.

Looking back, as I was saying, into the blank of my infancy, I recall that Somebody – who, I wonder, and which way did *She* go, when she died? – hummed the evening hymn to me, and I cried on the pillow: either with the remorseful consciousness of having kicked Somebody Else, or because still Somebody Else had hurt my feelings in the course of the day.

I can faintly remember learning the alphabet at my mother's knee. To this day, when I look upon the fat black letters in the primer, the puzzling novelty of their shapes, and the easy good nature of O and Q and S, seem to present themselves again before me as they used to do. 'A was an archer, and shot at a frog.' Of course he was. He was an apple-pie also, and there he is! He was a good many things in his time, was A, and so were most of his friends, except X, who had so little versatility, that I never knew him to get beyond Xerxes or Xanthippe – like Y, who was always confined to a Yacht or a Yew Tree; and Z condemned for ever to be a Zebra or a Zany.

I remember my poor mother, God forgive her, putting me on

a low wall with an iron railing on the top and making me cheer the Prince Regent, who was driving by.

What Party can that have been, and what New Year's Day can that have been, which first rooted the phrase, 'A New Year's day Party' in my mind? So far back do my recollections of childhood extend, that I have a vivid remembrance of the sensation of being carried downstairs in a woman's arms, and holding tight to her, in the terror of seeing the steep perspective below. Hence, I may have been carried into this Party, for anything I know; but, somehow or other, I most certainly got there, and was in a doorway looking on; and in that look a New Year's Party revealed itself to me, as a very long row of ladies and gentlemen sitting against a wall, all drinking at once out of little glass cups with handles, like custard-cups. What can this Party have been? I am afraid it must have been a dull one, but I *know* it came off. Where can this Party have been? I have not the faintest notion where, but I am absolutely certain it was some-where. Why the company should all have been drinking at once, and especially why they should all have been drinking out of custard-cups, are points of fact over which the Waters of Oblivion have long rolled. I doubt if they can have been drink-ing the Old Year out and the New One in, because they were not at supper and had no table before them. There was no speech-making, no quick movement and change of action, no demonstration of any kind. They were all sitting in a long row against the wall – very like my first idea of the good people in Heaven, as I derived it from a wretched picture in a Prayer Book – and they had all got their heads a little thrown back, and were all drinking at once. It is possible enough that I, the baby, may have been caught up out of bed to have a peep at the company, and that the company may happen to have been thus occupied for the flash and space of a moment only. But it has always seemed to me as if I looked at them for a long time – hours – during which they did nothing else; and to this present time, a casual mention in my hearing, of a Party on a New Year's Day, always revives that picture.

On what other early New Year's Day can I possibly have been an innocent accomplice in the secreting – in a coal cellar too – of a man with a wooden leg! There was no man with a wooden leg, in the circle of my acknowledged and lawful relations and friends. Yet, I clearly remember that we stealthily conducted the man with the wooden leg – whom we knew intimately – into the coal cellar, and that, in getting him over the coals to hide him behind some partition there was beyond, his wooden leg bored itself in among the coals, and his hat flew off, and he fell backwards and lay prone: a spectacle of helplessness. I clearly remember that his struggles to get up among the small coals, and to obtain any purchase on himself in those slippery and shifting circumstances, were a work of exceeding difficulty, involving delay and noise that occasioned us excessive terrors. I have not the least idea who 'we' were, except that I had a little sister for another innocent accomplice, and that there must have been a servant girl for principal: neither do I know whether the man with the wooden leg robbed the house, before or afterwards, or otherwise nefariously distinguished himself. Nor, how a cat came to be connected with the occasion, and had a fit, and ran over the top of a door. But, I know that some awful reason compelled us to hush it all up, and that we were 'never told'. For many years, I had this association with a New Year's day entirely to myself, until at last, the anniversary being come round again, I said to my little sister, as she and I sat by chance among our children, 'Do you remember the New Year's day of the man with the wooden leg?' Whereupon, a thick black curtain which had overhung him from her infancy, went up, and she saw just this much of the man, and not a jot more. (A day or before her death, that little sister told me that, in the night, the smell of the fallen leaves in the woods where we had habitually walked as very young children, had come upon her with such strength of reality that she had moved her head to look for strewn leaves on the floor at her bedside.)

What else do I remember? Let me see.

Toys

All toys at first, I find. There is the Tumbler with his hands in his pockets, who wouldn't lie down, but whenever he was put upon the floor, persisted in rolling his fat body about, until he rolled himself still, and brought those lobster eyes of his to bear upon me – when I affected to laugh very much, but in my heart of hearts was extremely doubtful of him. Close behind him is that infernal snuff-box, out of which there sprang a demoniacal Counsellor in a black gown, with an obnoxious head of hair, and a red cloth mouth, wide open, who was not to be endured on any terms, but could not be put away either; for he used suddenly, in a highly magnified state, to fly out of Mammoth Snuff-boxes in dreams, when least expected. Nor is the frog with cobbler's wax on his tail, far off; for there was no knowing where he wouldn't jump; and when he flew over the candle, and came upon one's hand with that spotted back – red on a green ground – he was horrible. The cardboard lady in a blue silk skirt, who was stood up against the candlestick to dance, was milder, and was beautiful; but I can't say as much for the larger cardboard man, who used to be hung against the wall and pulled by a string; there was a sinister expression in that nose of his; and when he got his legs round his neck (which he very often did), he was ghastly, and not a creature to be alone with.

When did that dreadful Mask first look at me? Who put it on, and why was I so frightened that the sight of it is an era in my life? It is not a hideous visage in itself; it is even meant to be droll; why then were its stolid features so intolerable? Surely not because it hid the wearer's face. An apron would have done as much; and though I should have preferred even the apron away, it would not have been absolutely insupportable, like the mask. Was it the immovability of the mask? The doll's face was immovable, but I was not afraid of *her*. Perhaps that fixed and set change coming over a real face, infused into my quickened heart some remote suggestion and dread of the universal change that is to come on every face, and make it still? Nothing reconciled me to it. No drummers, from whom proceeded a melancholy chirping on the turning of a handle; no regiment of soldiers, with a mute band, taken out of a box, and fitted, one by one, upon a stiff and lazy little set of lazy-tongs; no old woman, made of wires and a brown-paper composition, cutting up a pie for two small children; could give me a permanent comfort, for a long time. Nor was it any satisfaction to be shown the Mask, and see that it was made of paper, or to have it locked up and be assured that no one wore it. The mere recollection of that fixed face, the mere knowledge of its existence anywhere, was sufficient to wake me in the night all perspiration and horror, with, 'O I know it's coming! O the mask!'

I never wondered what the dear old donkey with the panniers – there he is! – was made of, then! His hide was real to the touch, I recollect. And the great black horse with the round red spots all over him – the horse that I could even get upon – I never wondered what had brought him to that strange condition, or thought that such a horse was not commonly seen at Newmarket. The four horses of no colour, next to him, that went into the waggon of cheeses, and could be taken out and stabled under the piano, appear to have bits of fur-tippet for their tails, and other bits for their manes, and to stand on pegs instead of legs, but it was not so when they were brought home for a Christmas present. They were all right, then; neither was their harness unceremoniously nailed into their chests, as appears to be the case now. The tinkling works of the music-cart, I *did* find out, to be made of quill toothpicks and wire; and I always thought that little tumbler in his shirt-sleeves, perpetually swarming up one side of a wooden frame, and coming down, head foremost, on the other, rather a weak-minded person – though good-natured; but the Jacob's Ladder, next him, made of little squares of red wood, that went flapping and clattering over one another, each developing a different picture, and the whole enlivened by small bells, was a mighty marvel and a great delight.

Ah! The Doll's house! – of which I was not a proprietor, but where I visited. I don't admire the Houses of Parliament half so much as that stone-fronted mansion with real glass windows, and doorsteps, and a real balcony – greener than I ever see now, except at watering places; and even they afford but a pale imitation. And though it *did* open all at once, the entire house-front (which was a blow, I admit, as cancelling the fiction of a staircase), it was but to shut it up again, and I could believe. Even open, there were three distinct rooms in it: a sitting-room and bedroom, elegantly furnished, and best of all, a kitchen, with uncommonly soft fire-irons, a plentiful assortment of diminutive utensils – oh, the warming pan! – and a tin man-cook in profile, who was always going to fry two fish. What Barmecide justice have I done to the noble feasts wherein the set of wooden platters figured, each with its own peculiar delicacy, as a ham or turkey, glued tight on to it, and garnished with something green, which I recollect as moss! Could all the Temperance Societies of these later days, united, give me such a tea-drinking as I have had through the means of yonder little set of blue crockery, which really would hold liquid (it ran out of the small wooden cask, I recollect, and tasted of matches), and which made tea, nectar. And if the two legs of the ineffectual little sugar-tongs did tumble over one another, and want purpose, like Punch's hands, what does it matter? And if I did once shriek out, as a poisoned child, and strike the fashionable company with consternation, by reason of having drunk a little teaspoon, inadvertently dissolved in too hot tea, I was never the worse for it, except by a powder!

O the wonderful Noah's Ark! It was not found seaworthy when put in a washing-tub, and the animals were crammed in at the roof, and needed to have their legs well shaken down before they could be got in, even there – and then, ten to one but they began to tumble out at the door, which was but imperfectly fastened with a wire latch – but what was *that* against it! Consider the noble fly, a size or two smaller than the elephant, the ladybird, the butterfly – all triumphs of art! Consider the goose, whose feet were so small, and whose balance was so indifferent, that he usually tumbled forward, and knocked down all the animal creation. Consider Noah and his family, like idiotic tobacco-stoppers: and how the leopard stuck to warm little fingers and how the tails of the larger animals used gradually to resolve themselves into frayed bits of string!

Last but far from least, the toy theatre – there it is, with its familiar proscenium, and ladies in feathers, in the boxes! – and all its attendant occupation with paste and glue, and gum, and water colours, in the getting-up of *The Miller and His Men*, and *Elizabeth, or the Exile of Siberia*. In spite of a few besetting accidents and failures (particularly an unreasonable disposition in the respectable Kelmar, and some others, to become faint in the legs, and double up, at exciting points of the drama),a teeming world of fancies so suggestive and all-embracing, that I see dark, dirty, real theatres in the day-time, adorned with these associations as with the freshest garlands of the rarest flowers, and charming me yet.

Books

I had plenty of the finest toys in the world, in short, and the most astonishing picture-books. Thin books in themselves, at first, but many of them, and with deliciously smooth covers of bright red or green. I date from the time of the Prince Regent, and remember picture-books about dandies -satires upon that eminent personage himself, possibly – but *I* never knew it. In those times there was a certain bright, smooth cover for picture-books, like a glorified surgical plaster. It has gone out this long, long time. The picture-book that seems to have been my first, was about one Mr Pillblister (in the medical profession, I presume, from the name) who gave a party. As the legend is impressed on my remembrance, it opened thus:

> Mr Pillblister
> And Betsy his sister
> Determined on giving a treat;
> Gay dandies they call
> To a supper and ball
> At their house in Great Camomile Street.

The pictures represented male dandies in every stage of preparation for this festival; holding on to bedposts to have their stays laced; embellishing themselves with artificial personal graces of many kinds; and enduring various humiliations in remote garrets. One gentleman found a hole in his stocking at the last moment:

> A hole in my stocking,
> Now how very shocking!
> Cries poor Mr Mopstaff enraged;
> It is always my fate,
> To be so very late,
> When at Mr Pillblister's engaged.

If I recollect right, they all got there at last, and passed a delightful evening. When first I came to London, I rejected the Tower, Westminster Abbey, St Paul's and the Monument, and entreated to be immediately taken to Great Camomile Street.

I was deeply impressed when I encountered, in an old spelling book, a touching instance of an old lion, of high moral dignity and stern principle, who felt it his imperative duty to devour a young man who had contracted a habit of swearing, as a striking example to the rising generation. But I have a distinct recollection (in my early days at school, when under the dominion of an old lady, who to my mind ruled the world with a birch) of feeling an intense disgust with printers and printing. I thought the letters were printed and sent there to plague me, and I looked upon the printer as my enemy. When I was taught to say my prayers I was told to pray for my enemies and I distinctly remember praying especially for the printer as my greatest enemy. I never now see a row of large, black, fat, staring Roman capitals, but this reminiscence rises up before me. As time wore on, however, and I became interested in story-books, this feeling of disgust became somewhat mitigated. I encountered a bean-stalk – the marvellous bean-stalk up which Jack climbed to the Giant's house! And now, these dreadfully interesting, double-headed giants, with their clubs over their shoulders, began to stride into my life in a perfect throng, drag-ging knights and ladies home for dinner by the hair of their heads. And Jack – how noble, with his sword of sharpness, and his shoes of swiftness! Again those old meditations come upon me as I gaze at him; and I debate within myself whether there was more than one Jack (which I am loth to believe possible), or only one genuine original admirable Jack, who achieved all the recorded exploits.

I have never grown out of the real original roaring giants. I have seen modern giants, for various considerations ranging from a penny to half-a-crown; but they have only had a head a-piece, and have been merely large men, and not always that. I have never outgrown the putting to myself of this suppositious case: Whether, if I, with a large company of brothers and sisters, had been put in his (by which I mean, of course, in Jack's) trying situation, I should have had at once the courage and the presence of mind to take the golden crowns (which it seems to me they always wore as night-caps) off the heads of the giant's children as they lay a-bed, and put them on my family; thus causing our treacherous host to batter his own offspring and spare us. I have never outgrown a want of confi-dence in myself, in this particular.

Yet, in the light of after-knowledge – and, in this particular, as a result of having become acquainted with a Kentucky Giant whose name is Porter, and who is of the modest height of seven feet eight inches in his stockings – it is clear to me that there never was a race of people who so completely gave the lie to history as these giants, or whom the chroniclers have so cruelly libelled. Instead of roaring and ravaging about the world, constantly catering for their cannibal larders, and perpetually going to market in an unlawful manner, they are the meekest people in any man's acquaintance; rather inclining to milk and vegetable diet, and bearing anything for a quiet life. So decidedly are amiability and mildness their characteristics, that I confess I look upon that youth who distinguished himself by the slaughter of these inoffensive persons as a false-hearted brigand, who, pretending to philanthropic motives, was secretly influenced only by the wealth stored up within their castles, and the hope of plunder. And I lean the more to this opinion from finding that even the historian of these exploits, with all his partiality for his hero, is fain to admit that the slaughtered monsters in question were of a very innocent and simple turn; extremely guileless and ready of belief; lending a credulous ear to the most improbable tales; suffering themselves to be easily entrapped into pits; and even (as in the case of the Welsh Giant) with an excess of the hospitable politeness of a landlord, ripping themselves open, rather than hint at the possibility of their guests being versed in the vagabond arts of sleight-of-hand and hocus-pocus.

Little Red Hiding Hood trips through the forest with her basket and comes to me one Christmas Eve to give me information of the cruelty and treachery of that dissembling Wolf who ate her grandmother, without making any impression on his appetite, and then ate her, after making that ferocious joke about his teeth. She was my first love. I felt that if I could have married Little Red Riding Hood, I should have known perfect bliss. But, it was not to be; and there was nothing for it but to look out the Wolf in the Noah's Ark there, and put him late in the procession on the table, as a monster who was to be degraded.

I may assume that I am not singular in entertaining a very great tenderness for the fairy literature of my childhood. What enchanted me then, and is captivating a million of young fancies now, has, at the same blessed time of life, enchanted vast hosts of men and women who have done their long day's work, and laid their grey heads down to rest. It would be hard to estimate the amount of gentleness and mercy that has made its way among us through these slight channels. Forbearance, courtesy, consideration for the poor and aged, kind treatment of animals, the love of nature, abhorrence of tyranny and brute force – many such good things have been first nourished in the child's heart by this powerful aid. It has greatly helped to keep us, in some sense, ever young, by preserving through our worldly ways one slender track not overgrown with weeds, where we may walk with children, sharing their delights.

I have never grown the thousandth part of an inch out of Robinson Crusoe. He fits me just as well, and in exactly the same way, as when I was among the smallest of the small. I have never grown out of his parrot, or his dog, or his fowling-piece, or the horrible old staring goat he came upon in the cave, or his rusty money, or his cap, or his umbrella. There has been no change in the manufacture of telescopes, since that blessed ship's spy-glass was made, through which, lying on his breast at the top of his fortification, with the ladder drawn up after him and all made safe, he saw the black figures of those Cannibals moving round the fire on the sea-sand, as the monsters danced themselves into an appetite for dinner. I have never grown out of Friday, or the excellent old father he was so glad to see, or the grave and gentlemanly Spaniard, or the reprobate Will Atkins, or the knowing way in which he and those other muti-neers were lured up into the Island when they came ashore there, and their boat was stove. I have got no nearer Heaven by the altitude of an atom, in respect of the tragi-comic bear whom Friday caused to dance upon a tree, or the awful array of howling wolves in the dismal weather, who were mad to make good entertainment of man and beast, and who were received with trains of gunpowder lain on fallen trees, and fired by the snapping of pistols; and who ran blazing into the forest dark-ness, or were blown up famously. Never sail I, idle, in a little boat, and hear the rippling water at the prow, and look upon the land, but I know that my boat-growth stopped for ever, when Robinson Crusoe sailed round the Island, and, having been nearly lost, was so affectionately awakened out of his sleep at home again by that immortal parrot, great progenitor of all the parrots I have ever known.

Hush! Again a forest, and somebody up a tree – not Robin Hood, nor Valentine, nor yet the Yellow Dwarf (I have passed him and all Mother Bunch's wonders, without a mention), but an Easter King with a glittering scimitar and turban. By Allah! *two* Eastern Kings, for I see another, looking over his shoulder! Down upon the grass, at the tree's foot, lies the full length of a coal-black Giant, stretched asleep, with his head in a lady's lap; and near them is a glass box, fastened with four locks of shining steel, in which he keeps the lady prisoner when he is awake. I see the four keys at his girdle now. The lady makes signs to the two kings in the tree, who softly descend. It is the setting-in of the bright *Arabian Nights*, all about scimitars and slippers and turbans, and dwarfs and giants and genii and fairies, and blue-beards and riches and caverns: all new and all true.

Oh, now all common things become uncommon and enchanted to me. All lamps are wonderful; all rings are talismans. Common flower-pots are full of treasure, with a little earth scattered on the top; trees are for Ali Baba to hide in; beefsteaks are to throw down into the Valley of Diamonds, that the precious stones may stick to them, and be carried by the eagles to their nests, whence the traders, with loud cries, will scare them. Tarts are made, according to the recipe of the Vizier's son of Bussorah, who turned pastrycook after he was set down in his drawers at the gate of Damascus; cobblers are all Mustaphas, and in the habit of sewing up people cut into four pieces, to whom they are taken blindfold.

Any iron ring let into stone is the entrance to a cave which only waits for the magician, and the little fire, and the necro-mancy, that will make the earth shake. All the dates imported come from the same tree as that unlucky date, with whose shell the merchant knocked out the eye of the genie's invisible son. All olives are of the stock of that fresh fruit, concerning which the Commander of the Faithful overheard the boy conduct the fictitious trial of the fraudulent olive merchant; all apples are akin to the apple purchased (with two others) from the Sultan's gardener for three sequins, and which the tall black slave stole from the child. All dogs are associated with the dog, really a transformed man, who jumped upon the baker's counter, and put his paw on the piece of bad money. All rice recalls the rice which the awful lady, who was a ghoul, could only peck by grains, because of her nightly feasts in the burial-place. My very rocking horse – there he is, with his nostrils turned completely inside-out, indicative of Blood! – should have a peg in his neck, by virtue thereof to fly away with me, as the wooden horse did with the Prince of Persia, in the sight of all his father's Court.

When I wake in bed, at daybreak, on the cold dark winter mornings, the white snow dimly beheld, outside, through the frost on the window-pane, I hear Dinarzade, 'Sister, sister, if you are yet awake, I pray you finish the story of the Young King of the Black Islands.' Scheherazade replies, 'If my lord the Sultan will suffer me to live another day, sister, I will not only finish that, but tell you a more wonderful story yet.' Then, the gracious Sultan goes out, giving no orders for the execution, and we all three breathe again. I tremble to think of Cassim

Baba cut into quarters, hanging in the Robbers' cave, or have some small misgivings that the fierce little old woman with the crutch, who used to start out of the box in the merchant Abudah's bedroom, might, one of these nights, be found upon the stairs, in the long, cold, dusky journey to bed.

For the little reader of story-books, by the firelight, the most testing time of all came about twilight, in the dead winter time, when the shadows closed in and gathered like mustering swarms of ghosts. When they stood lowering, in corners of rooms, and frowned out from behind half-opened doors when they had full possession of unoccupied apartments. When they danced upon the floors, and walls, and ceilings of inhabited chambers, while the fire was low, and withdrew like ebbing waters when it sprang into a blaze. When they frantically mocked the shapes of household objects, making the nurse an ogress, the rocking-horse a monster, the wondering child half-scared and half-amused, a stranger to itself – the very tongs upon the hearth, a straddling giant with his arms a-kimbo, evidently smelling the blood of Englishmen, and wanting to grind people's bones to make his bread.

I recollect, in short, everything I read as a very small boy as perfectly as I forget everything I read now.

Mr Barlow

A great reader of fiction at an unusually early age, therefore, it seems as though I had been born under the superinten-dence of the estimable but terrific gentleman whose name stands at the head of this section of my recollections. The instructive monomaniac, Mr Barlow, will be remembered as the tutor of Master Harry Sandford and Master Tommy Merton. He knew everything, and didactically improved all sorts of occasions, from the consumption of a plate of cher-ries to the contemplation of a starlight night. What youth came to without Mr Barlow was displayed in *The History of Sandford and Merton*, by the example of a certain awful Master Mash. This young wretch wore buckles and powder, conducted himself with insupportable levity at the theatre, had no idea of facing a mad bull single-handed (in which I think him less reprehensible, as remotely reflecting my own character), and was a frightful instance of the enervating effects of luxury upon the human race.

Strange destiny on the part of Mr Barlow, to go down to posterity as childhood's experience of a bore! Immortal Mr Barlow, boring his way through the verdant freshness of ages!

My personal indictment against Mr Barlow is one of many counts. I will proceed to set forth a few of the injuries he has done me.

In the first place, he never made or took a joke. This insensibility on Mr Barlow's part not only cast its own gloom over my boyhood, but blighted even the sixpenny jest books of the time; for, groaning under a moral spell constraining me to refer all things to Mr Barlow, I could not choose but ask myself in a whisper when tickled by a printed jest, 'What would *he* think of it? What would *he* see in it?' The point of the jest immediately became a sting, and stung my conscience. For my mind's eye saw him stolid, frigid, perchance taking from its shelf some dreary Greek book, and translating at full length what some dismal sage said (and touched up afterwards, perhaps, for publication), when he banished some unlucky joker from Athens.

The incompatibility of Mr Barlow with all other portions of my young life but himself, the adamantine inadaptability of the man to my favourite fancies and amusements, is the thing for which I hate him most. What right had he to bore his way into my *Arabian Nights*? Yet he did. He was always hinting doubts of the veracity of Sinbad the Sailor. If he could have got hold of the Wonderful Lamp, I knew he would have trimmed it and lighted it, and delivered a lecture over it on the qualities of sperm-oil, with a glance at the whale-fisheries. He would so soon have found out – on mechanical principles – the peg in the neck of the Enchanted Horse, and would have turned it the right way in so workmanlike a manner, that the horse could never have got any height into the air, and the story couldn't have been. He would have proved, by map and compass, that there was no such kingdom as the delightful kingdom of Casgar, on the frontiers of Tartary. He would have caused the hypocritical young prig Harry to make an experiment – with the aid of a temporary building in the garden and a dummy – demonstrating that you couldn't let a choked hunchback down an Eastern chimney with a cord, and leave him upright on the hearth to terrify the Sultan's purveyor.

But the weightiest charge of all my charges against Mr

Barlow is, that he still walks the earth in various disguises, seeking to make a Tommy of me, even in my maturity. Irrepressible, instructive monomaniac, Mr Barlow fills my life with pitfalls, and lies hiding at the bottom to burst out upon me when I least expect him.

Frightening encounters

At this point I begin to see, cowering among my recollections – it may be born of turkey, or of pudding, or mince pie, or of these many fancies, jumbled with Robinson Crusoe on his desert island, Philip Quarll among the monkeys, Sandford and Merton with Mr Barlow, Mother Bunch and the Mask – or it may be the result of indigestion, assisted by imagination and over-doctoring – a prodigious nightmare.

It is so exceedingly indistinct, that I don't know why it's frightful – but I know it is. I can only make out that it is an immense array of shapeless things, which appear to be planted on a vast exaggeration of the lazy-tongs that used to bear the toy soldiers, and to be slowly coming close to my eyes, and receding to an immeasurable distance. When it comes closest, it is worse. In connection with it I descry remembrances of winter nights incredibly long; of being sent early to bed, as a punishment for some small offence, and waking in two hours, with a sensation of having been asleep two nights; of the leaden hopelessness of morning ever dawning; and the oppression of a weight of remorse.

There was also a figure that I once saw, just after dark, chalked upon a door in a little back lane near a country church – my first church. How young a child I may have been at the time I don't know, but it horrified me intensely – in connection with the churchyard, I suppose, for it smoked a pipe, and had a big hat with each of its ears stretching out in a horizontal line under the brim, and was not in itself more oppressive than a mouth from ear to ear, a pair of goggle eyes, and hands like two bunches of carrots, five in each, can make it – that is still vaguely alarming to me to recall (as I have often done) the running home, the looking behind, the horror of its following me; though whether disconnected from the door, or door and all, I can't say, and perhaps never could.

Plays and players

The first play! The promise; the hope deferred; the saving-clause of 'no fine weather, no play'; the more than Murphian, or H.P. of Bermondsey Square, scrutiny of the weather during the day! Willingly did I submit, at five o'clock that evening, to the otherwise, and at any other time, detestable ordeal of washing, and combing, and being made straight. I did not complain when the soap got into my eyes; I bore the scraping of the comb, and the rasping of the brush, without a murmur: I was going to the play, and I was happy. Dressed, of course, an hour too soon; drinking tea as a mere form and ceremony – for the tea might have been hay and hot water (not impossible), and the bread and butter might have been sawdust, for anything I could taste of it; sitting with petful impatience in the parlour, trying on the first pair of white kid gloves, making sure that the theatre would be burnt down, or mamma prevented, by some special interference of malignant demons, from having her dress fastened; or that (to a positive certainty) a tremendous storm of hail, rain, sleet, and thunder would burst out as we stepped into the cab, and send us, theatreless, to bed.

I went to the play, and was happy. The sweet, dingy, shabby little country theatre, I declared, and believed, to be much larger than either Drury Lane or Covent Garden, of which little Master Cheesewright – whose father was a tailor, and always had orders – was wont to brag! dear, narrow, uncomfortable, faded-cushioned, flea-haunted, single tier of boxes! The green curtain, with a hole in it, through which a bright eye peeped; the magnificent officers, in red and gold coats (it was a garrison town, of course), in the stage-box, who volunteered, during the acts, the popular catch of –

> Ah! how, Sophia, can you leave
> Your lover, and of hope bereave?

– for our special amusement and delectation, as I thought then, but, as I am inclined to fear now, under the influence of wine! The pit, with so few people in it; with the lady, who sold apples and oranges, siting in a remote corner, like Pomona in the sulks. And the play when it did begin – stupid, badly acted, badly got up as it very likely was. Our intense, fear-stricken admiration of the heroine, when she let her back hair down, and went mad, in blue. The buff-boats of Digby the manager. The funny man (there never was such a funny man) in a red scratch wig, who, when imprisoned in the deepest dungeon beneath the castle moat, sang a comic song about a leg of mutton. The sorry quadrille band in the orchestra pit, to our ears as scientifically melodious as though Costa had been conductor; Sivori, first fiddle; Richardson, flute; or Bottsini, double bass. The refreshment, administered to me by kind hands during the intervals of performance, never to be forgotten – oranges, immemorial sponge-cakes. The admonitions to 'sit up', the warning not to 'talk loud', in defiance of which (seeing condonatory smiles on the faces of those I loved) I screamed outright with laughter, when the funny man, in the after-piece, essaying to scale a first front door by means of a rope ladder, fell, ladder and all, to the ground. The final fall of the green curtain, followed by an aromatic perfume of orange-peel and lamp-oil, and the mysterious appearance of ghostly brown Holland draperies from the private boxes. Shawling, cloaking, home, and more primaries – for then it was when I for the first time 'sat up late', and for the first time ever tasted sandwiches after midnight, or imbibed a sip, a very small sip, of hot something and water.

Yet again, I find myself before that vast green curtain. Yet again, the music plays, amidst a buzz of voices, and that fragrant smell of orange-peel and oil. Anon, the magic bell commands the music to cease, and yet again The Play begins! The devoted dog of Montargis avenges the death of his master, foully murdered in the Forest of Bondy; and a humorous Peasant with a red nose and a very little hat, whom I take from this hour forth to my bosom as a friend (I think he was a Waiter or an Hostler at a village inn, but many years have passed since he and I have met), remarks that the sassigassity of that dog is indeed surprising; and evermore this jocular conceit will live in my remembrance fresh and unfading, overtopping all possible jokes, unto the end of time. Or now, I learn with bitter tears how poor Jane Shore, dressed all in white, and with her brown hair hanging down, went starving through the streets; or how George Barnwell killed the worthiest uncle that ever man had, and was afterwards so sorry for it that he ought to have been let off.

Richard III, in a very uncomfortable cloak, first appeared to me at this theatre, and made my heart leap with terror by backing up against the stage-box in which I was posted, while struggling for life against the virtuous Richmond. It was within these walls that I learnt as from a page of English history, how that fearful King slept in war-time on a sofa much too short for him, and how fearfully his conscience troubled his boots. There, too, I first saw the funny countryman, but countryman of noble principles, in a flowered waistcoat, crunch up his little hat and throw it on the ground, and pull off his coat, saying, 'Dom thee, squire, coom on with thy fistes then!' At which the lovely young woman who kept company with him (and who went out gleaning, in a narrow white muslin apron with five beautiful bars of five different-coloured ribbons across it) was so frightened for his sake, that she fainted away. Many wondrous secrets of Nature did I come to the knowledge of in that sanctuary: of which not the least terrific were, that the witches in *Macbeth* bore an awful resemblance to the Thane and other proper inhabitants of Scotland; and that the good King Duncan couldn't rest in his grave, but was constantly coming out of it and calling himself somebody else.

Pantomimes and clowns

Comes swift to comfort me, the Pantomime – stupendous Phenomenon! – when clowns are shot from loaded mortars into the great chandelier, bright constellation that it is; when Harlequins, covered all over with scales of pure gold, twist and sparkle, like amazing fish; when Pantaloon (whom I deem it no irreverence to compare in my own mind to my grandfather) puts red-hot pokers in his pocket, and cries, 'here's somebody coming!' or taxes the Clown with petty larceny, by saying, 'Now, I sawed you do it!'; when Everything is capable, with the greatest ease, of being changed into Anything; and 'Nothing is, but thinking makes it so.' Now, too, I perceive my first experience of the dreary sensation – often to return in after-life – of being unable, next day, to get back to the dull, settled world; of wanting to live for ever in the bright atmosphere I have quitted; of doting on the little Fairy, with the wand like a celestial Barber's Pole, and pining for a Fairy immortality along with her. Ah, she comes back, in many shapes, as my eye wanders down the highways and byways of my life, and goes as often, and has never yet stayed by me!

I also conceived a strong veneration for Clowns, and an

intense anxiety to know what they did with themselves out of pantomime time, and off the stage. I pestered my relations and friends with questions out of number concerning these gentry; whether their appetite for sausages and suchlike wares was always the same, and if so, at what expense they were maintained; whether they were ever taken up for pilfering other people's goods, or were forgiven by everybody because it was only done in fun; how it was that they got such beautiful complexions, and where they lived; and whether they were born Clowns, or gradually turned into Clowns as they grew up. On these and a thousand other points my curiosity was insatiable. Nor were my speculations confined to Clowns alone: they extended to Harlequins, Pantaloons, and Columbines, all of whom I believed to be real and veritable personages, existing in the same forms and characters all the year round. How often have I wished that the Pantaloon were my godfather! and how often thought that to marry a Columbine would be to attain the highest pitch of all human felicity!

The delights – the ten thousand million delights of a pantomime – come streaming upon me now – even of the pantomime which came lumbering down in Richardson's wagons at fairtime to the dull little town in which I had the honour to be brought up, and which a long row of small boys, with frills as white as they could be washed, and hands as clean as they would come, were taken to behold the glories of, in fair daylight.

I feel again all the pride of standing in a body on the platform, the observed of all observers in the crowd below, while the junior usher pays away twenty-four ninepences to a stout gentleman under a Gothic arch, with a hoop of variegated lamps swinging over his head. Again I catch a glimpse (too brief, alas!) of the lady with a green parasol in her hand, on the outside stage of the next show but one, who supports herself on one foot, and on the back of a majestic horse, blotting-paper coloured and white; and once again my eyes open wide with wonder, and my heart throbs with emotion, as I deliver my cardboard check into the very hands of the Harlequin himself, who, all glittering with spangles, and dazzling with many colours, deigns to give me a word of encouragement and commendation as I pass into the booth.

What was this – even this – to the glories of the inside, where, amid the smell of sawdust and orange-peel, sweeter far than violets to youthful noses, the first play being over, the lovers united, the ghost appeased, the baron killed, and everything made comfortable and pleasant – the pantomime itself begins! What words can describe the deep gloom of the opening scene, where a crafty magician holding a young lady in bondage was discovered, studying an enchanted book to the soft music of a gong! – or in what terms can I express the thrill of ecstasy with which, his magic power opposed by superior art, I beheld the monster himself converted into Clown! What mattered it that the stage was three yards wide, and four deep? *I* never saw it. I had no eyes, ears, or corporeal senses, but for the pantomime. And when its short career was ran, and the baron previously slaughtered, coming forward with his hand upon his heart, announced that for that favour Mr Richardson returned his most sincere thanks, and the performances would commence again in a quarter of an hour, what jest could equal the effects of the baron's indignation and surprise, when the Clown, unexpectedly peeping from behind the curtain, requested the audience 'not to believe it, for it was all gammon!' Who but a Clown could have called forth the roar of laughter that succeeded; and what witchery but a Clown's could have caused the junior usher himself to declare aloud, as he shook his sides and smote his knee in a moment of irrepressible joy, that that was the very best thing he had ever heard said!

The golden sounds of the overture in the first metropolitan pantomime, I remember, were alloyed by Mr Barlow. Click click, ting ting, bang bang, weedle weedle, bang! I recall the chilling air that ran across my frame and cooled my hot delight, as the thought occurred to me, 'This would never do for Mr Barlow!' After the curtain drew up, dreadful thoughts of Mr Barlow's considering the costumes of the Nymphs of the Nebula as being sufficiently opaque, obtruded themselves on my enjoyment. In the clown I perceived two persons; one a fascinating unaccountable creature of a hectic complexion, joyous in spirits though feeble in intellect, with flashes of brilliancy; the other a pupil for Mr Barlow. I thought how Mr Barlow would secretly rise early in the morning, and butter the pavement for *him*, and, when he had brought him down, would look severely out of his study window and ask *him* how he enjoyed the fun.

I thought how Mr Barlow would heat all the pokers in the house, and singe him with the whole collection, to bring him better acquainted with the properties of incandescent iron, on which he (Barlow) would fully expatiate. I pictured Mr Barlow's instituting a comparison between the clown's conduct at his studies – drinking up the ink, licking his copy-book, and using his head for blotting-paper – and that of the already mentioned young prig of prigs, Harry, sitting at the Barlovian feet, sneakingly pretending to be in a rapture of youthful knowledge. I thought how soon Mr Barlow would smooth the clown's hair down, instead of letting it stand erect in three tufts; and how, after a couple of years or so with Mr Barlow, he would keep his legs close together when he walked, and would take his hands out of his big loose pockets, and wouldn't have a jump left in him.

I was brought up to town in 1819 and 1820 to behold the splendour of Christmas pantomimes and the humour of Grimaldi, in whose honour I am informed I clapped my hands with great precocity, but I had not arrived at man's estate when he left the stage and my recollections of his acting are, to my loss, but shadowy and imperfect.

Even in what are generally held to be years of greater maturity, I have betaken myself not infrequently to that jocund world of Pantomime, where there is no affliction or calamity that leaves the least impression; where a man may tumble into the broken ice, or dive into the kitchen fire, and only be the droller for the accident; where babies may be knocking about and sat upon, or choked with gravy spoons, in the process of feeding, and yet no Coroner be wanted, nor anybody made uncomfortable; where workmen may fall from the top of a house to the bottom, or even from the bottom of a house to the top, and sustain no injury to the brain, need no hospital, leave no young children; where everyone, in short, is so superior to the accidents of life, though encountering them at every turn, that I suspect this to be the secret (though many persons may not present it to themselves) of the general enjoyment which an audience of vulnerable spectators, liable to pain and sorrow, find in this class of entertainment.

The Harlequin's Wand

When I was a little animal revolting to the sense of sight (for I date from the period when small boys had a dreadful, high-shouldered sleeved strait-waistcoat put upon them by their keepers, over which their dreadful little trousers were buttoned tight, so that they roamed about disconsolate, with their hands in their pockets, like dreadful little pairs of tongs that were vainly looking for the rest of the fire-irons); when I was the object of just contempt and horror to all well-constituted minds, and when, according to the best of my remembrance and self-examination in the past, even my small shirt was an airy supposition which had no sleeves to it and stopped short at my chest; when I was this exceedingly uncomfortable and disreputable father of my present self, I remember to have been taken, upon a New Year's day, to the Bazaar in Soho Square, London, to have a present bought for me. A distinct impression yet lingers in my soul that a grim and unsympathetic old personage of the female gender, flavoured with musty dry lavender, dressed in black crape, and wearing a pocket in which something clinked at my ear as we went along, conducted me on this occasion to the World of Toys. I remember to have been incidentally escorted a little way down some conveniently retired street diverging from Oxford Street, for the purpose of being shaken; and nothing has ever slaked the burning thirst for vengeance awakened in me by this female's manner of insisting upon wiping my nose herself (I had a cold and a pocket-handkerchief), on the screw principle. For many years I was unable to excogitate the reason why she should have undertaken to make me a present. In the exercise of a matured judgment, I have now no doubt that she had done something bad in her youth and that she took me out as an act of expiation.

Nearly lifted off my legs by this adamantine woman's grasp of my glove (another fearful invention of those dark ages – a muffler, and fastened at the wrist like a handcuff), I was hauled through the Bazaar. My tender imagination (or conscience) represented certain small apartments in corners, resembling wooden cages, wherein I have since seen reason to suppose that ladies' collars and the like are tried on, as being, either dark places of confinement for refractory youth, or dens in which the lions were kept who fattened on boys who said they didn't care. Suffering tremendous terrors from the vicinity of these avenging mysteries, I was put before an expanse of toys, apparently about a hundred and twenty acres in extent, and was asked what I would have to the value of half-a-crown? Having first selected every object at half-a-guinea, and then staked all the aspirations of my nature on every object at five shillings, I hit, as a last resource, upon a Harlequin's Wand – painted parti-coloured, like the Harlequin himself.

Although of a highly hopeful and imaginative temperament, I had no fond belief that the possession of this talisman would enable me to change Mrs Pipchin at my side into anything agreeable. When I tried the effect of the wand upon her, behind her bonnet, it was rather as a desperate experiment founded on the conviction that she could change into nothing worse, than with any latent hope that she would change into something better. Howbeit, I clung to the delusion that when I got home I should do something magical with this wand; and I did not resign all hope of it until I had, by many trials, proved the wand's total incapacity. It had no effect on the staring obsti-nacy of my rocking-hose; it produced no live Clown out of the hot beefsteak-pie at dinner; it could not even influence the minds of my honoured parents to the extent of suggesting the decency and propriety of their giving me an invitation to sit up to supper.

The failure of this wand is my very first memorable associa-tion with a New Year's Day. Other wands have failed me since, but the Day itself has become their substitute, and is always potent. It is the best Harlequin's Wand I have ever had. It has wrought strange transformations – no more of them – its power of reproducing the Past is admirable. Nothing ever goes wrong with that trick. I throw up and catch my little wand of New Year's Day, beat the dust of years from the ground at my feet with it, twinkle it a little, and Time reverses his hour-glass, and flies back, much faster than he ever flew forward.

My nurse's stories

It would be difficult to overstate the intensity and accuracy of an intelligent child's observations. At that impressible time of life, it must sometimes produce a fixed impression. If the fixed impression be of an object terrible to the child, it will be (for want of reasoning upon) inseparable from great fear. Force the child at such a time, be Spartan with it, send it into the dark against its will, and you had better murder it.

I can see back to very early days indeed, when my bad dreams – they were frightful, though my more mature understanding has never made out why – were of an interminable sort of rope-making, with long minute filaments for strands, which, when they were spun home together close to my eyes, occasioned screaming.

But when revisiting the associations of my childhood as recorded in the prologue to these notes, my experience in this wise was made quite inconsiderable and of no account, by the quantity of places and people – utterly impossible places and people, but none the less alarmingly real – that I found I had been introduced to by my nurse before I was six years old, and used to be forced to go back to at night without at all wanting to go. If we all knew our own minds (in a more enlarged sense than the popular acceptation of that phrase), I suspect we should find our nurses responsible for most of the dark corners we are forced to go back to against our wills.

The first diabolical character who intruded himself on my peaceful youth was a certain Captain Murderer. This wretch must have been an offshoot of the Blue Beard family, but I had no suspicion of the consanguinity in those times. His warning name would seem to have awakened no general prejudice against him, for he was admitted into the best society and possessed immense wealth. Captain Murderer's mission was matrimony, and the gratification of a cannibal appetite with tender brides. On his marriage morning, he always caused both sides of the way to church to be planted with curious flowers; and when his bride said, 'Dear Captain Murderer, I never saw flowers like these before: what are they called?' he answered, 'They are called Garnish for house-lambs', and laughed at his ferocious practical-joke in a horrid manner, disquieting the minds of the noble bridal company, with a very sharp show of teeth, then displayed for the first time. He made love in a coach and six, and married in a coach and twelve, and all his horses were milk-white horses with one red spot on the back which he caused to be hidden by the harness. For, the spot *would* come there, though every horse was milk-white when Captain Murderer bought him. And the spot was young bride's blood. (To this terrific point I am indebted for my personal experience of a shudder and cold beads on the forehead.) When Captain Murderer had made an end of feasting and revelry, and had dismissed the noble guests, and was alone with his wife on the day month after their marriage, it was his whimsical custom to produce a golden rolling-pin and a silver pie-board. Now, there was a special feature in the Captain's courtships, that he always asked if the young lady could make pie-crust; and if she couldn't by nature or education, she was taught. Well. When the bride saw Captain Murderer produce the golden rolling-pin and silver pie-board, she remembered this, and turned up her laced silk sleeves to make a pie. The Captain brought out a silver pie-dish of immense capacity, and the Captain brought out flour and butter and eggs and all things needful, except the inside of the pie: of materials for the staple of the pie itself, the Captain brought out none. Then said the lovely bride, 'Dear Captain Murderer, I see no meat.' The Captain humorously retorted, 'Look in the glass.' She looked in the glass, but still she saw no meat, and then the Captain roared with laughter, and suddenly frowning and drawing his sword, bade her roll out the crust. So she rolled out the crust, dropping large tears upon it all the time because he was so cross, and when she had lined the dish with crust all ready to fit the top, the Captain called out, 'I see the meat in the glass!' And the bride looked up at the glass, just in time to see the Captain cutting her head off; and he chopped her in pieces, and peppered her, and salted her, and put her in the pie, and sent it to the baker's, and ate it all, and picked the bones.

The young woman who brought me acquaintance with Captain Murderer had a fiendish enjoyment of my terrors, and used to begin, I remember – as a sort of introductory overture – by clawing the air with both hands, and uttering a long low hollow groan. So acutely did I suffer from this ceremony in combination with this infernal Captain, that I sometimes used to plead I thought I was hardly strong enough and old enough to hear the story again just yet. But, she never spared me one word of it, and indeed commended to my lips the awful chalice which featured in the tale as the only preservative known to science against 'The Black Cat' – a weird and glaring-eyed supernatural Tom, who was reputed to prowl about the world by night, sucking the breath of infancy, and who was endowed with a special thirst (as I was given to understand) for mine.

This female bard – may she have been repaid my debt of obligation to her in the matter of nightmares and perspirations! – reappears in my memory as the daughter of a shipwright. Her name was Mercy, though she had none on me. She was a sallow woman with a fishy eye, an aquiline nose, and a green gown, one of whose stories featured a brave and lovely servant-maid (whom the aquiline-nosed woman, though not at all answering the description, always mysteriously implied to be herself).

She made a standing pretence which greatly assisted in forcing me back to a number of hideous places that I would by all means have avoided. This pretence was, that all her ghost stories had occurred to her own relations. Politeness towards a meritorious family, therefore, forbade my doubting them, and they acquired an air of authentication that impaired my digestive powers for life. There was a narrative concerning an unearthly animal foreboding death, which appeared in the open street to a parlour-maid who 'went to fetch the beer' for supper; first (as I now recall it) assuming the likeness of a black dog, and gradually rising on its hind-legs and swelling into the semblance of some quadruped greatly surpassing a hippopotamus: which apparition – not because I deemed it to be in the least improbable, but because I felt it to be really too large to bear – I feebly endeavoured to explain away. But, on Mercy's retorting with wounded dignity that the parlour-maid was her own sister-in-law, I perceived there was no hope, and resigned myself to this zoological phenomenon as one of my many pursuers. There was another narrative describing the apparition of a young woman who came out of a glass-case and haunted another young woman until the other young woman questioned it and elicited that its bones (Lord! To think of its being particular about its bones!) were buried under the glass-case, whereas she required them to be interred, with every Undertaking solemnity up to twenty-four pound ten, in another particular place. This narrative I considered I had a personal interest in disproving, because we had glass-cases at home, and how, otherwise, was I to be guaranteed from the intrusion of young women requiring *me* to bury them up to twenty-four pound ten, when I had only twopence a week? But my remorseless nurse cut the ground from under my tender feet, by informing me that She was the other young woman; and I couldn't say 'I don't believe you'; it was not possible.

This same narrator, who had a Ghoulish pleasure, I have long been persuaded, in terrifying me to the utmost confines of my reason, had another authentic anecdote within her own experience, founded, I now believe, upon *Raymond and Agnes, or the Bleeding Nun*. She said it happened to her brother-in-law, who was immensely rich – which my father was not; and immensely tall – which my father was not. It was always a point with this Ghoul to present my dearest relations and friends to my youthful mind under circumstances of disparaging contrast. The brother-in-law was riding once through a forest on a magnificent horse (we had no magnificent horse at our house), attended by a favourite and valuable Newfoundland dog (we had no dog), when he found himself benighted, and came to an Inn. A dark woman opened the door, and he asked her if he could have a bed there. She answered yes, and put his horse in the stable, and took him into a room where there were two dark men. While he was at supper, a parrot in the room began to talk, saying, 'Blood, blood! Wipe up the blood!' Upon which one of the dark men wrung the parrot's neck and said he was fond of roasted parrots, and he meant to have this one for breakfast in the morning. After eating and drinking heartily, the immensely rich, tall brother-in-law went up to his bed; but he was rather vexed, because they had shut his dog in the stable, saying that they never allowed dogs in the house. He sat very quiet for more than an hour, thinking and thinking, when, just as his candle was burning out, he heard a scratch at the door. He opened the door, and there was his Newfoundland dog! The dog came softly in, smelt about him, went straight to some straw in the corner which the dark men had said covered apples, tore the straw away, and disclosed two sheets steeped in blood. Just at that moment the candle went out, and the brother-in-law, looking through a chink in the door, saw the two dark men stealing upstairs; one armed with a dagger that long (about five feet); the other carrying a chopper, a sack, and a spade. Having no remembrance of the close of this adventure, I suppose my faculties to have been always so frozen with terror at this stage of it, that the power of listening stagnated within me for some quarter of an hour.

Such are a few of the journeys that I was forced to make, against my will, when I was very young and unreasoning.

Birthdays

I can very well remember being taken out to visit some peach-faced creature in a blue sash, and shoes to correspond, whose life I supposed to consist entirely of birthdays. Upon seed-cake, sweet wine and shining presents, that glorified young person seemed to me to be excessively reared. At so early a stage of my travels did I assist at the anniversary of her nativity (and become enamoured of her), that I had not yet acquired the recondite knowledge that a birthday is the common property of all who are born, but supposed it to be a special gift bestowed by the favouring Heavens on that one distinguished infant. There was no other company, and we sat in a shady bower – under a table, as my better (or worse) knowledge leads me to believe – and were regaled with saccharine substances and liquids, until it was time to part. A bitter powder was administered to me next morning, and I was wretched. On the whole, a pretty accurate foreshadowing of my more mature experiences in such wise!

Then came the time when, inseparable from one's own birthday, was a certain sense of merit, a consciousness of well-earned distinction. When I regarded my birthday as a graceful achievement of my own, a monument of my perseverance, independence, and good sense, redounding greatly to my honour. This was at about the period when Olympia Squires became involved in the anniversary. Olympia was most beautiful (of course), and I loved her to that degree, that I used to be obliged to get out of my little bed in the night, expressly to exclaim to Solitude, 'O, Olympia Squires!' Visions of Olympia, clothed entirely in sage-green, from which I infer a defectively educated taste on the part of her respected parents, who were necessarily unacquainted with the South Kensington Museum, still arise before me. Truth is sacred, and the visions are crowned by a shining white beaver bonnet, impossibly suggestive of a little feminine postboy.

My memory presents a birthday when Olympia and I were taken by an unfeeling relative – some cruel uncle, or the like – to a slow torture called an Orrery (a clockwork model of the planetary system). The terrible instrument was set up at the local Theatre, and I had expressed a profane wish in the morning that it was a Play: for which a serious aunt had probed my conscious deep, and my pocket deeper, by reclaiming a bestowed half-crown. It was a venerable and a shabby Orrery, at least one thousand stars and twenty-five comets behind the age. Nevertheless, it was awful. When the low-spirited gentleman with a wand said 'Ladies and gentlemen' (meaning particularly

Olympia and me) 'the lights are about to be put out, but there is not the slightest cause for alarm', it was very alarming. Then the planets and stars began. Sometimes they wouldn't come on, sometimes they wouldn't go off, sometimes they had holes in them, and mostly they didn't seem to be good likenesses. All this time the gentleman with the wand was going on in the dark (tapping away at the heavenly bodies between whiles, like a wearisome woodpecker), about a sphere revolving on its own axis eight hundred and ninety-seven thousand millions of times – or miles – in two hundred and sixty-three thousand five hundred and twenty-four millions of something elses, until I thought if this was a birthday it were better never to have been born. Olympia, also, became much depressed, and we both slumbered and woke cross, and still the gentleman was going on in the dark – whether up in the stars, or down on the stage, it would have been hard to make out, if it had been worth trying – cyphering away about planes of orbits, to such an infamous extent that Olympia, stung to madness, actually kicked me.

A pretty spectacle, when the lights were turned up again, and all the schools in the town (including the National, who had come in for nothing, and serve them right, for they were always throwing stones) were discovered with exhausted counte-nances, screwing their knuckles into their eyes, or clutching their heads of hair. A pretty birthday speech when Dr Sleek of the City-free bobbed up his powdered head in the stage-box, and said that before this assembly dispersed he really must beg to express his entire approval of a lecture as improving, as informing, as devoid of anything that could call a blush into the cheek of youth, as any it had ever been his lot to hear delivered. A pretty birthday altogether, when Astronomy couldn't leave poor small Olympia Squires and me alone, but must put an end to our loves! For, we never got over it; the threadbare Orrery outwore our mutual tenderness; the man with the wand was too much for the boy with the bow.

My preparatory school

It seems as if my schools were doomed to be the sport of change. I have faint recollections of a Preparatory Day-School, which I have sought in vain, and which must have been pulled down to make a new street, ages ago. I have dim impressions, scarcely amounting to a belief, that it was over a dyer's shop. I know that you went up steps to it; that you frequently grazed your knees in doing so; that you generally got your leg over the scraper, in trying to scrape the mud off a very unsteady little shoe. The mistress of the Establishment holds no place in my memory; but rampant upon one's eternal doormat, in an eternal entry long and narrow, is a puffy pug-dog, with a personal animosity towards me, who triumphs over Time. The bark of that baleful Pug, a certain radiating way he had of snapping at my undefended legs, the ghastly grinning of his most black muzzle and white teeth, and the insolence of his crisp tail curled like a pastoral crook, all live and flourish. From an otherwise unaccountable association of him with a fiddle, I conclude that he was of French extraction, and his name 'Fidèle'. He belonged to some female, chiefly inhabiting a back-parlour, whose life appears to me to have been consumed in sniffing, and in wearing a brown beaver bonnet. For her, he would sit up and balance cake upon his nose, and not eat it until twenty had been counted. To the best of my belief I was once called in to witness this performance; when, unable, even in his milder moments, to ensure my presence, he instantly made at me, cake and all.

Why a something in mourning, called 'Miss Frost', should still connect itself with my preparatory school, I am unable to say. I retain no impression of the beauty of Miss Frost – if she were beautiful; or of the mental fascinations of Miss Frost – if she were accomplished; yet her name and her black dress hold an enduring place in my remembrance. An equally impersonal boy, whose name has long since shaped itself unalterably into 'Master Mawls', is not to be dislodged from my brain. Retaining no vindictive feelings towards Mawls – no feeling whatever, indeed – I infer that neither he nor I can have loved Miss Frost. My first impression of Death and Mourning is associated with this formless pair. We all three nestled awfully in a corner one wintry day, when the wind was blowing shrill, with Miss Frost's pinafore over our heads; and Miss Frost told us in a whisper about somebody being 'screwed down'. It is the only distinct recollection I preserve of these impalpable creatures, except a suspicion that the manners of Master Mawls were susceptible of much improvement. Generally speaking, I may observe that whenever I see a child intently occupied with its nose, to the exclusion of all other subjects of interest, my mind reverts, in a flash, to Master Mawls.

Pulpit passions

Whenever religion is resorted to, as a strong drink, and as an escape from the dull monotonous round of home, those of its minsters who pepper the highest will be the surest to please. They who strew the Eternal Path with the greatest amount of brimstone, and who most ruthlessly tread down the flowers and leaves that grow by the wayside, will be voted the most right-eous; and they who enlarge with the greatest pertinacity on the difficulty of getting into heaven, will be considered by all true believers certain of going there: though it will be hard to say by what process of reasoning this conclusion is arrived at. It is so at home, and it is so abroad.

Half the misery and hypocrisy of the Christian world arises (as I take it) from a stubborn determination to refuse the New Testament as a sufficient guide in itself, and to force the Old Testament into alliance with it – whereof comes all manner of camel-swallowing and of gnat-straining.

I have no curiosity, these days, to hear powerful preachers. Time was, when I was dragged by the hair of my head, as one may say, to hear too many. On summer evenings, when every flower, and tree, and bird, might have been better addressed by my soft young heart, I have in my day been caught in the palm of a female hand by the crown, have been violently scrubbed from the neck to the roots of the hair as a purification for the Temple, and have then been carried off highly charged with spontaneous electricity, to be steamed like a potato in the unventilated breath of the powerful Boanerges Boiler and his congregation, until what small mind I had was quite steamed out of me. In which pitiable plight I have been haled out of the place of meeting, at the conclusion of the exercise, and cate-chised respecting Boanerges Boiler, his fifthly, his sixthly, and his seventhly, until I have regarded that reverend person in the light of a most dismal and oppressive Charade.

Time was, when I was carried off to platform assemblages at which no human child, whether of wrath or grace, could possi-bly keep its eyes open, and when I felt the fatal sleep stealing over me, and when I gradually heard the orator in possession, spinning and humming like a great top, until he rolled, collapsed, and tumbled over, and I discovered to my burning shame and fear, that as to that last stage it was not he, but I.

I have sat under Boanerges when he has specifically addressed himself to us – us, the infants – and at this present writing I hear his lumbering jocularity (which never amused us, though we basely pretended that it did), and I behold his big round face, and I look up the inside of his outstretched coat-sleeve as if he were a telescope with the stopper on, and I hate him with an unwholesome hatred for two hours. Through such means did it come to pass that I knew the powerful preacher from beginning to end, all over and all through, while I was very young, and that I left him behind me at an early period of life. Peace be with him! More peace than he ever brought to me!

Other recollections

What else do I remember? Let me see.

I recollect when I was a very young child indeed having a fancy that the reflection of the moon in water was a path to Heaven, trodden by the spirits of good people on their way to God; and this old feeling often came over me again in after-life, when I watched it on a tranquil sea at night.

I remember the school in Chatham, presided over by a little pale clergyman, where I began an irregular, rambling education. (On the night before we came away from that town my good master came flitting among the packing cases to give me Goldsmith's *Bee* as a keepsake. Which I kept for his sake, and its own, a long time afterwards.) My notions of the theological positions to which my Catechism bound me were not at all accurate; for I have a lively remembrance that I supposed my declaration that I was to 'walk in the same all the days of my life' laid me under an obligation always to go through the town from our house in one particular direction, and never to vary it by turning down by the wheelwright's or up by the mill.

I remember the inn where my friends used to put up, and where we used to go to see parents, and to have salmon and fowls, and to be tipped. It had an ecclesiastical sign – 'The

Mitre' – and a bar that seemed to be the next best thing to a bishopric, it was so snug. I loved the landlord's youngest daughter to distraction – but let that pass. It was in this inn that I was cried over by my rosy little sister, because I had acquired a black eye in a fight.

I remember tasting my first oyster. A remarkable sensation! I feel it slipping down my throat now, like a sort of maritime castor-oil, and am again bewildered by an unsatisfactory doubt whether it really *was* the oyster which made that mysterious disappearance, or whether I am going to begin to taste it presently.

I remember to have had my ears boxed for informing a lady visitor who made a morning call at our house, that a certain ornamental object on the table, which was covered with marbled paper, 'wasn't marble'. Years of reflection upon this injury have fully satisfied me that the honest object in question never imposed upon anybody; further, that my honoured parents, though both of a sanguine temperament, never can have conceived it possible that it might, could, should, would, or did, impose upon anybody. Yet, I have no doubt that I had my ears boxed for violating a tacit compact in the family and among the family visitors, to blink the stubborn fact of the marbled paper, and to agree upon a fiction of real marble.

I remember the first funeral I attended. It was a fair representative funeral after its kind, being that of the husband of a married servant, once my nurse. She married for money. Sally Flanders, after a year or two of matrimony, became the relict of Flanders, a small master builder; and either she or Flanders had done me the honour to express a desire that I should 'follow'. I may have been seven or eight years old – young enough, certainly, to feel rather alarmed by the expression, as not knowing where the invitation was held to terminate, and how far I was expected to follow the deceased Flanders. Consent being given by the heads of houses, I was jobbed up into what was pronounced at home decent mourning (comprehending somebody else's shirt, unless my memory deceives me), and was admonished that if, when the funeral was in action, I put my hands in my pockets, or took my eyes out of my pocket-handkerchief, I was personally lost, and my family disgraced.

On the eventful day, having tried to get myself into a disastrous frame of mind, and having formed a very poor opinion of myself because I couldn't cry, I repaired to Sally's. Sally was an excellent creature, and had been a good wife to old Flanders, but the moment I saw her I knew that she was not in her own natural state. She formed a sort of Coat of Arms, grouped with a smelling-bottle, a handkerchief, an orange, a bottle of vinegar. Flanders's sister, her own sister, Flanders's brother's wife and two neighbouring gossips – all in mourning, and all ready to hold her whenever she fainted. At sight of poor little me she became much agitated (agitating me much more), and having exclaimed, 'O here's dear Master Charles!' became hysterical, and swooned, as if I had been the death of her. An affecting scene followed, during which I was handed about and poked at her by various people, as if I were the bottle of salts. Reviving a little, she embraced me, said, 'You knew him well, dear Master Charles, and he knew you!' and fainted again: which, as the rest of the Coat of Arms soothingly said, 'done her credit'. Now, I knew that she needn't have fainted unless she liked, and that she wouldn't have fainted unless it had been expected of here, quite as well as I know it at this day. It made me feel uncomfortable and hypocritical besides. I was not sure but that it might be manners in *me* to faint next, and I resolved to keep my eye on Flanders's uncle, and if I saw any signs of his going in that direction, to go too, politely. But Flanders's uncle (who was a weak little retail grocer) had only one idea, which was that we all wanted tea; and he handed us cups of tea all round, incessantly, whether we refused or not. There was a young nephew of Flanders's present, to whom Flanders, it was rumoured, had left nineteen guineas. He drank all the tea that was offered him, this nephew – amounting, I should say, to several quarts – and ate as much plum-cake as he could possibly come by; but he felt it to be decent mourning that he should now and then stop in the midst of a lump of cake, and appear to forget that his mouth was full, in the contemplation of his uncle's memory.

I felt all this to be the fault of the undertaker, who was handing us gloves on a tea-tray, as if they were muffins, and tying us into cloaks (mine had to be pinned up all round, it was so long for me), because I knew that he was making game. So, when we got out into the streets, and I constantly disarranged the procession by tumbling on all the people behind me because my cloak was so long, I felt that we were all making game. I was truly sorry for Flanders, but I knew that it was no reason why we should be trying (the women with their heads in hoods like coal-scuttles with the black side outward) to keep in step with a man in a scarf, carrying a thing like a mourning spy-glass, which he was going to open presently and sweep the horizon with. I knew that we should not all have been speaking in one particular key-note struck by the undertaker, if we had not been making game.

When we returned to Sally's, it was all of a piece. The continued impossibility of getting on without plum-cake; the ceremonious apparition of a pair of decanters containing port and sherry and cork; Sally's sister at the tea-table, clinking the best crockery and shaking her head mournfully every time she looked down into the teapot, as if it were the tomb; the Coat of Arms again, and Sally as before; lastly, the words of consolation administered to Sally when it was considered right that she should 'come round nicely'; which were, that the deceased had had 'as com-for-ta-ble a funeral as comfort-able could be!'

Other funerals have I seen with grown-up eyes, since that day, of which the burden has been the same childish burden. Making game. Real affliction, real grief and solemnity, have been outraged, and the funeral has been 'performed'. The waste for which the funeral customs of many tribes of savages are conspicuous, has attended these civilised obsequies; and once, and twice, have I wished in my soul that if the waste must be, that they would let the undertaker bury the money, and let me bury the friend.

The scenes of my childhood

What man is there, over whose mind a bright spring morning does not exercise a magic influence – carrying him back to the days of his childish sports, and conjuring up before him the old green field with its gently-waving trees, where the birds sang as he has never heard them since – where the butterfly fluttered far more gaily than he ever sees him now, in all his ramblings – where the air blew more freshly over greener glass, and sweeter-smelling flowers – where everything wore a richer and more brilliant hue than it is ever dressed in now! Such are the deep feelings of childhood, and such are the impressions which every object stamps upon the heart! The hardy traveller wanders through the maze of thick and pathless woods, where the sun's rays never shone, and Heaven's pure air never played; he stands on the brink of the roaring waterfall, and, giddy and bewildered, watches the foaming mass as it leaps from stone to stone, and from crag to crag; he lingers in the fertile plains of a land of perpetual sunshine, and revels in the luxury of their balmy breath. But what are the deep forests, or the thundering waters, or the richest landscapes that bounteous nature ever spread, to charm the eyes, and captivate the senses of man, compared with the recollection of the old scenes of his early youth? Magic scenes indeed; for the fancies of childhood dressed them in colours brighter than the rainbow, and almost as fleeting!

The sleepy old town of Rochester, the place with which my childhood is inseparably associated, is exactly forty-two miles and three-quarters from Hyde Park Corner. As I peeped about its old corners with interest and wonder when I was a very little child, few people can find a greater charm in that ancient city than I do. It has a long, straggling, quiet High Street, full of gables with old beams and timbers carved into strange faces. It is oddly garnished with a queer old clock that projects over the pavement out of a grave red-brick building, as if Time carried on an active stroke of work in Rochester, in the old days of the Romans, and the Saxons, and the Normans; and down to the times of King John, when the rugged castle – I will not undertake to say how many years old then – was abandoned to the centuries of weather which have so defaced the dark apertures in its walls, that the ruin looks as if the rooks and daws had pecked its eyes out.

From the balustrades of Rochester Bridge, on a fine sunny morning, one could contemplate a charming scene. On the left of the spectator lay the ruined wall, broken in many places, and in some, overhanging the narrow beach below in rude and heavy masses. Huge knots of sea-weed hung upon the jagged and pointed stones, trembling in every breath of wind; and the green ivy clung mournfully round the dark and ruined battlements. Behind it rose the ancient castle, its towers roofless, and its massive walls crumbling away, but telling us proudly of its own might and strength, as when, seven hundred years ago, it rang with the clash of arms, or resounded with the noise of feasting and revelry. On either side, the banks of the Medway,

covered with cornfields and pastures, with here and there a
windmill, or a distant church, stretched away as far as the eye
could see, presenting a rich and varied landscape, rendered
more beautiful by the changing shadows which passed swiftly
across it, as the thin and half-formed clouds skimmed away in
the light of the morning sun. The river, reflecting the clear blue
of the sky, glistened and sparkled as it flowed noiselessly on;
and the oars of the fishermen dipped into the water with a clear
and liquid sound, as the heavy but picturesque boats glided
slowly down the stream.

A little way out of Rochester, on the road to Gravesend and
not thirty miles from London, one came to some very pretty
country and to Gad's Hill – Shakespeare's Gads Hill, where
Falstaff engaged in the robbery on the men with the treasure.
On the summit, with a noble prospect at the side and behind,
looking down into the valley of the Medway, there stood what I
used to look upon as a wonderful mansion (which God knows it
isn't) when I was a very odd little child. (The spot where the
robbery was committed was before the door and a little rustic
ale house called 'The Sir John Falstaff' was over the way – had
been over the way, ever since, in honour of the event.) It was a
quaint little country house of Queen Anne's time, composed of
grave red brick, which on closer acquaintance I would find to be
old-fashioned, plain and comfortable. Cobham Woods and Park
were behind the house; the distant Thames in front; the
Medway, with Rochester, and its old castle, and cathedral, on
one side. I much admired this stupendous property when I was
a very little child indeed, not more than half as old as nine, and
it used to be a treat for me to be brought to look at it. I thought
it the most beautiful house (I suppose because of its famous old
cedar trees) ever seen and it was certainly the great landmark
of the whole neighbourhood. The spot and the very house are
literally 'a dream of my childhood'. My father, seeing me so
extraordinarily fond of it, often said to me, 'If you are very
persevering, and work hard, you might some day come to live in
it.' When I was nine I came by myself to gaze at it. I knew, of
course, very queer small boy that I was, that my father's predic-
tion was impossible, but I now have every reason to believe that
what he said was true.

I was familiar with the intricacies of Chatham Dockyard and
fascinated, in particular, by a Chinese Enchanter's Car. There
is a great reservoir of water where timber is steeped in various

Gad's Hill Place, Rochester.

temperatures, as a part of its seasoning process. Above it, on a tramroad supported by pillars, is the Car, which fishes the logs up, when sufficiently steeped, and rolls smoothly away with them to stack them. I used to think that I should like to play at Chinese Enchanter, and to have that apparatus placed at my disposal by a beneficent country.

Satisfaction is demanded

It was on a New Year's day that I fought a duel. Furious with love and jealousy. I 'went out' with another gentleman of honour, to assert my passion for the loveliest and falsest of her sex. I estimate the age of that young lady to have been about nine – my own age, about ten. I knew the Queen of my soul, as 'the youngest Miss Clickitt but one'. I had offered marriage, and my proposals had been very favourably received, though not definitely closed with. At which juncture, my enemy – Paynter, by name – arose out of some abyss or cavern, and came between us. The appearance of the fiend Paynter, in the Clickitt Paradise,

was altogether so mysterious and sudden, that I don't know
where he came from; I only know that I found him, on the surface
of this earth, one afternoon late in the month of December,
playing at hot boiled beans and butter with the youngest Miss
Clickitt but one. His conduct on that occasion was such, that I
sent a friend to Paynter. After endeavouring with levity to evade
the question, by pulling the friend's hat off and throwing it into
a cabbage-garden, Paynter referred my messenger to his cousin
– a goggle-eyed Being worthy of himself. Preliminaries were
arranged, and by my own express stipulation the meeting was
appointed for New Year's Day, in order that one of us might quit
this state of existence on a day of mark.

I passed a considerable portion of the last evening of the old
year in arranging my affairs. I addressed a pathetic letter, and
a goldfinch, to the youngest Miss Clickitt but one (to be delivered into her own hands by my friend, in case I should fail), and
I wrote another letter for my sister, and made a disposition of
my property: which consisted of books, some coloured drawings
of Bamfylde Moore Carew, Mrs Shipton, and others, in a florid
state of art, and a rather choice collection of marbles. While
engaged in these last duties, I suffered the keenest anguish,
and wept abundantly. The combat was to begin with fists, but
was to end anyhow. Dark presentiments overshadowed my
mind, because I had heard, on reliable authority, that Paynter
(whose father was paymaster of some regiment stationed in the
seaport where the conflict impended) had a dirk and meant the
worst. I had no other arms, myself, than a blank cartridge, of
which ammunition we used to get driblets from the soldiers
when they practised, by following them up with tobacco, and
bribing them with pipes-full screwed in old copies, to pretend
to load and not to do it. This cartridge my friend and second
had specially recommended me, on the combat's assuming a
mortal appearance, to explode on the fell Paynter: which I, with
some indefinite view of blowing that gentleman up, had undertaken to do, though the engineering details of the operation
were not at all adjusted.

We met in a sequestered trench, among the fortifications.
Paynter had access to some old military stores, and appeared
on the ground in the regulation-cap of a full-grown Private of
the Second Royal Veteran Battalion – I see the boy now, coming
from among the stinging-nettles in an angle of the trench, and
making my blood run cold by his terrible appearance.

Preliminaries were arranged, and we were to begin the struggle – this again was my express stipulation – on the word being given, 'The youngest Miss Clickitt but one!' At this crisis, a difference of opinion arose between the seconds, touching the exact construction of that article in the code of honour which prohibits 'hitting below the waistcoat'; and I rather think it arose from *my* second's having manoeuvred the whole of *my* waistcoat into the neighbourhood of my chin. However it arose, expressions were used which Paynter, who I found had a very delicate sense of humour, could not permit to pass. He immediately dropped his guard, and appealed to me whether it was not our duty most reluctantly to forego our own gratification until the two gentlemen in attendance on us had established their honour? I warmly assented; I did more; I immediately took my friend aside, and lent him the cartridge. But, so unworthy of our confidence were those seconds that they declined, in spite alike of our encouragements and our indignant remonstrances, to engage. This made it plain both to Paynter and myself, that we had but one painful course to take; which was, to leave them ('with loathing', Paynter said, and I highly approved), and go away arm in arm. He gave me to understand as we went along that he too was a victim of the youngest Miss Clickitt but one, and I became exceedingly fond of him before we parted.

My father's library

My father had invested in a small collection of books (*Cooke's Pocket Library*) which were kept in a little room upstairs, to which I had access (for it adjoined my own) and which nobody else in our house ever troubled. From that blessed little room, Roderick Random, Peregrine Pickle, Humphrey Clinker, Tom Jones, the Vicar of Wakefield, Don Quixote, Gil Blas, and Robinson Crusoe, came out, a glorious host, to keep me company. They kept alive my fancy, and my hope of something beyond that place and time – they, and the *Arabian Nights*, and the *Tales of the Genii* – and did me no harm; for whatever harm was in some of them was not there for me; *I* knew nothing of it. It is astonishing to me now, how I found time, in the midst of my porings and blunderings over heavier themes, to read these books as I did. It is curious to me how I could ever have consoled myself under my small troubles (which were great troubles to me), by impersonating my favourite characters in them – as I did. I have been Tom Jones (a child's Tom Jones, a harmless creature) for a week together. I have sustained my own idea of Roderick Random for a month at a stretch, I verily believe.

In one sense, at any rate, I have never grown up, for my growth stopped when the great Haroun Alraschid spelt his name so, and when nobody had ever heard of a Jin. When the Sultan of the Indies was a mighty personage, to be approached respectfully even on the stage; and when all the dazzling wonders of those many nights held far too high a place in the imagination to be burlesqued and parodied. When Blue Beard, condescending to come out of book at all, came over mountains, to the music of his own march, on an elephant, and knew no more of slang than of Sanscrit. My growth stopped, when Don Quixote might have been right after all in going about to succour the distressed, and when the priest and the barber were no more justified in burning his books than they would have been in making a bonfire of our own two bedroom shelves. When Gil Blas had a heart, and was, somehow or other, not at all worldly that I knew of: and when it was a wonderful accident that the end of that interesting story in the *Sentimental Journey*, commencing with the windy night, and the notary; and the Pont Neuf, and the hat blown off, was not to be found in our Edition, though I looked for it a thousand times.

I had a greedy relish for a few volumes of *Voyages* and *Travels* – I forget what, now – that were on those shelves; and for days and days I can remember to have gone about my region of the house, armed with the centre-piece out of an old pair of boot-trees – the perfect realisation of Captain Somebody, of the Royal British Navy, in danger of being beset by savages, and resolved to sell his life at a great price. The Captain never lost his dignity, from having his ears boxed with the Latin Grammar. I did; but the Captain was a Captain and a hero, in despite of all the grammars and languages in the world, dead or alive.

When I think of it, the picture always arises in my mind, of a summer evening, the boys at play in the churchyard, and I sitting on my bed, reading as if for life. Every barn in the neighbourhood, every stone in the church, and every foot of the churchyard, had some association of its own, in my mind, connected with these books, and stood for some locality made famous in them. I have seen Tom Pipes go climbing up the church-steeple; I have watched Strap, with the knapsack on his back, stopping to rest himself upon the wicket-gate; and I *know* that Commodore Trunnion held that club with Mr Pickle, in the parlour of our little village alehouse.

I was thus well-versed in most of our English novelists before I was ten years old, one of the consequences being that – driven by a spirit of emulation – I wrote tragedies and got other children to act them. I became a writer, therefore, when I was a mere baby, and always an actor from the same age.

My departure for London

As I left Chatham in the days when there were no railroads in the land, I left it in a stage-coach. Through all the years that have since passed, have I ever lost the smell of the damp straw in which I was packed – like game – and forwarded, carriage paid, to the Cross Keys, Wood Street, Cheapside, London? There was no other inside passenger, and I consumed my sandwiches in solitude and dreariness and it rained hard all the way, and I thought life sloppier than I had expected to find it.

PART TWO

BOYHOOD

'I am not a lonely man, though I was once a
lonely boy; but that was long ago.'
– *'Railway Dreaming', May 1850*

I go astray

I was a very small boy indeed, both in years and stature, when
my family took up residence in Bayham Street, in Camden
Town. I became, for a time, a little companion and nurse to one
of my uncles, through a weary illness, and shall never forget the
many proofs that he gave me, in later days, of his interest and
affection. One of the earliest things that happened to me after
our arrival was that I got lost one day in the City of London. I
was taken out by Somebody (shade of Somebody forgive me for
remembering no more of thy identity!), as an immense treat, to
be shown the outside of St Giles's Church. I had romantic ideas
in connection with that religious edifice; firmly believing that
all the beggars who pretended through the week to be blind,
lame, one-armed, deaf and dumb, and otherwise physically
afflicted, laid aside their pretences every Sunday, dressed
themselves in holiday clothes, and attended divine service in
the temple of their patron saint. I had a general idea that the
reigning successor of Bamfylde Moore Carew acted as a sort of
church-warden on these occasions, and sat in a high pew with
red curtains.

It was in the spring-time when these tender notions of mine,
bursting forth into new shoots under the influence of the
season, became sufficiently troublesome to my parents and
guardians to occasion Somebody to volunteer to take me to see
the outside of St Giles's Church, which was considered likely (I
suppose) to quench my romantic fire, and bring me to a practical state. We set off after breakfast. I have an impression that
Somebody was got up in a striking manner – in cord breeches
of fine texture and milky hue, in long jean gaiters, in a green

coat with bright buttons, in a blue neckerchief, and a monstrous short-collar. I think he must have newly come (as I had myself) out of the hop-grounds of Kent. I considered him the glass of fashion and the mould of form: a very Hamlet without the burden of his difficult family affairs.

We were conversational together, and saw the outside of St Giles's Church with sentiments of satisfaction, much enhanced by a flag flying from the steeple. I infer that we then went down to Northumberland House in the Strand to view the celebrated lion over the gateway. At all events, I know that in the act of looking up with mingled awe and admiration at that famous animal I lost Somebody.

The child's unreasoning terror of being lost, comes as freshly on me now as it did then. I verily believe that if I had found myself astray at the North Pole instead of in the narrow, crowded, inconvenient street over which the lion in those days presided, I could not have been more horrified. But, this first fright expended itself in a little crying and tearing up and down; and then I walked, with a feeling of dismal dignity upon me, into a court, and sat down on a step to consider how to get through life.

To the best of my belief, the idea of asking my way home never came into my head. It is possible that I may, for the time, have preferred the dismal dignity of being lost; but I have a serious conviction that in the wide scope of my arrangements for the future, I had no eyes for the nearest and most obvious course. I was but very juvenile; from eight to nine years old, I fancy.

I had one and fourpence in my pocket, and a pewter ring with a bit of red glass in it on my little finger. This jewel had been presented to me by the object of my affections, on my birthday, when we had sworn to marry, but had foreseen family obstacles to our union, in her being (she was six years old) of the Wesleyan persuasion, while I was devotedly attached to the Church of England. The one and fourpence were the remains of half-a-crown presented on the same anniversary by my god-father – a man who knew his duty and did it.

Armed with these amulets, I made up my little mind to seek my fortune. When I had found it, I thought I would drive home in a coach and six, and claim my bride. I cried a little more at the idea of such a triumph, but soon dried my eyes and came out of the court to pursue my plans. These were, first to go (as a species of investment) and see the Giants in Guildhall, out of whom I felt it not improbable that some prosperous adventure would arise; failing that contingency, to try about the City for any opening of a Whittington nature; baffled in that too, to go into the army as a drummer.

So, I began to ask my way to Guildhall: which I thought meant, somehow, Gold or Golden Hall; I was too knowing to ask my way to the Giants, for I felt it would make people laugh. I remember how immensely broad the streets seemed now I was alone, how high the houses, how grand and mysterious everything. When I came to Temple Bar, it took me half an hour to stare at it, and I left it unfinished even then. I had read about heads being exposed on the top of Temple Bar, and it seemed a wicked old place, albeit a noble monument of architecture and a paragon of utility. When at last I got away from it, behold I came, the next minute, on the figures at St Dunstan's! Who could see those obliging monsters strike upon the bells and go? Between the quarters there was the toyshop to look at – still there, at this present writing, in a new form – and even when that enchanted spot was escaped from, after an hour and more, then St Paul's arose, and how was I to get beyond its dome, or to take my eyes from its cross of gold? I found it a long journey to the Giants, and a slow one.

I came into their presence at last, and gazed up at them with dread and veneration. They looked better-tempered, and were altogether more shiny-faced, than I had expected; but they were very big, and, as I judged their pedestals to be about forty feet high, I considered that they would be very big indeed if they were walking on the stone pavement. I was in a state of mind as to these and all such figures, which I suppose holds equally with most children. While I knew them to be images made of something that was not flesh and blood, I still invested them with attributes of life – with consciousness of my being there, for example, and the power of keeping a sly eye upon me. Being very tired I got into the corner under Magog, to be out of the way of his eye, and fell asleep.

When I started up after a long nap, I thought the giants were roaring, but it was only the City. The place was just the same as when I fell asleep: no beanstalk, no fairy, no princess, no dragon, no opening in life of any kind. So, being hungry, I thought I would buy something to eat, and bring it in there and eat it, before going forth to seek my fortune on the Whittington plan.

I was not ashamed of buying a penny role in a baker's shop, but looked into a number of cooks' shops before I could muster courage to go into one. At last I saw a pile of cooked sausages in a window with the label, 'Small Germans, A Penny'. Emboldened by knowing what to ask for, I went in and said, 'If you please will you sell me a small German?' which they did, and I took it, wrapped in paper in my pocket, to Guildhall.

The Giants were still lying by, in their sly way, pretending to take no notice, so I sat down in another corner, when what should I see before me but a dog with his ears cocked. He was a black dog, with a bit of white over one eye, and bits of white and tan in his paws, and he wanted to play – frisking about me, rubbing his nose against me, dodging at me sideways, shaking his head and pretending to run away backwards, and making himself good-naturedly ridiculous, as if he had no consideration for himself, but wanted to raise my spirits. Now, when I saw this dog I thought of Whittington, and felt that things were coming right; I encouraged him by saying, 'Hi boy!' 'Poor fellow!' 'Good dog!' and was satisfied that he was to be my dog for ever afterwards, and that he would help me to seek my fortune.

Very much comforted by this (I had cried a little at odd times ever since I was lost), I took the small German out of my pocket, and began my dinner by biting off a bit and throwing it to the dog, who immediately swallowed it with a one-sided jerk, like a pill. While I took a bit myself, and he looked me in the face for a second piece, I considered by what name I should call him. I thought 'Merrychance' would be an expressive name, under the circumstances: and I was elated, I recollect, by inventing such a good one, when Merrychance began to growl at me in a most ferocious manner.

I wondered he was not ashamed of himself, but he didn't care for that; on the contrary he growled a good deal more. With his mouth watering, and his eyes glistening, and his nose in a very damp state, and his head very much on one side, he sidled about on the pavement in a threatening manner and growled at me, until he suddenly made a snap at the small German, tore it out of my hand, and went off with it. He never came back to me to help me to seek my fortune. From that hour to the present, when I am forty years of age, I have never seen my faithful Merrychance again.

I felt very lonely. Not so much for the loss of the small

German, though it was delicious (I knew nothing about highly-peppered horse at that time), as on account of Merrychance's disappointing me so cruelly; for I had hoped we would do every friendly thing but speak, and perhaps even come to that. I cried a little more, and began to wish that the object of my affections had been lost with me, for company's sake. But, then I remembered that *she* could not go into the army as a drummer; and I dried my eyes and ate my loaf. Coming out, I met a milkwoman, of whom I bought a pennyworth of milk; quite set up again by my repast, I began to roam about the City, and to seek my fortune in the Whittington direction.

When I go into the City now, it makes me sorrowful to think that I am quite an artful wretch. Strolling about it as a lost child, I thought of the British Merchant and the Lord Mayor, and was full of reverence. Strolling about it now, I laugh at the sacred liveries of state, and get indignant with the corporation as one of the strongest practical jokes of the present day. What did I know then, about the multitude who are always being disappointed in the City; who are always expecting to meet a party there, and to receive money there, and whose expectations are never fulfilled? What did I know then, about that wonderful person, the friend in the City, who is to do so many things for so many people; who is to get this one into a post at home, and that one into a post abroad; who is to settle with this man's creditors, provide for that man's son, and see that other man paid; who is to 'throw himself' into this grand Joint Stock certainty, and who is to put his name down on that Life Assurance Directory, and never does anything predicted of him? What did I know, then, about him as the friend of gentlemen, Mosaic Arabs and others, usually to be seen at races, and chiefly residing in the neighbourhood of Red Lion Square; and as being unable to discount the whole amount of that paper in money, but as happening to have by him a case of remarkable fine sherry, a dressing-case, and a Venus by Titian, with which he would be willing to make up the balance? Had I ever heard of him, in those innocent days, as confiding information (which never by any chance turned out to be in the remotest degree correct) to solemn bald men, who mysteriously imparted it to breathless dinner tables? No. Had I ever learned to dread him as a shark, disregard him as a humbug, and know him for a myth? Not I. Had I ever heard of him as associated with tightness in the money market, gloom in consols, the exportation of gold, or that rock ahead in everybody's course, the bushel of wheat? Never. Had I the least idea what was meant by such terms as jobbery, rigging the market, cooking accounts, getting up a dividend, making things pleasant and the like? Not the slightest. Should I have detected in Mr Hudson himself, a staring carcase of golden veal? By no manner of means. The City was to me a vast emporium of precious stones and metals, casks and bales, honour and generosity, foreign fruits and spices. Every merchant and banker was a compound of Mr FitzWarren and Sinbad the Sailor. Smith, Payne and Smith, when the wind was fair for Barbary and the captain present, were in the habit of calling their servants together (the cross cook included) and asking them to produce their little shipments. Glyn and Halifax had personally undergone great hardships in the valley of diamonds. Baring Brothers had seen Rocs' eggs and travelled with caravans. Rothschild had sat in the Bazaar at Baghdad with rich stuffs for sale; and a veiled lady from the Sultan's harem, riding on a donkey, had fallen in love with him.

Thus I wandered about the City, like a child in a dream, staring at the British merchants, and inspired by a mighty faith in the marvellousness of everything. Up courts and down courts – in and out of yards and little squares – peeping into counting-house passages and running away – poorly feeding the echoes in the court of the South Sea House with my timid steps – roaming down into Austin Friars, and wondering how the Friars used to like it – ever staring at the British merchants, and never tired of the shops – I rambled on, all through the day. In such stories as I made, to account for the different places, I believed as devoutly as in the City itself. I particularly remember that when I found myself on 'Change, and saw the shabby people sitting under the placards about ships, I settled that they were Misers, who had embarked all their wealth to go and buy gold-dust or something of that sort, and were waiting for their respective captains to come and tell them that they were ready to sail. I observed that they all munched dry biscuits, and I thought it was to keep off sea-sickness.

This was very delightful; but it still produced no result according to the Whittington precedent. There was a dinner preparing at the Mansion House, and when I peeped in at a grated kitchen window, and saw the men cooks at work in their white caps, my heart began to beat with hope that the Lord

Mayor, or the Lady Mayoress, or one of the young Princesses their daughters, would look out of an upper apartment and direct me to be taken in. But, nothing of the kind occurred. It was not until I had been peeping in some time that one of the cooks called to me (the window was open) 'Cut away, you sir!' which frightened me so, on account of his black whiskers, that I instantly obeyed.

After that, I came to the India House, and asked a boy what it was, who made faces and pulled my hair before he told me, and behaved altogether in an ungenteel and discourteous manner. Sir James Hogg himself might have been satisfied with the veneration in which I held the India House. I had no doubt of its being the most wonderful, the most magnanimous, the most incorruptible, the most practically disinterested, the most in all respects astonishing, establishment on the face of the earth. I understood the nature of an oath, and would have sworn it to be one entire and perfect chrysolite.

Thinking much about boys who went to India, and who immediately, without being sick, smoked pipes like curled-up bell-ropes, terminating in a large cut-glass sugar basin upside down, I got among the outfitting shops. There, I read the list of things that were necessary for an India-going boy, and when I came to 'one brace of pistols', thought what happiness to be reserved for such a fate! Still no British merchant seemed at all disposed to take me into his house. The only exception was a chimney-sweep – he looked at me as if he thought me suitable to his business; but I ran away from him.

I suffered very much, all day, from boys; they chased me down turnings, brought me to bay in doorways, and treated me quite savagely, though I am sure I gave them no offence. One boy, who had a stub of black-lead pencil in his pocket, wrote his mother's name and address (as he said) on my white hat, outside the crown. MRS BLORES, WOODEN LEG WALK, TOBACCO-STOPPER ROW, WAPPING. And I couldn't rub it out.

I recollect resting in a little churchyard after this persecution, disposed to think upon the whole, that if I and the object of my affections could be buried there together, at once, it would be comfortable. But, another nap, and a pump, and a bun, and above all a picture that I saw, brought me round again.

I must have strayed by that time, as I recall my course, into

Goodman's Fields, or somewhere thereabouts. The picture represented a scene in a play then performing at a theatre in that neighbourhood which is no longer in existence. It stimulated me to go to that theatre and see that play. I resolved, as there seemed to be nothing doing in the Whittington way, that on the conclusion of the entertainments I would ask my way to the barracks, knock at the gate, and tell them that I understood they were in want of drummers, and there I was. I think I must have been told, but I know I believed, that a soldier was always on duty, day and night, behind every barrack-gate, with a shilling; and that a boy who could by any means be prevailed on to accept it, instantly became a drummer, unless his father paid four hundred pounds.

I found out the theatre – of its external appearance I only remember the loyal initials G.R. untidily painted in yellow ochre on the front – and waited, with a pretty large crowd, for the opening of the gallery doors. The greater part of the sailors and others composing the crowd were of the lowest description, and their conversation was not improving; but I understood little or nothing of what was bad in it then, and it had no depraving influence on me. I have wondered since, how long it would take, by means of such association, to corrupt a child nurtured as I had been, and innocent as I was.

Whenever I saw that my appearance attracted attention, either outside the doors or afterwards within the theatre, I pretended to look out for somebody who was taking care of me, and from whom I was separated, and to exchange nods and smiles with that creature of my imagination. This answered very well. I had my sixpence clutched in my hand ready to pay; and when the doors opened, with a clattering of bolts, and some screaming from women in the crowd, I went on with the current like a straw. My sixpence was rapidly swallowed up in the money-taker's pigeon hole, which looked to me like a sort of mouth, and I got into the freer staircase above and ran on (as everybody else did) to get a good place. When I came to the back of the gallery, there were very few people in it, and the seats looked so horribly steep, and so like a diving arrangement to send me, head foremost, into the pit, that I held by one of them in a terrible fright. However, there was a good-natured baker with a young woman, who gave me his hand, and we all three scrambled over the seats together down into the corner of the first row. The baker was very fond of the young woman, and kissed her a good deal in the course of the evening.

I was no sooner comfortably settled, than a weight fell upon my mind, which tormented it most dreadfully, and which I must explain. It was a benefit night – the benefit of the comic actor – a little fat man with a very large face and, as I thought then, the smallest and most diverting hat that ever was seen. The comedian, for the gratification of his friends and patrons, had undertaken to sing a comic song on a donkey's back, and afterwards to give away the donkey so distinguished, by lottery. In this lottery, every person admitted to the pit and gallery had a chance. On paying my sixpence, I had received the number, forty-seven; and I now thought, in a perspiration of terror, what should I ever do if that number was to come up the prize, and I was to win the donkey!

It made me quite tremble all over to think of the possibility of my good fortune. I knew I never could conceal the fact of my holding forty-seven, in case the number came up, because, not to speak of my confusion, which would immediately condemn me, I had shown my number to the baker. Then, I pictured to myself the being called upon to come down on the stage and receive the donkey. I thought how all the people would shriek when they saw that it had fallen to a little fellow like me. How should I lead him out – for of course he wouldn't go? If he began to bray, what should I do? If he kicked, what would become of me? Suppose he backed into the stage-door, and stuck there, with me upon him? For I felt that if I won him, the comic actor would have me on his back, the moment he could touch me. How was I to feed him? Where was I to stable him? It was bad enough to have gone astray by myself, but to go astray with a donkey, too, was a calamity more tremendous than I could bear to contemplate.

These apprehensions took away all my pleasure in the first piece. When the ship came on – a real man-of-war she was called in the bills – and rolled prodigiously in a very heavy sea, I couldn't, even in the terrors of the storm, forget the donkey. It was awful to see the sailors pitching about, with telescopes and speaking-trumpets (they looked very tall indeed aboard the man-of-war), and it was awful to suspect the pilot of treachery, though impossible to avoid it, for when he cried – 'We are lost! To the raft, to the raft! A thunderbolt has struck the main-mast!' – I myself saw him take the main-mast out of its socket and drop it overboard; but even these impressive circumstances paled before my dread of the donkey. Even, when the good sailor (and he was very good) came to good fortune, and the bad sailor (and he was very bad) threw himself into the ocean from the summit of a curious rock, presenting something of the appearance of a pair of steps. I saw the dreadful donkey through my tears.

At last the time came when the fiddler struck up the comic song, and the dreaded animal, with new shoes on, as I inferred from the noise they made, came clattering in with the comic actor on his back. He was dressed out with ribbons (I mean the donkey was) and as he persisted in turning his tail to the audience, the comedian got off him, turned about, and with his face that way, sang the song three times, amid thunders of applause. All this time, I was fearfully agitated; and when two pale people, a good deal splashed with the mud of the streets, were invited out of the pit to superintend the drawing of the lottery, and were received with a round of laughter from everybody else, I could have begged and prayed them to have mercy on me, and not draw number forty-seven.

But I was soon put out of my pain now, for a gentleman behind me, in a flannel jacket and a yellow neck-kerchief, who had eaten two fried soles and all his pocket-fulls of nuts before the storm began to rage, answered to the winning number, and went down to take possession of the prize. The gentleman had appeared to know the donkey, rather, from the moment of his entrance, and had taken a great interest in the proceedings; driving him to himself, if I use an intelligible phrase, and saying, almost in my ear, when he made any mistake, 'Kum up, you precious Moke. Kum up!' He was thrown by the donkey on first mounting him, to the great delight of the audience (including myself), but rode him off with great skill afterwards, and soon returned to his seat quite calm. Calmed myself by the immense relief I had sustained, I enjoyed the rest of the performance very much indeed. I remember there were a good many dances, some in fetters and some in roses, and one by a most divine little creature, who made the object of my affections look but commonplace. In the concluding drama she reappeared as a boy (in arms, mostly), and was fought for, several times. I rather think a Baron wanted to drown her, and was on various occasions prevented by the comedian, a ghost, a Newfoundland dog, and a church bell. I only remember beyond this, that I wondered where the Baron expected to go, and that he went there in a shower of sparks. The lights were turned out while the sparks died out, and it appeared to me as if the whole play – ship, donkey, men and women, divine little creature, and all – were a wonderful firework that had gone off, and left nothing but dust and darkness behind it.

It was late when I got out into the streets, and there was no moon, and there were no stars, and the rain fell heavily. When I emerged from the dispersing crowd, the ghost and the baron had an ugly look in my remembrance; I felt unspeakably forlorn; and now, for the first time, my little bed, and the dear familiar faces came before me, and touched my heart. By daylight, I had never thought of the grief at home. I had never thought of my mother. I had never thought of anything but adapting myself to the circumstances in which I found myself, and going to seek my fortune.

For a boy who could do nothing but cry, and run about, saying, 'O I am lost!' to think of going into the army was, I felt sensible, out of the question. I abandoned the idea of asking my way to the barracks – or rather the idea abandoned me – and ran about, until I found a watchman in his box. It is amazing to me, now, that he should have been sober; but I am inclined to think he was too feeble to get drunk.

This venerable man took me to the nearest watch-house – I say he took me, but in fact I took him, for when I think of us in the rain, I recollect that we must have made a composition like a vignette of Infancy leading Age. He had a dreadful cough, and was obliged to lean against a wall, whenever it came on. We got at last to the watch-house, a warm and drowsy sort of place embellished with great-coats and rattles hanging up. When a paralytic messenger had been sent to make inquiries about me, I fell asleep by the fire, and awoke no more until my eyes opened on my father's face. This is literally and exactly how I went astray. They used to say I was an odd child, and I suppose I was. I am an odd man perhaps.

Shade of Somebody, forgive me for the disquiet I must have caused thee! When I stand beneath the Lion, even now, I see thee rushing up and down, refusing to be comforted. I have gone astray since, many times, and farther afield. May I therein have given less disquiet to others, than herein I gave to thee!

Our neighbourhood

The area in which we were now living was as shabby, dingy, damp, and mean a neighbourhood, as one would desire not to see. Its poverty was not of the demonstrative order. It shut the street-doors, pulled down the blinds, screened the parlour-windows with the wretchedest plants in pots, and made a desperate attempt to keep up appearances. The genteeler part of the inhabitants, in answering knocks, got behind the door to keep out of sight, and endeavoured to diffuse the fiction that a servant of some sort was the ghostly warder. Lodgings were let, and many more were *to* let; but with this exception, signboards and placards were discouraged. A few houses that became afflicted in their lower extremities with eruptions of mangling and clear-starching, were considered a disgrace to the neighbourhood. The working bookbinder with the large door-plate was looked down upon for keeping fowls, who were always going in and out. A corner house with 'Ladies School' on a board over the first floor windows, was barely tolerated for its educational facilities; and Miss Jamanne the dress-maker, who inhabited two parlours, and kept an obsolete work of art representing the Fashions, in the window of the front one, was held at a marked distance by the ladies of the neighbourhood – who patronised her, however, with far greater regularity than they paid her.

In those days, the neighbourhood was as quiet and dismal as any neighbourhood about London. Its crazily built houses – the largest, eight-roomed – were rarely shaken by any conveyance heavier than the spring van that came to carry off the goods of a 'sold-up' tenant. To be sold up was nothing particular. The whole neighbourhood felt itself liable, at any time, to that common casualty of life. A man used to come into the neighbourhood regularly, delivering the summonses for rates and taxes as if they were circulars. We never paid anything until the last extremity, and Heaven knows how we paid it then. The streets were positively hilly with the inequalities made in them by the man with the pickaxe who cut off the company's supply of water to defaulters. It seemed as if nobody had any money but old Mrs Frowze, who lived with her mother at Number fourteen Little Twig Street, and who was rumoured to be immensely rich; though I don't see why, unless it was that she never went out of doors, and never wore a cap, and never brushed her hair, which was immensely dirty.

As to visitors, we really had no visitors at that time. Stabber's Band used to come every Monday morning and play for three-quarters of an hour on one particular spot by the 'Norwich Castle'; but how they first got into the habit of coming, or even how we knew them to be Stabber's Band, I am unable to say. It was popular in the neighbourhood, and we used to contribute to it: dropping our halfpence into an exceedingly hard hat with a warm handkerchief in it, like a sort of bird's-nest (I am not aware whether it was Mr Stabber's hat or not), which came regularly round. They used to open with 'Begone, dull Care!' and to end with a tune which the neighbourhood recognised as 'I'd rather have a Guinea than a One-pound Note'. I think any reference to money, that was not a summons or an execution, touched us melodiously. As to Punches, they knew better than to do anything but squeak and drum in the neighbourhood, unless a collection was made in advance – which never succeeded. Conjurors and strong men strayed amongst us, at long intervals; but, I never saw a donkey go up once. Even costermongers were shy of us, as a bad job: seeming to know instinctively that the neighbourhood ran stores with Mrs Slaughter, Greengrocer, etc., of Great Twig Street, and consequently didn't dare to buy a ha'porth elsewhere: or very likely being told so by young Slaughter, who managed the business and was always lurking in the Coal Department, practising Ramoo Samee with three potatoes.

As to shops, we had no shops either, worth mentioning. We had the 'Norwich Castle', Truman Hanbury and Buxton, by J. Wigzell: a violent landlord, who was constantly eating in the bar, and constantly coming out with his mouth full and his hat on, to stop his amiable daughter from giving more credit; and we had Slaughter's; and we had a jobbing tailor's (in a kitchen), and a toy and hardbake (in a parlour), and a Bottle Rag Bone Kitchen-stuff and Ladies' Wardrobe, and a tobacco and weekly paper. We used to run to the door and windows to look at a cab, it was such a rare sight.

Chimney sweeps

A mystery hung over the sweeps in those days. Legends were in existence of wealthy gentlemen who had lost children, and who, after many years of sorrow and suffering, had found them in the character of sweeps. Stories were related of a young boy who, having been stolen from his parents in his infancy, and devoted to the occupation of chimney-sweeping, was sent, in the course of his professional career, to sweep the chimney of his mother's bedroom; and how, being hot and tired when he came out of the chimney, he got into the bed he had so often slept in as an infant, and was discovered and recognised therein by his mother, who once every year of her life, thereafter, requested the pleasure of the company of every London sweep, at half-past one o'clock, to roast beef, plum pudding, porter and sixpence.

Such stories as these, and there were many such, threw an air of mystery round the sweeps, and produced from them some of those good effects which animals derive from the doctrine of the transmigration of souls. No one (except the masters) thought of ill-treating a sweep, because no one knew who he might be, or what nobleman's or gentleman's son he might turn out. Chimney-sweeping was, by many believers in the marvellous, considered as a sort of probationary term, at an earlier or later period of which, divers young noblemen were to come into possession of their rank and titles: and the profession was held by them in great respect accordingly.

I remember a little sweep about my own age, with curly hair and white teeth, whom I devoutly and sincerely believed to be the lost son and heir of some illustrious personage – an impression which was resolved into an unchangeable conviction of my infant mind, by the subject of my speculations informing me, one day, in reply to my question, propounded a few moments before his ascent to the summit of the kitchen chimney, 'that he believed he'd been born in the vurkis, but he'd never know'd his father'. I felt certain, from that time forth, that he would one day be owned by a lord; and I never heard the church-bells ring, or saw a flag hoisted in the neighbourhood, without thinking that the happy event had at last occurred, and that his long-lost parent had arrived in a coach-and-six, to take him home to Grosvenor Square. He never came, however; and, at the present moment, the young gentleman in question is settled down as a master sweep in the neighbourhood of Battle Bridge, his distinguishing characteristics being a decided antipathy to washing himself, and the possession of a pair of legs very inadequate to the support of his unwieldy and corpulent body.

I consoled myself as best I could for this disappointment, but the time came, eventually, when I could not disguise from myself the fact that whole families of sweeps were regularly born of sweeps, in the rural districts of Somers Town and Camden Town – that the eldest son succeeded to the father's business, that the other branches assisted him therein, and commenced on their own account; that their children, again, were educated to the profession; and that about their identity there could be no mistake whatever.

The Field of the Forty Footsteps

My first remembrance of a certain spot in north-western London, which I have reason for recalling, is of a very uninviting piece of wet waste ground, and a miserable pool of water; it looked like a rather barbarous place of execution, with its poles and cross-poles erected for the beating of carpets; and it was overrun with nettles and dockweed. Associated with this place was a story, captivating enough to my boyish imagination, concerning 'The Field of the Forty Footsteps'; a part of the place so called, as I remember, because of a duel that was traditionally supposed to have been fought there between two brothers, one of whom, advancing upon the other certain paces as he retreated, to wound him mortally, the grass got trodden down by forty dreadful footsteps, upon which the grass grew never more. I remember to have gone, accompanied by an adventurous young Englishman of my own age, about eleven, with whom I had certain designs to seek my fortune in the neighbourhood of the Spanish Main, as soon as we should have accumulated forty shillings each and a rifle, which we never did.

I remember to have gone, accompanied by this young pirate, to inspect this ground. I also remember to have counted forty places on which the grass indubitably did not grow – though whether grass grew anywhere thereabouts for a few feet together, without being chequered with bald patches, I will not say. This 'Field of Forty Footsteps' was close to the site on which was afterwards built University College, and formed, generally, a part of the open space of ground on which now stands University College Hospital.

Unforgettable scenes and unshakeable convictions

There are real people and places that I have never outgrown, though they themselves may have passed away long since: which I always regard with the eye and mind of childhood. I recall a dusty, dry old shop in Long Acre, where, displayed in the windows, in tall slim bottles, were numerous preparations, looking, at first sight, like unhealthy maccaroni. On a nearer inspection these were found to be tapeworms, extracted from the internal mechanisms of certain ladies and gentlemen who were delicately referred to, on these bottles, by initial letters. Doctor Gardner's medicine had effected these wonderful results; but, the Doctor, probably apprehensive that his patients might 'blush to find it fame', enshrined them in his museum, under a thin cloud of mystery. I have a lively remembrance of a white basin, which, in the days of my boyhood, remained, for eight or ten years, in a conspicuous part of the museum, and was supposed to contain a specimen so recent that there had not yet been time for its more elaborate preservation. It bore, as I remember, the label, 'This singular creature, with ears like a mouse, was last week found destroying the inside of Mr O—— in the City Road'. But, this was an encroachment on the province of the legitimate tapeworms. That species were all alike except in length. The smallest, according to the labels, measured, to the best of my recollection, about two hundred yards.

I miss a tea-tray shop, for many years at the corner of Bedford Street and King Street, Covent Garden, where there was a tea-tray in the window representing, with an exquisite art that I have not yet outgrown either, the departure from home for school at breakfast time, of two boys – one used to it; the other, not. There was a charming mother in a bygone fashion, evidently much affected though trying to hide it; and a little sister, bearing, as I remember, a basket of fruit for the consolation of the unused brother: what time the used one, receiving advice I opine from his grandmother, drew on his glove in a manner I once considered unfeeling, but which I was afterwards inclined to hope might be only his brag. There were some corded boxes, and faithful servants; and there was a breakfast-table, with accessories (an urn and plate of toast particularly) my admiration of which, as perfect illusions, I never have outgrown and never shall outgrow.

I shall never forget the mingled feelings of awe and respect with which I used to gaze on the exterior of Newgate at this time. How dreadful its rough heavy walls, and low massive doors, appeared to me – the latter looking as if they were made for the express purpose of letting people in, and never letting them out again. Then the fetters over the debtors' door, which I used to think were a *bona fide* set of irons, just hung up there for convenience sake, ready to be taken down at a moment's notice, and riveted on the limbs of some refractory felon! I was never tired of wondering how the hackney-coachmen on the opposite stand could cut jokes in the presence of such horrors, and drink pots of half-and-half so near the last drop.

Often did I stray here, in sessions time, to catch a glimpse of the whipping-place, and that dark building on one side of the yard, in which is kept the gibbet with all its dreadful apparatus, and on the door of which I half expected to see a brass plate, with the inscription 'Mr Ketch'; for I never imagined that the distinguished functionary could by possibility live anywhere else! The days of these childish dreams have passed away, and with them many other boyish dreams of a gayer nature. But I still retain so much of my original feeling, that to this hour I never pass the building without something like a shudder and have never outgrown its rugged walls, or any other prison on the outside. All within, is still the same blank of remorse and misery.

I have never outgrown the whole region of Covent Garden. I preserve it as a fine, dissipated, insoluble mystery. I believe that the gentleman mentioned in Colman's *Broad Grins* still lives in King Street. I have a general idea that the passages at the Old Hummums lead to groves of gorgeous bedrooms, eating out the whole of the adjacent houses: where Chamberlains who have never been in bed themselves for fifty years, show any country gentleman who rings at the bell, at any hour of the night, to luxurious repose in palatial apartments fitted up after the Eastern manner. (I have slept in there in my time, but that makes no difference.) There is a fine secrecy and mystery about the Piazza – how you get up to those rooms above it, and what reckless deeds are done there. (I know some of those apartments very well, but that does not signify in the least.) I have not outgrown the two great Theatres. Ghosts of great names are always getting up the most extraordinary pantomimes in them, with scenery and machinery on a tremendous scale. I have no doubt that the critics sit in the pit of both houses, every night. Even as I write in my commonplace office I behold, from the window, four young ladies with peculiarly limp bonnets, and of a yellow or drab style of beauty, making for the stage-door of the Lyceum Theatre, in the dirty little fog-choked street over the way. Grown-up wisdom whispers that these are beautiful fairies by night, and that they will find Fairy Land dirty even to their splashed skirts, and rather cold and dull (notwithstanding its mixed gas and daylight), this easterly morning. But, I don't believe it.

There was a poor demented woman, who used to roam about the City, dressed all in black with cheeks staringly painted, and thence popularly known as *Rouge et Noire*; whom I have never outgrown by the height of a mustard seed. The story went that her only brother, a Bank-clerk, was sentenced to death for forgery; and that she, broken-hearted creature, lost her wits on the morning of his execution, and ever afterwards, while her confused dream of life lasted, flitted thus among the busy money-changers. A story, alas! all likely enough; but, likely or unlikely, true or untrue, never to take other shape in my mind. Evermore she wanders, as to my stopped growth, among the crowd, and takes her daily loaf out of the shop-window of the same charitable baker, and between whiles sits in the old Bank office awaiting her brother. 'Is he come yet?' Not yet, poor soul. 'I will go walk for an hour and come back.' It is then she passes my boyish figure in the street, with that strange air of vanity upon her, in which the comfortable self-sustainment of sane vanity (God help us all!) is waiting, and with her wildly-seeking, never resting eyes. So she returns to his old Bank office, asking 'Is he come yet?' Not yet, poor soul! So she goes home, leaving word that indeed she wonders he has been away from her so long, and that he must come to her however late at night he may arrive. He will come to thee, O stricken sister, with thy best friend – foe to the prosperous and happy – not to such as thou!

Another very different person who stopped my growth, I associate with Berners Street, Oxford Street; whether she was constantly on parade in that street only, or was ever to be seen elsewhere, I am unable to say. The White Woman is her name. She is dressed entirely in white, with a ghastly white plaiting round her head and face, inside her white bonnet. She even carries (I hope) a white umbrella. With white boots I know she picks her way through the winter dirt. She is a conceited old creature, cold and formal in manner, and evidently went simpering mad on personal grounds alone – no doubt because a wealthy Quaker wouldn't marry her. This is her bridal dress. She is always walking up here, on her way to church to marry the false Quaker. I observe in her mincing step and fishy eye that she intends to lead him a sharp life. I stopped growing when I got at the conclusion that the Quaker had had a happy escape of the White Woman.

Right thankful I am to have stopped my growth at so many points – for each of these has a train of its own belonging to it. Not to be too wise, not to be too stately, not to be too rough with innocent fancies, or to treat them with too much lightness – which is as bad – are points to be remembered that they may do us all good in our years to come.

My education is neglected

In the little world in which children have their existence, whosoever brings them up, there is nothing so finely perceived and so finely felt, as injustice. It may be only small injustices that the child can be exposed to, but the child is small, and its world is small, and its rocking-horse stands as many hands high, according to scale, as a big-boned Irish hunter.

I know my father to have been as kindhearted and generous a man as ever lived in the world. Everything that I can remember of his conduct to his wife, or children, or friends, in sickness or affliction, is beyond all praise. By me, as a sick child, he watched night and day, unweariedly and patiently, many days and nights. He never undertook any business, charge or trust, that he did not zealously, conscientiously, punctually, honourably discharge. His industry was always untiring. He was proud of me in his way, and had a great admiration of my comic singing. But, in the ease of his temper, and the straitness of his means, he appeared to have utterly lost at this time the idea of educating me at all, and to utterly put from him the notion that I had any claim upon him, in that regard, whatever. So I degenerated into cleaning his boots of a morning, and my own; and making myself useful in the work of the little house; and looking after my younger brothers and sisters (we were now six in all), and going on such poor errands as arose out of our poor way of living.

It is a most miserable thing to feel ashamed of home. There may be bleak ingratitude in the thing, and the punishment may be retributive and well-deserved: but, that it is a miserable thing, I can testify. I had believed in our Chatham home. I had believed in the best parlour as a most elegant saloon; I had believed in the front door, as a mysterious portal of the Temple of State whose solemn opening was attended with a sacrifice of roast fowls; I had believed in the kitchen as a chaste though not magnificent apartment. Within a single year all this was changed. Now, it was all coarse and common.

As I thought, in the little back garret in Bayham Street, of all I had lost in losing Chatham, what would I have given, if I had had anything to give, to have been sent back to any other school, to have been taught something somewhere!

My poor mother tried to exert herself in an attempt to recoup the family fortunes. She resolved to set up a school (the success of which, so I thought, might even result in my going to school myself) and we moved to Gower Street North and the centre of the street door was perfectly covered with a great brass plate on which was engraved MRS DICKENS ESTABLISHMENT. I left, at a great many other doors, a great many circulars calling attention to the merits of the establishment. Yet nobody ever came to school, nor do I recollect that anybody ever proposed to come, or that the least preparation was made to receive anybody. But I know that we got on very badly with the butcher and baker; that very often we had not too much for dinner; and that at last my father was arrested.

I am employed at a blacking warehouse

James Lamert, a relative who had lived with us in Bayham Street, seeing how I was employed from day to day, and knowing what our domestic circumstances then were, proposed that I should go into a blacking warehouse, to be as useful as I could, at a salary, I think, of six shillings a week.

16 Bayham Street, Camden Town.

I am not clear whether it was six or seven. I am inclined to believe, from my uncertainty on this head, that it was six at first and seven afterwards. At any rate the offer was accepted very willingly by my father and mother, and on a Monday morning I went down to the blacking warehouse to begin my business life.

This speculation, of which James Lamert himself was the chief manager, was a rivalry of 'Warren's Blacking, 30, Strand' – at that time very famous. One Jonathan Warren (the famous one was Robert), living at 30, Hungerford Stairs, or Market, Strand (for I forget which it was called then), claimed to have been the original inventor or proprietor of the blacking recipe, and to have been deposed or ill-used by his renowned relation. At last he put himself in the way of selling his recipe, and his name and his 30, Hungerford Stairs, Strand (30, Strand, very large, and the intermediate direction very small), for an annuity: and he set forth by his agents that a little capital would make a great business of it. The man of some property was found in George Lamert, the cousin and brother-in-law of James. He bought this right and title, and went into the blacking business and the blacking premises – in an evil hour for me, as I often bitterly thought.

It is wonderful to me how I could have been so easily cast away at such an age. It is wonderful to me that, even after my descent into the poor little drudge I had been since we came to London, no one had compassion enough on me – a child of singular abilities, quick, eager, delicate, and soon hurt, bodily or mentally – to suggest that something might have been spared, as certainly it might have been, to place me at any common school. My father and mother were quite satisfied. They could hardly have been more so if I had been twenty years of age, distinguished at a grammar school, and going to Cambridge.

The blacking warehouse was the last house on the left-hand side of the way at old Hungerford Stairs. It was a crazy, tumble-down old house, abutting of course on the river, and literally overrun with rats. Its wainscoted rooms and its rotten floors and staircase, with the old grey rats swarming down in the cellars, and the sound of their squeaking and scuffling coming up the stairs at all times, and the dirt and decay of the place rise up visibly before me as if I were there again. The counting-house was on the first floor, looking over the coal-barges on the river. There was a recess in it, in which I was to sit and work. My work was to cover the pots of paste-blacking, first with a piece of oil-paper and then with a piece of blue paper, to tie them round with a string, and then to clip the paper close and neat all round, until it looked as smart as a pot of ointment from the apothecary's shop. When a certain number of grosses of pots had attained this pitch of perfection, I was to paste on each a painted label, and then go on again with more pots. Two or three other boys were kept at a similar duty downstairs on similar wages. One of them came up, in a ragged apron and a paper cap, on the first Monday morning, to show me the trick of using the string and tying the knot. His name was Bob Fagin, and I took the liberty of using his name long afterwards in *Oliver Twist*.

Our relative had kindly arranged to teach me something in the dinner-hour; from twelve to one, I think it was, every day. But an arrangement so incompatible with counting-house business soon died away, from no fault of his or mine; and for the same reason my small work-table and my grosses of pots, my papers, string, scissors, paste-pots and labels, by little and little, vanished out of the recess in the counting-house, and kept company with the other small work-tables, grosses of pots, papers, string, scissors and paste-pots downstairs. It was not long before Bob Fagin and I, and another boy whose name was Paul Green but who was currently believed to have been christened Poll (a belief which I transferred, long afterwards, to Mr Sweedlepipe, in *Martin Chuzzlewit*), worked generally side by side. Bob Fagin was an orphan and lived with his brother-in-law – a waterman. Poll Green's father had the additional distinction of being a fireman, and was employed at Drury Lane Theatre, where another relation of Poll's, I think his little sister, did imps in the pantomimes.

No words can express the secret agony of my soul as I sunk into this companionship; compared these every-day associates with those of my happier childhood; and felt my early hopes of growing up to be a learned and distinguished man crushed in my breast. The deep remembrance of the sense I had of being utterly neglected and hopeless – of the shame I felt in my position – of the misery it was to my young heart to believe that, day by day, what I had learned and thought and delighted in, and raised my fancy and my emulation up, was passing away from me, never to be brought back any more – cannot be written. My whole nature was so penetrated with the grief and humiliation of such considerations that, even now – famous and caressed and happy – I often forget in my dreams that I have a dear wife and children – even that I am a man – and wander desolately back to that time of my life.

Old Hungerford Stairs, where the blacking warehouse was 'the last house on the left-hand side of the way'.

My father's imprisonment

I had long been aware that my father's affairs were in a far from satisfactory state and an awful document referred to as 'the deed', which I now know to have been a composition with his various creditors, looms large in my recollections of those times. At last my father's affairs came to a crisis. Eleven days after I had started work at the blacking factory he was arrested early one morning for debt and carried over to the Marshalsea prison. He told me, as he went out of the house, that the God of day had now gone down upon him – and I really thought his heart was broken and mine too.

On the first Sunday after he was taken there, I was to go and see him, and have dinner with him. I was to ask my way to such a place, and just short of that place I should see another place, and just short of that I should see a yard, which I was to cross, and keep straight on until I saw a turnkey. All this I did; and when at last I did see (poor little fellow that I was!), and thought how, when Roderick Random was in a debtors' prison, there was a man there with nothing on him but an old rug, the turnkey swam before my dimmed eyes and my beating heart.

My father was waiting for me in the lodge, and we went up to his room (on the top storey but one) and cried very much. And he told me, I remember, to take warning by the Marshalsea, and to observe that if a man had twenty pounds a year, and spent nineteen pounds nineteen shillings and sixpence, he would be happy; but that a shilling spent the other way would make him wretched. I see the fire we sat before, now; with two bricks inside the rusted grate, one on each side, to prevent its burning too many coals. Some other debtor shared the room with him, who came in by-and-by; and as the dinner was a joint-stock repast, I was sent up to 'Captain Porter' in the room overhead, with Mr Dickens's compliments, and I was his son, and could he, Captain P., lend me a knife and fork?

Captain Porter lent me the knife and fork, with his compliments in return. There was a very dirty lady in his little room; and two wan girls, his daughters, with shock heads of hair. I thought I should not have liked to borrow Captain Porter's comb. The Captain himself was in the last extremity of shabbiness; and if I could draw at all, I would draw an accurate portrait of the old brown greatcoat he wore, with no other coat below it. His whiskers were large. I saw his bed rolled up in a corner; and what plates, and dishes, and pots he had, on a shelf; and I knew (God knows how) that the two girls with shock heads were Captain Porter's natural children, and that the dirty lady was not married to Captain P. My timid, wondering station on his threshold was not occupied more than a couple of minutes, I dare say; but I came down again to the room below with all this as surely in my knowledge as the knife and fork were in my hand.

There was something gipsy-like and agreeable in the dinner, after all. I took back Captain Porter's knife and fork early in the afternoon, and went home to comfort my mother with an account of my visit.

Almost everything, by degrees, was sold or pawned. My father's books went first. I carried them, one after another, to a bookstall in the Hampstead Road – one part of which, near our house, was almost all bookstalls and bird-shops then – and sold them for whatever they would bring. The keeper of this bookstall, who lived in a little house behind it, used to get tipsy every night, and to be violently scolded by his wife every

The register of the Marshalsea Prison recording the admission of John Dickens.

morning. More than once, when I went there early, I had audience of him in a turn-up bedstead, with a cut in his forehead or a black-eye, bearing witness to his excesses over-night (I am afraid he was quarrelsome in his drink), and he with a shaking hand, endeavouring to find the needful shillings in one or other of the pockets of his clothes, which lay on the floor, while his wife, with a baby in her arms and her shoes down at heel, never left off rating him. Sometimes he had lost his money, and then he would ask me to call again; but his wife had always got some – had taken his, I dare say, while he was drunk – and secretly completed the bargain on the stairs, as we went down together.

At the pawnbroker's shop, too, I began to be very well known. The principal gentleman who officiated behind the counter, took a great deal of notice of me; and often got me, I recollect, to decline a Latin noun or adjective, or to conjugate a Latin verb, in his ear, while he transacted my business.

I don't know how the household furniture came to be sold for the family benefit, or who sold it, except that *I* did not. A sale

84

was held at Gower Street North, however, and my own little bed was so superciliously looked upon by a Power unknown to me hazily called 'the Trade', that a brass coal-scuttle, a roasting-jack, and a birdcage, were obliged to be put in to make a lot of it, and then it went for a song. So I heard mentioned, and I wondered what song, and I thought what a dismal song it must have been to sing!

Our furniture was carried away in a van, all that was left being my parents' bed, a few chairs and the kitchen-table. With these possessions my mother and my brothers and sisters – excepting Fanny, who had been elected a pupil of the Royal Academy of Music some time before – encamped, as it were, with a young servant girl from Chatham Workhouse, in the two parlours of the emptied house. It was a long way to go and return within the dinner-hour, and usually I either carried my dinner with me or went and bought it at some neighbouring shop. In the latter case it was commonly a saveloy and a penny loaf; sometimes a fourpenny plate of beef from a cook's shop; sometimes a plate of bread and cheese and a glass of beer, from a miserable old public-house over the way – *The Swan* if I remember, or *The Swan and* something else that I have forgotten. Once I remember tucking my own bread – which I had brought from home in the morning – under my arm, wrapped up in a piece of paper like a book, and going into the best dining-room in Johnson's à *la mode* beef-house in Clare Court, Drury Lane, and magnificently ordering a small plate of à *la mode* beef to eat with it. What the waiter thought of such a strange little apparition coming in all alone I don't know; but I can see him now, staring at me as I ate my dinner, and bringing the other waiter in to look. I gave him a halfpenny and I wish now that he hadn't taken it.

My solitary life

At last my mother resolved to move into the prison, where my father had now secured a room to himself. The key of the house was sent back to the landlord, who was very glad to get it, and I (small Cain that I was, except that I had never done harm to anyone) was handed over as a lodger to a reduced old lady, long known to our family, in Little College Street, Camden Town, who took children in to board, and had once done so at Brighton; and who, with a few alterations and embellishments, unconsciously began to sit for Mrs Pipchin in *Dombey* when she took in me.

She had a little brother and sister under her care then, somebody's natural children (who were very irregularly paid for), and a widow's little son. The two boys and I slept in the same room. My own exclusive breakfast, of a penny cottage loaf and a pennyworth of milk, I provided for myself. I kept another small loaf and a quarter of a pound of cheese on a particular shelf of a particular cupboard, to make my supper on when I came back at night. They made a hole in the six or seven shillings I know well, and I was out at the blacking-warehouse all day and had to support myself upon that money all the week. I suppose my lodging was paid for by my father; I certainly did not pay for it myself, and I certainly had no other assistance whatever – the making of my clothes, I think, excepted – from Monday morning until Saturday night. No advice, no counsel, no encouragement, no consolation, no support, from anyone that I can call to mind, so help me God!

Sundays Fanny and I passed in the prison. I was at the academy in Tenterden Street, Hanover Square, at nine o'clock in the morning to fetch her, and we walked back there together at night.

I was so young and childish and so little qualified – how could I be otherwise? – to undertake the whole charge of my existence, that, in going to Hungerford Square of a morning, I could not resist the stale pastry put out at half-price on trays at the confectioners' doors in Tottenham Court Road, and I often spent on that the money I should have kept for my dinner. Then I went without my dinner, or bought a roll or a slice of pudding. There were two pudding shops between which I was divided according to my finances. One was in a court close to St Martin's Church (at the back of the church), which is now removed altogether. The pudding at that shop was made with currants and was rather a special pudding, but was dear – two penn'orth not being larger than a penn'orth of more ordinary pudding. A good shop for the latter was in the Strand, somewhere near where the Lowther Arcade is now. It was a stout, hale pudding, heavy and flabby, with great raisins in it stuck in whole at great distances apart. It came up hot at about noon every day, and many and many a day did I dine off it.

We had half-an-hour, I think, for tea. When I had money enough I used to go to a coffee-shop, and have half-a-pint of coffee and a slice of bread and butter. When I had no money I took a turn in Covent Garden Market and stared at the pine-apples. The coffee-shops to which I most resorted were, one in Maiden Lane; one in a court (non-existent now) close to Hungerford Market; and one in St Martin's Lane, of which I only recollect that it stood near the church, and that in the door there was an oval glass plate, with 'Coffee-room' painted on it, addressed towards the street. If I ever find myself in a very different kind of coffee-room now, but where there is such an inscription on glass, and read it backwards on the wrong side 'moor-eeffoC' (as I often used to do then, in a dismal reverie), a shock goes through my blood.

I know I do not exaggerate, unconsciously and unintention-ally, the scantiness of my resources and the difficulties of my life. I know that if a shilling or so were given to me by anyone I spent it in a dinner or tea. I know that I worked from morning to night, with common men and boys, a shabby child. I know that I tried, but ineffectively, not to anticipate my money, and to make it last the week through; by putting it away in the drawer I had in the counting-house, wrapped into six little parcels, each parcel containing the same amount, and labelled with a different day. I know that I have lounged about the streets insufficiently and unsatisfactorily fed. I know that, but for the mercy of God, I might easily have been, for any care that was taken of me, a little robber or a little vagabond.

But I held some station at the blacking-warehouse too. Besides that my relative at the counting house did what a man so occupied, and dealing with a thing so anomalous could, to treat me as one upon a different footing from the rest, I never said, to man or boy, how it was that I came to be there, or gave the least indication of being sorry that I was there. That I suffered in secret, and that I suffered exquisitely, no one ever knew but I. How much I suffered, it is, as I have said already, utterly beyond my power to tell. No man's imagination can overlap the reality. But I kept my own counsel, and I did my work. I knew from the first that if I could not do my work as well as any of the rest, I could not hold myself above slight and contempt. I soon became at least as expeditious and as skilful with my hands as either of the other boys. Though perfectly familiar with them, my conduct and manners were different enough from theirs to place a space between us. They and the men always spoke of me as 'the young gentleman'. A certain one (a soldier once) called Thomas, who was the foreman, and another named Harry, who was the carman, and wore a red jacket, used to call me 'Charles' sometimes, in speaking to me; but I think it was mostly when we were very confidential, and when I had made some efforts to entertain them over our work with the remnants of some of the old readings, which were fast perishing out of my mind. Poll Green uprose once, and rebelled against the 'young gentleman' usage, but Bob Fagin settled him speedily.

My rescue from this kind of existence I considered quite hopeless, and abandoned, as such, altogether; though I am solemnly convinced that I never, for one hour, was reconciled to it, or was otherwise than miserably unhappy. I felt keenly, however, the being so cut off from my parents, my brothers, and sisters; and, when my day's work was done, going home to such a miserable blank; and *that*, I thought, might be corrected. One Sunday night I remonstrated with my father on this head, so pathetically and with so many tears, that his kind nature gave way. He began to think that it was not quite right. I do believe he had never thought so before, or thought about it. It was the first remonstrance I had ever made about my lot, and perhaps it opened up a little more than I intended. A back-attic was found for me at the house of an insolvent court agent, who lived in Lant Street in the Borough, where Bob Sawyer lodged many years afterwards. A bed and bedding were sent over for me, and made up on the floor. The little window had a pleasant prospect of a timber-yard; and when I took possession of my new abode, I thought it was a Paradise.

Bob Fagin was very good to me on the occasion of a bad attack of my old disorder. I suffered such excruciating pain that time, that they made a temporary bed of straw in my old recess in the counting-house, and I rolled about on the floor, and Bob filled empty blacking-bottles with hot water, and applied relays of them to my side half the day. I got better, and quite easy towards evening; but Bob (who was much bigger and older than I) did not like the idea of my going home alone, and took me under his protection. I was too proud to let him know about the prison; and after making several efforts to get rid of him, to all of which Bob Fagin in his goodness was deaf, shook hands with him on the steps of a house near Southwark Bridge on the

Surrey side, making believe that I lived there. As a finishing piece of reality in case of his looking back, I knocked at the door, I recollect, and asked, when the woman opened it, if that was Mr Robert Fagin's house.

My usual way home was over Blackfriars Bridge, and down that turning in the Blackfriars Road which has Rowland Hill's chapel on one side, and the likeness of a golden dog licking a golden pot over a shop door on the other. There are a good many little low-browed old shops in that street, of a wretched kind; and some are unchanged now. I looked into one a few weeks ago, where I used to buy boot-laces on Saturday nights, and saw the corner where I once sat down on a stool to have a pair of ready-made half-boots fitted on. I have been seduced more than once, in that street on a Saturday night, by a show-van at a corner; and have gone in, with a very motley assemblage, to see the Fat Pig, the Wild Indian, and the Little Lady. There were two or three hat-manufactories there then (I think they are there still); and among the things which, encountered anywhere, or under any circumstances, will instantly recall that time, is the smell of hat-making.

It was necessary, as a matter of form, that the clothes I wore should be seen by the official appraiser. I had a half-holiday to enable me to call upon him, at his own time, at a house somewhere beyond the Obelisk. I recollect his coming out to look at me with his mouth full, and a strong smell of beer upon him, and saying good-naturedly that 'that would do', and 'it was all right'. Certainly the hardest creditor would not have been disposed (even if he had been legally entitled) to avail himself of my poor white hat, little jacket, or corduroy trousers. But I had a fat old silver watch in my pocket, which had been given me by my grandmother before the blacking days, and I had entertained my doubts, as I went along, whether that valuable possession might not bring me over the twenty pounds. So I was greatly relieved, and made him a bow of acknowledgment as I went out.

I never, happily for me no doubt, made a single acquaintance, or spoke to any of the many boys whom I saw daily in going to the warehouse, in coming from it, and in prowling about the streets at meal-times. I led the same secretly unhappy life; but I led it in the same lonely, self-reliant manner. The only changes I am conscious of are, firstly, that I had grown more shabby, and secondly, that I was now relieved of much of the weight of my parents' cares; for some relatives or friends had engaged to help them at their present pass, and they lived more comfortably in the prison than they had lived for a long while out of it. I used to breakfast with them now, in virtue of some arrangement, of which I have forgotten the details. I forget, too, at what hour the gates were opened in the morning, admitting of my going in; but I know that I was often up at six o'clock, and that my favourite lounging-place in the interval was old London bridge, where I was wont to sit in one of the stone recesses, watching the people going by, or to look over the balustrades at the sun shining in the water, and lighting up the golden flame on top of the Monument. The Chatham work-house girl met me here sometimes, to be told some astonishing fictions respecting the wharves and the Tower; of which I can say no more than that I hope I believed them myself. In the evening I used to go back to the prison, and walk up and down the parade with my father.

I was fond of wondering about the Adelphi, because it was a mysterious place, with those dark arches. I see myself emerging one evening from some of these very arches, at a little public-house close to the river, with an open space before it; where some coal-heavers were dancing; to look at whom I sat down upon a bench. I wonder what they thought of me!

I was such a little fellow, with my poor white hat, little jacket, and corduroy trousers, that frequently, when I went in the bar of a strange public-house for a glass of ale or porter to wash down the saveloy and the loaf I had eaten in the street, they didn't like to give it to me. I remember, one evening (I had been somewhere for my father, and was going back to the Borough, over Westminster Bridge), that I went into a public-house in Parliament Street, which is still there though altered, at the corner of the short street leading into Cannon Row, and said to the landlord behind the bar, 'What is your very best – the VERY *best* – ale, a glass?' For, the occasion was a festive one, for some reason, I forget why. It may have been my birth-day, or someone else's. 'Twopence,' says he. 'Then', says I, 'just draw me a glass of that, if you please, with a good head to it.' The landlord looked at me, in return, over the bar, from head to foot, with a strange smile on his face, and instead of drawing the beer, looked round the screen and said something to his wife, who came out from behind it, with her work in her hand, and joined him in surveying me. Here we stand, all three, before me now, in my study in Devonshire Place. The landlord, in his shirt-sleeves, leaning against the bar window-frame; his wife, looking over the little half-door; and I, in some confusion, looking up at them from outside the partition. They asked me a good many questions, as what my name was, how old I was, where I lived, how I was employed, etc., etc. To all of which, that I might commit nobody, I invented appropriate answers. They served me with the ale, though I suspect it was not the strongest on the premises; and the landlord's wife, opening the little half-door and bending down, gave me a kiss that was half-admiring and half-compassionate, but all womanly and good, I am sure.

I call to mind that my father, about this time, composed a petition praying for the boon of a bounty to the prisoners to enable them to drink His Majesty's health on His Majesty's birthday. It was arranged that a great signing ceremony should be held. I mention the circumstance because it illustrates, to me, my early interest in observing people. When I went to the Marshalsea of a night, I was always delighted to hear from my mother what she knew about the histories of the different debtors in the prison; and when I heard of this approaching ceremony, I was so anxious to see them all come in, one after another (though I knew the greater part of them already, to speak to, and they me), that I got leave of absence on purpose, and established myself in a corner, near the petition. It was stretched out, I recollect, on a great ironing-board, under the window, which in another part of the room made a bedstead at night. The internal regulations of the place, for cleanliness and order, and for the government of a common-room in the ale-house, where hot water and some means of cooking, and a good fire, were provided for all who paid a very small subscription, were excellently administered by a governing committee of debtors, of which my father was chairman for the time being. As many of the principal officers of this body as could be got into the small room without filling it up, supported him, in front of the petition; and my old friend Captain Porter (who had washed himself, to do honour to so solemn an occasion) stationed himself close to it, to read it to all who were unacquainted with its contents.

The door was then thrown open, and they began to come in, in a long file; several waiting on the landing outside, while one entered, affixed his signature, and went out. To everybody in

This scene from David Copperfield is based on that described by Dickens as having taken place 'at a public-house in Parliament Street'.

succession, Captain Porter said, 'Would you like to hear it read?'
If he weakly showed the least disposition to hear it, Captain
Porter, in a loud sonorous voice, gave him every word of it. I
remember a certain luscious roll he gave to such words as
'Majesty – gracious Majesty – your gracious Majesty's unfortunate subjects – your Majesty's well-known munificence' – as if
the words were something real in his mouth, and delicious to
taste; my poor father meanwhile listening with a little of an
author's vanity, and contemplating (not severely) the spikes on
the opposite wall. Whatever was comical in this scene, and whatever was pathetic, I sincerely believe I perceived in my corner,
whether I demonstrated it or not, quite as well as I should
perceive it now. I made out my own little character and story for
every man who put his name to the sheet of paper. I might be
able to do that now, more truly, not more earnestly, or with a
closer interest. Their different peculiarities of dress, of face, of
gait, of manner, were written indelibly upon my memory. I would
rather have seen it than the best play ever played; and I thought
about it afterwards, over the pots of paste-blacking, often and
often. When I looked, with my mind's eye, into the Fleet Prison
during Mr Pickwick's incarceration, I wonder whether half-a-
dozen men were wanting from the Marshalsea crowd that came
filing in again, to the sound of Captain Porter's voice!

Some of my readers may have an interest in being informed
whether or no any portions of the Marshalsea Prison are yet
standing. I myself did not know until 1857, when I went to look.
I found the outer front courtyard metamorphosed into a butter
shop; and then I almost gave up every brick of the jail for lost.
Wandering, however, down a certain adjacent 'Angel Court,
leading to Bermondsey', I came to 'Marshalsea Place': the
houses which I recognised, not only as the great block of the
former prison, but as preserving the rooms that arose in my
mind's eye when I became Little Dorrit's biographer.

A little further on, I found the older and smaller wall, which
used to enclose the pent-up inner prison where nobody was put,
except for ceremony. Whosoever goes into Marshalsea Place,
turning out of Angel Court, leading to Bermondsey, will find his
feet on the very paving-stones of the extinct Marshalsea jail; will
see its narrow yard to the right and to the left, very little altered
if at all, except that the walls were lowered when the place got
free; will look upon the rooms in which the debtors lived; will
stand among the crowding ghosts of many miserable years.

My father is released and so am I

My father eventually obtained his freedom. I re-joined my family in the Little College Street lodgings and we subsequently moved to a small house in Somers Town. Before that move took place we saw my sister presented with one of the prizes given to the pupils of the Royal Academy of Music. I could not bear to think of myself – beyond the reach of all such honourable emulation and success. The tears ran down my face. I felt as if my heart were rent. I prayed, when I went to bed that night, to be lifted out of the humiliation and neglect in which I was. I never had suffered so much before. There was no envy in this.

I am not sure that it was before this time, or after it, that the blacking-warehouse was removed to Chandos Street, Covent Garden. It is no matter. Next to the shop at the corner of Bedford Street in Chandos Street are two rather old-fashioned houses and shops adjoining one another. They were one then, or thrown into one, for the blacking business; and had been a butter shop. Opposite to them was, and is, a public-house, where I got my ale, under these new circumstances. The stones in the street may be smoothed by my small feet going across to it at dinner-time, and back again. The establishment was larger now, and we had one or two new boys. Bob Fagin and I had attained great dexterity in tying up the pots. I forget how many we could do in five minutes. We worked, for the light's sake, near the second window as you come from Bedford Street; and we were so brisk at it, that the people used to stop and look in. Sometimes there would be quite a little crowd there. I saw my father coming in at the door one day when we very busy, and I wondered how he could bear it.

Now, I generally had my dinner in the warehouse. Sometimes I brought it with me from home, so I was better off. I see myself coming across Russell Square from Somers Town, one morning, with some cold hotch-potch in a small basin tied up in a handkerchief. I had the same wanderings about the street as I used to have, and was just as solitary and self-dependent as before; but I had not the same difficulty in merely living. I never, however, heard a word of being taken away, or of being otherwise than quite provided for.

At last, one day, my father and the relative so often mentioned, quarrelled; quarrelled by letter, for I took the letter from my father to him which caused the explosion, but quarrelled very fiercely. It was about me. It may have had some backward reference, in part, for anything I know, to my employment at the window. All I am certain of is, that, soon after I had given him the letter, my cousin (for he was a sort of cousin, by marriage) told me that he was very much insulted about me; and that it was impossible to keep me after that. I cried very much, partly because it was so sudden, and partly because in his anger he was violent about my father, though gentle to me. Thomas, the old soldier, comforted me, and said he was sure it was for the best. With a relief so strange that it was like oppression, I went home.

My mother set herself to accommodate the quarrel, and did so next day. She brought home a request for me to return next morning, and a high character of me, which I am very sure I deserved. My father said I should go back no more, and should go to school. I do not write resentfully or angrily, for I know how all these things have worked together to make me what I am; but I never afterwards forgot, I never can forget, that my mother was warm for my being sent back.

From that hour until this at which I write, no word of that part of my childhood, which I have now gladly brought to a close, has passed my lips to any human being. I have no idea how long it lasted, whether for a year, or much more, or less. From that hour until this, my father and mother have been stricken dumb upon it. I have never heard the least allusion to it, however far off and remote, from either of them. I have never, until I now impart to this paper, in any burst of confidence with anyone, my own wife not excepted, raised the curtain I then dropped, thank God.

Until old Hungerford Market was pulled down, until old Hungerford Stairs were destroyed, and the very nature of the ground changed, I never had the courage to go back to the place where my servitude began. I never saw it. I could not endure to go near it. For many years, when I came near to Robert Warren's in the Strand, I crossed over to the opposite side of the way to avoid a certain smell of the cement they put upon the blacking-corks, which reminded me of what I once was. It was a very long time before I liked to go up Chandos Street. My old way home by the Borough made me cry, after my eldest child could speak.

In my walks at night I have walked there often, since then,

and by degrees I have come to write this. It does not seem a tithe of what I might have written, or of what I meant to write.

My education is resumed

There was a school in the Hampstead Road kept by Mr Jones, a Welshman, to whom my father despatched me to ask for a card of terms. The boys were at dinner, and Mr Jones was carving for them, with a pair of holland sleeves on, when I acquitted myself of this commission. He came out, and gave me what I wanted; and hoped I should become a pupil. I did. At seven o'clock one morning, very soon afterwards, I went as a day scholar to Mr Jones's establishment, which was in Mornington Place, and had its classroom sliced away by the Birmingham railway, when that change came about. The schoolroom, however, was not threatened by directors or civil engineers then, and there was a board over the door graced with the words 'Wellington House Academy'.

It seemed to me so long since I had been among such boys, or among any companions of my own age except Bob Fagin and Poll Green, that I felt as strange as ever I had done in my life. I was so conscious of having passed through scenes of which they could have no knowledge, and of having acquired experiences foreign to my age, appearance, and conditions as one of them, that I half believed it was an imposture to come there as an ordinary schoolboy. I had become, in the blacking warehouse time, however short or long it may have been, so unused to the sports and games of boys that I knew I was awkward and inexperienced in the commonest things belonging to them. My mind ran upon what they would think, if they knew of my familiar acquaintance with the Marshalsea. What would they say, who made so light on money, if they could know how I had scraped my halfpence together, for the purchase of my daily saveloy and beer, or my slices of pudding? But, within the space of a few short hours I began to feel my uneasiness softening away.

I was old enough to be put into Virgil when I went there, and to get Prizes for a variety of polishing on which the dust has long accumulated. It was a school of some celebrity in its neighbourhood – nobody could have said why – and I had the honour to attain and hold the eminent position of first boy. The master was supposed among us to know nothing, and one of the ushers (Mr Taylor) was supposed to know everything. I am still inclined to think the first-named supposition perfectly correct.

I have a general idea that the respected proprietor of Our School had been in the leather trade, and had bought us – meaning Our School – of another proprietor who was immensely learned. Whether this belief had any real foundation, I am not likely ever to know now. What I *do* know is that he was by far the most ignorant man I have ever had the pleasure to encounter and one of the worst-tempered men perhaps who ever lived. The only branches of education with which he showed the least acquaintance were ruling and corporally punishing. He was always ruling ciphering-books with a bloated mahogany ruler, or smiting the palms of offenders with the same diabolical instrument, or viciously drawing a pair of pantaloons tight with one of his large hands, and caning the wearer with the other. I have no doubt whatever that this occupation was the principal solace of his existence. It was his business to make as much out of us and to put as little into us as possible, and he eventually sold us at a figure which I remember we used to delight to estimate as amounting to exactly £2.4s.6d. a head.

I don't like that sort of school, because I don't see what business the master had at the top of it instead of the bottom, and because I never could understand the wholesomeness of the moral preached by the abject appearance and degraded condition of the teachers who plainly said to us every day, 'Boys, never be learned; whatever you are, above all things, be warned from that in time by our sunken cheeks, by our poor pimply noses so cruelly eruptive in the frosty mornings, by our meagre diet, by our acid beer, and by our extraordinary suits of clothes, of which no human being can say whether they are snuff-coloured turned black, or black turned snuff-coloured, a point upon which we ourselves are perfectly unable to offer any ray of enlightenment, it is so very long since they were undarned and new.' I don't like that sort of school, because I have never yet lost my ancient suspicion touching that curious coincidence that the boy with four brothers to come always gets the prizes. In fact, and in short, I do not like that sort of school, which is a pernicious and abominable humbug altogether.

Again, I don't like that sort of school, a ladies' school, with which Our School used to dance on Wednesdays, where the

97

Charles Dickens aged about twelve.

young ladies, as I look back upon them now, seem to me always to have been in new stays and disgrace – the disgrace chiefly concerning a place of which I know nothing at this day, that bounds Timbuctoo on the north-west – and where memory always depicts the youthful enthraller of my first affection as for ever standing against a wall, in a curious machine of wood, which confined her innocent feet in the first dancing position, while those arms which should have encircled my jacket, those precious arms, were pinioned behind her by an instrument of torture called a backboard, fixed in the manner of a double direction post.

A profound respect for money pervaded Our School, which was, of course, derived from its Chief. I remember an idiotic goggle-eyed boy, with a big head and half-crowns without end, who suddenly appeared as a parlour-boarder, and was rumoured to have come by sea from some mysterious part of the earth where his parents rolled in gold. He was usually called 'Mr' by the Chief, and was said to feed in the parlour on steaks and gravy; likewise to drink currant wine. And he openly stated that if rolls and coffee were ever denied to him at breakfast, he would write home to that unknown part of the globe from which he had come, and cause himself to be recalled to the regions of gold. He was put into no form or class, but learnt alone, as little as he liked – and he liked very little – and there was a belief among us that this was because he was too wealthy to be 'taken down'. His special treatment, and our vague association of him with the sea, and with storms, and sharks, and Coral Reefs occasioned the wildest legends to be circulated as to his history. A tragedy in blank verse was written on the subject – if my memory does not deceive me, by the hand that now chronicles these recollections – in which his father figured as Pirate, and was shot for a voluminous catalogue of atrocities: first imparting to his wife the secret of the cave in which his wealth was stored, and from which his only son's half-crowns now issued. Dumbledon (the boy's name) was represented as 'yet unborn' when his brave father met his fate; and the despair and grief of Mrs Dumbledon at that calamity was movingly shadowed forth as having weakened the parlour-boarder's mind. This production was received with great favour, and was twice performed with closed doors in the dining-room. But it got wind, and was seized as libellous, and brought the unlucky poet into severe affliction. Some two years afterwards, all of a sudden one day, Dumbledon vanished. It was whispered that the Chief himself had taken him down to the Docks, and re-shipped him for the Spanish Main; but nothing certain was ever known about his disappearance. At this hour, I cannot thoroughly disconnect him from California.

Our School was rather famous for mysterious pupils. There was another – a heavy young man, with a large double-cased silver watch, and a fat knife the handle of which was a perfect tool-box – who unaccountably appeared one day at a special desk of his own, erected close to that of the Chief, with whom he held familiar converse. He lived in the parlour, and went out for his own walks, and never took the least notice of us – even of me, the first boy – unless to give us a deprecatory kick, or grimly to take our hats off and throw them away, when he encountered us out of doors, which unpleasant ceremony he always performed as he passed – not even condescending to stop for the purpose. Some of us believed that the classical attainments of this phenomenon were terrific, but that his penmanship and arithmetic were defective, and he had come there to mend them; others, that he was going to set up a school, and had paid the Chief 'twenty-five pund down', for leave to see Our School at work. The gloomier spirits even said that he was going to buy us; against which contingency, conspiracies were set on foot for a general defection and running away. However, he never did that. After staying for a quarter, during which period, though closely observed, he was never seen to do anything but make pens out of quills, write small hand in a secret portfolio, and punch the point of the sharpest blade in his knife into his desk all over it, he too disappeared, and his place knew him no more.

There was another boy, a fair, meek boy, with a delicate complexion and rich curling hair, who, we found out, or thought we found out (I have no idea now, and probably had none then, on what grounds, but it was confidentially revealed from hand to mouth), was the son of a Viscount who had deserted his lovely mother. It was understood that if he had rights, he would be worth twenty thousand a year. And that if his mother ever met his father, she would shoot him with a silver pistol, always loaded to the muzzle, for that purpose. He was a very suggestive topic. So was a young Mulatto, who was always believed (though very amiable) to have a dagger upon him somewhere. But I think they were both outshone, upon the whole, by another boy who claimed to have been born upon the twenty-ninth of February, and to have only one birthday in five years. I suspect this to have been a fiction – but he lived upon it all the time he was at Our School.

The principal currency of Our School was slate pencil. It had some inexplicable value, that was never ascertained, never reduced to a standard. To have a great hoard of it was somehow to be rich. We used to bestow it in charity, and confer it as a precious boon upon our chosen friends. When the holidays were coming, contributions were solicited for certain boys whose relatives were in India, and who were appealed for under the generic name of 'Holiday-stoppers' – appropriate marks of remembrance that should enliven and cheer them in their homeless state. Personally, I always contributed these tokens of sympathy in the form of slate pencil, and always felt that it would be a comfort and a treasure to them.

Our School was remarkable for white mice. Red-polls, linnets, and even canaries, were kept in desks, drawers, hat-boxes, and other strange refuges for birds; but white mice were the favourite stock. The boys trained the mice much better than the masters trained the boys. I recall one white mouse, who lived in the cover of a Latin dictionary, who ran up ladders, drew Roman chariots, shouldered muskets, turned wheels, and even made a very creditable appearance on the stage as the Dog of Montargis. He might have achieved greater things, but for having the misfortune to mistake his way in a triumphal procession to the Capitol, when he fell into a deep inkstand, and was dyed black and drowned. The mice were the occasion of some most ingenious engineering, in the construction of their houses and instruments of performance. The famous one belonged to a company of proprietors, some of whom have since made Railroads, Engines, and Telegraphs; the chairman has erected mills and bridges in New Zealand.

The usher at Our School, who was considered to know everything as opposed to the Chief, who was considered to know nothing, was Mr Taylor, a bony, gentle-faced, clerical-looking young man in rusty black. It was whispered that he was sweet upon one of Maxby's sisters (Maxby lived close by, and was a day pupil), and further that he 'favoured Maxby'. As I remember, he taught Italian to Maxby's sisters on half-holidays. He once went to the play with them, and wore a white waistcoat and a rose: which was considered among us equivalent to a declaration. We were of opinion on that occasion, that to the last moment he expected Maxby's father to ask him to dinner at five o'clock, and therefore neglected his own dinner at half-past one, and finally got none. We exaggerated in our imaginations the extent to which he punished Maxby's father's cold meat at supper; and we agreed to believe that he was elevated with wine and water when he came home. But we all liked him; for he had a good knowledge of boys, and would have made it a much better school if he had had more power. He was writing master, mathematical master, English master, made out the bills, mended the pens, and did all sorts of things. He divided the little boys with the Latin master (they were smuggled through their rudimentary books, at odd times when there was little else to do), and he always called at parents' houses to inquire after sick boys, because he had gentlemanly manners. He was rather musical, and on some remote quarter-day had bought an old trombone; but a bit of it was lost, and it made the most extraordinary sounds when he sometimes tried to play it of an evening. His holidays never began (on account of the bills) until long after ours; but in the summer vacations he used to take pedestrian excursions with a knapsack; and at Christmas time he went to see his father at Chipping Norton, who we all said (on no authority) was a dairy-fed pork-butcher. Poor fellow! he was very low all day on Maxby's sister's wedding-day, and afterwards was thought to favour Maxby more than ever, though he had been expected to spite him. He has been dead these twenty years. Poor fellow!

My remembrance presents the Latin master (Mr Mandeville) as a colourless doubled-up near-sighted man with a crutch, who was always cold, and always putting onions into his ears for deafness, and always disclosing ends of flannel under all his garments, and almost always applying a ball of pocket-handkerchief to some part of his face with a screwing action round and round. He was a very good scholar, and took great pains where he saw intelligence and a desire to learn: otherwise, perhaps not. My memory presents him (unless teased into a passion) with as little energy as colour – as having been worried and tormented into monotonous feebleness – as having had the best part of his life ground out of him in a Mill of boys. I remember with terror how he fell asleep one sultry afternoon with the little smuggled class before him, and awoke not when the footsteps of the Chief fell heavy on the floor; how the Chief aroused him, in the midst of a dead silence, and said, 'Mr Mandeville, are you ill, sir?'; how he blushing replied, 'Sir, rather so'; how the Chief retorted with severity, 'Mr Mandeville, this is no place to be ill in' (which was very, very true), and walked back solemn as the ghost in *Hamlet*, until, catching a wondrous eye, he caned that boy for inattention, and happily expressed his feelings towards the Latin master through the medium of a substitute.

There was a fat little dancing master (Mr Shiers) who used to come in a gig, and taught the more advanced among us hornpipes (as an accomplishment in great social demand in after life); and there was a brisk little French master who used to come in the sunniest weather, with a handleless umbrella, and to whom the Chief was always polite, because (as we believed), if the Chief offended him, he would instantly address the Chief in French, and for ever confound him before the boys with his inability to understand or reply.

There was, besides, a serving man whose name was Phil. My retrospective glance presents Phil as a shipwrecked carpenter, cast away upon the desert island of a school, and carrying into practice an ingenious inkling of many trades. He mended whatever was broken, and made whatever was wanted. He was general glazier, among other things, and mended all the broken windows – at the prime cost (as was darkly rumoured among us) of ninepence, for every square charged three-and-six to parents. We had a high opinion of his mechanical genius, and generally held that the Chief 'knew something bad of him', and on pain of divulgence enforced Phil to be his bondsman. I particularly remember that Phil had a sovereign contempt for learning: which engenders in me a respect for his sagacity, as it implies his accurate observation of the relative positions of the Chief and the ushers. He was an impenetrable man, who waited at tables between whiles, and throughout 'the half' kept the boxes in severe custody. He was morose, even to the Chief, and never smiled, except at breaking-up, when, in acknowledgment of the toast, 'Success to Phil! Hooray!' he would slowly carve a grin out of his wooden face, where it would remain until we were all gone. Nevertheless, one time when we had the scarlet fever in the school, Phil nursed all the sick boys of his own accord, and was like a mother to them.

When shall I disconnect the combined smells of oranges, brown paper, and straw from birthdays at school, when the coming hamper cast its shadow before, and when a week of social harmony – shall I add of admiring and affectionate popularity – led me up to that Institution? What noble sentiments were expressed to me in the days before the hamper, what vows of friendship were sworn to me, what exceedingly old knives were given me, what generous avowals of having been in the wrong emanated from else obstinate spirits once enrolled among my enemies!

The birthday of the potted game, and guava jelly, is still made special to me by the noble conduct of Bully Gibson. Letters from home had mysteriously inquired whether I should be much surprised and disappointed if among the treasures in the coming hamper I discovered potted game, and guava jelly from the Western Indies. I had mentioned those hints in confidence to a few friends, and had promised to give away, as I now see reason to believe, a handsome covey of partridges potted, and about a hundredweight of guava jelly. It was now that Gibson, bully no more, sought me out in the playground. He was a big fat boy, with a big fat head and a big fat fist, and at the beginning of that Half had raised such a bump on my forehead that I couldn't get my hat of state on, to go to church. He said that after an interval of cool reflection (four months) he now felt this blow to have been an error of judgment, and that he wished to apologise for the same. Not only that, but holding down his big head between his two big hands in order that I might reach it conveniently, he requested me, as an act of justice which would appease his awakened conscience, to raise a retributive bump upon it, in the presence of witnesses. This handsome proposal I modestly declined, and he then embraced me, and we walked away conversing. We conversed respecting the West India Islands, and, in the pursuit of knowledge he asked me with much interest whether in the course of my reading I had met with any reliable description of the mode of manufacturing guava jelly; or whether I had ever happened to taste that conserve, which he had been given to understand was of rare excellence.

I wonder by what secret understanding our attention began to wander when we had pored over our books for some hours. I wonder by what ingenuity we brought on that confused state of mind when sense becomes nonsense, when figures wouldn't work, when dead languages wouldn't construe, when live languages wouldn't be spoken, when memory wouldn't come, when dullness and vacancy wouldn't go. I cannot remember that we ever conspired to be sleepy after dinner, or that we ever particularly wanted to be stupid, and to have flushed faces and hot beating heads, or to find blank hopelessness and obscurity this afternoon in what would become perfectly clear and bright in the freshness of tomorrow morning. We suffered for these things, and they made us miserable enough. Neither do I remember that we ever bound ourselves by any secret oath or other solemn obligation, to find the seats getting too hard to be sat upon after a certain time; or to have intolerable twitches in our legs, rendering us aggressive and malicious with those members; or to be troubled with a similar uneasiness in our elbows, attended with fistic consequences to our neighbours; or to carry two pounds of lead in the chest, four pounds in the head, and several active blue-bottles in each ear. Yet, for certain, we suffered under those distresses, and were always charged at for labouring under them, as if we had brought them on, of our own deliberate act and deed. As to the mental portion of them being my own fault in my own case – I should like to ask any well-trained and experienced teacher, not to say psychologist. And as to the physical portion – I should like to ask Professor Owen.

I used, when I was at school, to take in *The Terrific Register*, making myself unspeakably miserable, and frightening my very wits out of my head, for the small charge of a penny weekly; which considering that there was an illustration to every number, in which there was always a pool of blood, and at least one body, was cheap.

Christmas associations cluster thick. School-books shut up, Ovid and Virgil silenced; the Rule of Three, with its cool impertinent inquiries, long disposed of; Terence and Plautus acted no more, in an arena of huddled desks and forms, all chipped, and notched, and inked; cricket-bats, stumps and balls, left higher up, with the smell of trodden grass and the softened noise of shouts in the evening air.

There was another school not far off, and of course Our School could have nothing to say to that school. It is mostly the way with schools, whether of boys or men. Well! the railway has swallowed up ours, and the locomotives now run mostly over its ashes.

> So fades and languishes, grows dim and dies,
> All that this world is proud of,

– and is not proud of too. It has little reason to be proud of Our School and has done much better since in that way, and will do far better yet.

PART THREE

MANHOOD

'I devoted myself ... to the study of shorthand,
with a view to trying out what I could do as a
reporter – not for the newspapers, but legal
authorities – in our Ecclesiastical courts.'
– letter to J.H. Keunzel, July (?) 1838

I begin the world

I won prizes at school, and great fame, and was positively
assured that I was a very clever boy. I distinguished myself (as
at other places) like a brick. But I left school tolerably early, for
my father was not a rich man and I had to begin the world. I
began it in a solicitor's office (the solicitor being a friend of my
father), which is a very little world and a very dull one.

In the capacity of junior clerk, attired in Russian jacket and
soldierly young cap, I became familiar, for some two years, with
a set of chambers in Gray's Inn Square, since which time I have
looked upon Gray's Inn generally as one of the most depressing
institutions in brick and mortar known to the children of men.
Can anything be more dreary than its arid Square, Sahara
Desert of the law, with its ugly, old tiled-topped tenements, the
dirty windows, the bills 'To Let', 'To Let', the door-posts
inscribed like gravestones, the crazy gateway giving upon the
filthy Lane, the scowling iron-barred prison-like passages into
Verulam Buildings, the mouldy red-nosed ticket-porters with
little coffin plates, and why with aprons, the dray hard atomy-
like appearance of the whole dust-heap? When my travels tend
nowadays to this dismal spot, my comfort is its rickety state.
Imagination gloats over the fullness of time when the staircases
shall have quite tumbled down – they are daily wearing into an
ill-savoured powder, but have not quite tumbled down yet –
when the last old prolix bencher of all the olden time, shall have
been got out of a window by means of a Fire Ladder, and carried
off to the Holborn Union; when the last clerk shall have

107

engrossed the last parchment behind the last splash on the last of the mud-stained windows, which, all through the miry year, are pilloried out of recognition in Gray's Inn Lane. Then, shall a squalid little trench, with rank grass and a pump in it, lying between the coffee-house and South Square, be wholly given up to cats and rats, and not, as now, have its empire divided between those animals and a few briefless bipeds – surely called to the Bar by voices of deceiving spirits, seeing that they are wanted there by no mortal – who glance down, with eyes better glazed than their casements, from their dreary and lacklustre rooms. Then shall the way Nor' Westward, now lying under a short grim colonnade where in summer-time pounce flies from law-stationering windows into the eyes of laymen, be choked with rubbish and happily become impassable. Then shall the gardens where turf, trees, and gravel wear a legal livery of black, run rank, and pilgrims go to Gorhambury to see Bacon's effigy as he sat, and not come here (which in truth they seldom do) to see where he walked. Then, in a word, shall the old-established vendor of periodicals sit alone in his little crib of a shop behind the Holborn gate, like a lumbering Marius among the ruins of Carthage, who has sat heavy on a thousand million of similes.

I grow ambitious

I never had money help from any human creature after I was a child (and I would never have anything left to me but relations). Understandably, in all the golden fables I had read there was never gold enough for me. Fortunatus had only a life interest in his purse; and we all know too well that when he died, it vanished with him. Sinbad the Sailor, a munificent merchant in his way, gave the porter of Baghdad only a poor one hundred sequins every day after dinner. Aladdin sent his mother to propose for the Sultan's daughter, with a tolerable present of jewels, but still with no more than could be spread forth on a china dish and tied up in a napkin. The Genie of the Lamp considered it a reasonable exercise of his supernatural power, to serve refreshments on a 'large silver tray holding twelve covered dishes of the same metal, two flagons of wine, and two silver cups'. Ali Baba beheld in the robbers' cavern what his limited ideas conceived to be a pretty large amount of ready money in gold coin; yet he thought it a wonderful thing to carry off no more than his three asses could bear, under an outer load of wood and green boughs; and there was not so much of it but that his wife borrowed 'a small measure' – about the size of a banker's shovel, say – to measure it out. Prince Camarlalzaman (not to be learned, and call him Kummir al Zummaun) found, in the cave he accidentally opened on the gardener's ground, fifty brass urns, each with a cover on it, all full of gold dust. But, his share of gold dust, when he divided it with the gardener, was not such a great share after all, for it only half-filled fifty olive pots; and *that's* not much – in these times. Candide and Cacambo, when they came to the land of the red sheep, found the common children (in very ragged clothes of golden brocade) playing at quits with pretty large pieces of gold. But, they might find the common men in Australia and California playing a variety of games with the same bright metal, at the present hour. The double- and treble-headed giants whom courageously Jack destroyed, were believed in their pastoral days to be gigantically rich, although they had only stored up inexhaustible amounts of gold. Nay, the very gods of classical antiquity were represented as celestial in the possession of services of golden plate, and the lounging upon golden couches.

I repeat, in all these golden fables there was never gold enough for me. I always wanted more. I saw no reason why there should not be mountains and rivers of gold, instead of paltry little caverns and olive pots; why Jason and his men should not have sailed in search of flocks of golden fleeces rather than one. For, when imagination does begin to deal with what is so hard of attainment in reality, it might at least get out of bounds for once in a way, and let us have enough.

I didn't much like it in the solicitor's office, and after a couple of years (as well as I can remember) applied myself with a celestial or diabolical energy to the study of such things as would qualify me to be a first-rate parliamentary reporter – at that time a calling pursued by many clever men who were young at the Bar. I made enquiries as to how I could qualify myself for this pursuit and learnt that the mere mechanical acquisition necessary, except in rare cases, for thorough excellence in it, that is to say, a perfect and entire command of the mystery of shorthand writing and reading, was about equal in difficulty to the mastering of six languages; and that it might, perhaps, be attained, by dint of perseverance, in the course of a few years.

But I did not allow my resolution, with respect to the parliamentary debates, to cool. It was one of the irons I kept hot, and hammered at, with a perseverance I may honestly admire. I bought an improved scheme of the noble art and mystery of stenography (Thomas Gurney's *Brachygraphy, or an easy and compendious System of Shorthand* which cost me ten and sixpence) and plunged into a sea of perplexity that brought me, in a few weeks, to the confines of distraction. The changes that were rung upon dots, which in such a position meant such a thing, and in such another position something else, entirely different; the wonderful vagaries that were played by circles; the unaccountable consequences that resulted from marks like flies' legs; the tremendous effects of a curve in a wrong place; not only troubled my waking hours, but reappeared before me in my sleep. When I had groped my way, blindly, through these difficulties, and had mastered the alphabet, which was an Egyptian temple in itself, there then appeared a procession of new horrors, called arbitrary characters; the most despotic characters that I have ever known; who insisted, for instance, that a thing like the beginning of a cobweb, meant expectation, and that a pen-and-ink skyrocket stood for disadvantageous. When I had fixed these wretches in my mind, I found that they had driven everything else out of it; then, beginning again, I forgot them; while I was picking them up, I dropped the other fragments of the system; in short, it was almost heart-breaking.

I feel as if it were not for me to record how hard I worked at that tremendous shorthand. I will only add, to what I have already written of my perseverance at this time of my life, and of a patient and continuous energy which then began to be matured within me, and which I know to be the strong part of my character, if it have any strength at all, that there, on looking back, I find the source of my success. I have been very fortunate in worldly matters; many men have worked much harder, and not succeeded half so well; but I never could have done what I have done, without the habits of punctuality, order, and diligence, without the determination to concentrate myself on one object at a time, no matter how quickly its successor should come upon its heels, which I then formed. Heaven knows I write this in no spirit of self-laudation. The man who reviews

A specimen of Dickens's shorthand.

his own life, as I do mine, in going on here, from page to page, had need to have been a good man indeed, if he would be spared the sharp consciousness of many talents neglected, many opportunities wasted, many erratic and perverted feelings constantly at war within his breast, and defeating him. I do not hold one natural gift, I dare say, that I have not abused. My meaning simply is, that whatever I have tried to do in life, I have tried with all my heart to do well; that whatever I have devoted myself to, I have devoted myself to completely; that in great aims and in small, I have always been thoroughly in earnest. I have never believed it possible that any natural or improved ability can claim immunity from the companionship of the steady, plain, hard-working qualities, and hope to gain its end. There is no such thing as such fulfilment on this earth. Some happy talent, and some fortunate opportunity, may form the two sides of the ladder on which some men mount, but the rounds of that ladder must be made of stuff to stand wear and tear; and there is no substitute for thorough-going, ardent, and sincere earnestness. Never to put one hand to anything on which I could throw my whole self; and never to affect depreciation of my work, whatever it was; I find, now, to have been one of my golden rules.

I eventually tamed that savage stenographic mystery and found work at Doctors' Commons as a shorthand writer for the proctors. I lived in lodgings for a time with a law student, James Roney (a future Colonial Chief Justice!), and we gave our first dinner at the mansion of Mrs Rogers in Buckingham Street, Adelphi. I bought the soup myself (it was hard, and looked like a bit of a mantel-piece), and he provided some inheritance of family tea-spoons for the decoration of the festival. He had a great affection for me at that time, and always supposed I was to do some sort of wonders.

The work at Doctors' Commons was not a very good living (although not a *very* bad one) and was wearily uncertain; which made me think of the Theatre as a possible career in quite a business-like way. I went to some theatre every night, with a very few exceptions, for at least three years: really studying the bills first, and going to where there was the best acting: and always to see Charles Matthews wherever he played. I practised immensely (even such things as walking in and out, and sitting down in a chair); often four, five, six hours a day; shut up in my own room, or walking about in the fields. I prescribed to myself, too, a sort of Hamiltonian system for learning parts; and learnt a great number.

When I was about twenty, and knew three or four successive years of Matthews's *At Homes* from sitting in the pit to hear them, I wrote to George Bartley, who was stage-manager at Covent Garden, and told him how young I was, and exactly what I thought I could do; and that I believed I had a strong perception of character and oddity, and a natural power of reproducing in my own person what I observed in others. I recollect I wrote the letter from a little office I had at No. 5 Bell Yard, where the answer came also. There must have been something in my letter that struck the authorities, for Bartley wrote to me almost immediately to say that they were busy getting up *The Hunchback* (so they were!), but that they would communicate again with me in a fortnight. Punctual to the time another letter came, with an appointment to do anything of Matthews's I pleased before him and Charles Kemble, on a certain day at the theatre. My sister Fanny was in the secret, and was to go with me to play the songs. I was laid up when the day came with a terrible bad cold and inflammation of the face; the beginning, by-the-bye, of an annoyance in one ear to which I am subject to this day. I wrote to say so, and added that I would renew my application next season.

But I was meanwhile induced to join *The Mirror of Parliament*, a voluminous publication no longer in existence which was at that time devoted solely to the debates. I made a great splash in the gallery (at about eighteen, I suppose) and was then engaged by the *Morning Chronicle*, which had acquired a large circulation after being purchased by Sir John Easthope. I had a distinction in the little world of the newspaper, which made me like it; began to write; did not want money; had never thought of the stage but as the means of getting it and gradually left off turning my thoughts in the direction of the theatre and never resumed the idea. But years later, when engaged in amateur theatricals, I developed some wonderful thoughts on stage effects to the Master Carpenter at one of the theatres, and he shook his head with an intensely mournful air, and said 'Ah Sir, it's a universal observation in the profession, Sir, that it was a great loss to the public wen you took to writing books!'

A Reading Room encounter

I also devoted myself for some time to the acquirement of such general literature as I could pick up in the Library of the British Museum, but found my attention distracted by a shabby-genteel man; he was bodily present to my senses all day, and he was in my mind's eye all night. The man of whom Sir Walter Scott speaks in his *Demonology* did not suffer half the persecution from his imaginary gentleman-usher in black velvet that I sustained from my friend in quondam black cloth. He first attracted my notice, by sitting opposite to me in the Reading Room at the Museum; and what made the man more remarkable was, that he always had before him a couple of shabby-genteel books – two old dog's eared folios, in mouldy worm-eaten covers, which had once been smart. He was in his chair every morning, just as the clock struck ten; he was always the last to leave the room in the afternoon; and when he did, he quitted it with the air of a man who knew not where else to go for warmth and quiet. There he used to sit all day, as close to the table as possible, in order to conceal the lack of buttons on his coat: with his old hat carefully deposited at his feet, where he evidently flattered himself it escaped observation.

When I first saw this poor object, I thought it quite impossible that his attire could ever become worse. I even went so far as to speculate on the possibility of his shortly appearing in a decent second-hand suit. I knew nothing about the matter; he grew more and more shabby-genteel every day. The buttons dropped off his waistcoat one by one; then, he buttoned his coat; and when one side of the coat was reduced to the same condition as the waistcoat, he buttoned it over on the other side. He looked somewhat better at the beginning of the week than at the conclusion, because his neckerchief, though yellow, was not quite so dingy; and in the midst of all his wretchedness, he never appeared without gloves and straps. He remained in this state for a week or two. At length, one of the buttons on the back of the coat fell off, and then the man himself disappeared, and I thought he was dead.

I was sitting at the same table about a week after his disappearance, and as my eyes rested on his vacant chair, I insensibly fell into a train of meditation on the subject of his retirement from public life. I was wondering whether he had hung himself, or thrown himself off a bridge – whether he really was dead, or had only been arrested – when my conjectures were suddenly set at rest by the entry of the man himself. He had undergone some strange metamorphosis, and walked up the centre of the room with an air which showed he was fully conscious of the improvement in his appearance. It was very odd. His clothes were a fine, deep, glossy black; and yet they looked like the same suit; nay, there were the very darns with which old acquaintance had made me familiar. The hat, too – nobody could mistake the shape of that hat, with its high crown gradually increasing in circumference towards the top. Long service had imparted to it a reddish-brown tint; but now it was as black as the coat. The truth flashed suddenly upon me – they had been 'revived'. It is a deceitful liquid that black and blue reviver; I have watched its effect on many a shabby-genteel man. It betrays its victims into a temporary assumption of importance: possibly into the purchase of a new pair of gloves, or a cheap stock, or some other trifling article of dress. It elevates their spirits for a week, only to depress them, if possible, below their original level. It was so in this case; the transient dignity of the unhappy man decreased, in exact proportion as the 'reviver' wore off. The knees of the unmentionables, and the elbows of the coat, and the seams generally, soon began to get alarmingly white. The hat was once more deposited under the table, and its owner crept into his seat as quietly as ever.

There was a week of incessant rain and mist. At its expiration the 'reviver' had entirely vanished, and the shabby-genteel man never afterwards attempted to effect any improvement in his outward appearance.

Doctors' Commons

If, walking without any definite object through St Paul's Churchyard, a little while ago, one happened to turn down a street entitled 'Paul's Chain', and kept straight forward for a few hundred yards, one found oneself, as a natural consequence, in Doctors' Commons – familiar by name to everybody, at that time, as the place where they granted marriage-licences to love-sick couples, and divorces to unfaithful ones; registered the wills of people who had any property to leave, and punished hasty gentlemen who called ladies by unpleasant names.

Crossing a quiet and shady courtyard, paved with stone, and frowned upon by old red brick houses, on the doors of which were painted the names of sundry learned civilians, one came at length to the building known as the 'Prerogative Office' and walked into a room which was a long, busy-looking place, in which a few clerks were engaged in copying or examining deeds. Down the centre of the room were several desks nearly breast high, at each of which, three or four people were standing, poring over large volumes, searching for wills. It was curious to contrast the lazy indifference of the attorneys' clerks who were making a search for some legal purpose, with the air of earnestness and interest which distinguished the strangers to the place, who were looking up the will of some deceased relative; the former pausing every now and then with an impatient yawn, or raising their heads to look at the people who passed up and down the room; the latter stooping over the book, and running down column after column of names in the deepest abstraction.

The maxim that out of evil cometh good, is abundantly proved by the records of the Prerogative Office. Some immensely rich old gentleman or lady, surrounded by needy relatives, makes, upon a low average, a will a-week. The old gentleman or lady, never very remarkable in the best of times for good temper, is full of aches and pains from head to foot; full of fancies and caprices; full of spleen, distrust, suspicion, and dislike. To cancel old wills, and invent new ones, is at last the sole business of such a testator's existence; and relations and friends (some of whom have been bred up distinctly to inherit a large share of the property, and have been, from their cradles, especially disqualified from devoting themselves to any useful pursuit, on that account) are so often and so unexpectedly and summarily cut down, and reinstated, and cut off again, that the whole family, down to the remotest cousin, is kept in a perpetual fever. At length it becomes plain that the old lady or gentleman has not long to live; and the plainer this becomes, the more clearly the old lady or gentleman perceives that everybody is in a conspiracy against their poor dying relative; wherefore the old lady or gentleman makes another last will – positively the last this time – conceals the same in a china teapot, and expires next day. Then it turns out, that the whole of the real and personal estate is divided between half-a-dozen charities; and that the dead and gone testator has in pure spite helped to do a great deal of good, at the cost of an immense amount of evil passion and misery.

One naturally fell into a chain of reflection, walking homewards, upon the curious old records of likings and dislikings; of jealousies and revenges; of affection defying the power of death, and hatred pursued beyond the grave, which these depositories contain; silent but striking tokens, some of them, of excellence of heart, and nobleness of soul; melancholy examples, others, of the worst passions of human nature. How many men as they lay speechless and helpless on the bed of death, would have given worlds but for the strength and power to blot out the silent evidence of animosity and bitterness, which now stands registered against them in Doctors' Commons!

I recall my first visit to one of the Courts, passing through the aforementioned paved courtyard formed of the grave houses, which I inferred, from the Doctors' names upon the doors, to be the official abiding-places of the learned advocates, and into a large dull room, not unlike a chapel to my thinking, on the left hand. The upper part of this room was fenced off from the rest; and there, on the two sides of a raised platform of the horse-shoe form, sitting on easy old-fashioned dining-room chairs, were sundry gentlemen in red gowns and grey wigs, whom I found to be the Doctors aforesaid. Blinking over a little desk like a pulpit-desk, in the curve of the horse-shoe, was an old gentleman, whom, if I had seen him in an aviary, I should certainly have taken for an owl, but who, I learned, was the presiding judge. In the space within the horse-shoe, lower than these, that is to say on about the level of the floor, were sundry other gentlemen dressed in black gowns with white fur upon them, sitting at a long green table. Their cravats were in general stuff, I thought, and their looks haughty; but in this last respect, I presently conceived I had done them an injustice, for when two or three of them had to rise and answer a question of the presiding dignitary, I never saw anything more sheepish. The public, represented by a boy with a comforter, and a shabby-genteel man secretly eating crumbs out of his coat pockets, was warming itself at a stove in the centre of the Court. The languid stillness of the place was only broken by the chirping of this fire and by the voice of one of the Doctors, who was wandering slowly through a perfect library of evidence, and stopping to put up, from time to time, at little roadside inns of argument on the journey. Altogether, I have never, on any occasion, made one at such a cosy, dosey, old-fashioned, time-forgotten, sleepy-headed little family-party in all my life, and I felt it would be quite a soothing opiate to belong to it in any character – except perhaps as a suitor.

Early attachments

I don't believe, I can't believe, the man who tells me he has never been in love, and can't remember with delicious, and yet melancholy distinctness, all about it. I don't care whether it was the little girl with plaited tails, in frilled trousers, and a pinafore (though I never truly loved another) or your school-master's daughter, or the lady who attended to the linen department, who you thought a Houri, but who was, probably, some forty years of age. You may have loved Fanny, Maria, Louisa, Sarah, Martha, Harriet, or Charlotte, or fancied that you loved them since then; but in your heart of hearts you still keep the portrait of your first love, bright.

I broke my heart into the smallest pieces, many times between thirteen and three-and-twenty. Twice, I was very horribly in earnest; and once I really set upon the cast for six or seven long years, all the energy and determination of which I am owner. But it went the way of nearly all such things at last, though I think it kept me steadier than the working of my nature was, to many good things for the time. If anyone had interfered with my very small Cupid, I don't know what absurdity I might not have committed in assertion of his proper liberty; but having plenty of rope he hanged himself, beyond all chance of restoration.

By first love, I mean what is commonly known as 'calf love'. Our reminiscences of real first love are indissolubly connected with a disreslish for our victuals, and a wild desire to dress, regardless of expense; of dismal wailings in secret; of a demoniacal hatred of all fathers, cousins, and brothers; of hot summer days passed in green fields, staring at the birds on the boughs, and wishing – oh how devoutly wishing! – that we were twenty-one years of age.

I mind when I, turned of eighteen, went with my Angelica one Sunday morning to a City church on account of a shower, and when I said to my Angelica, 'Let the blessed event,

Angelica, occur at no altar but this!' and when my Angelica consented that it should occur at no other – which it certainly never did, for it never occurred anywhere. And O, Angelica, what has become of you, this present Sunday morning, when I can't attend to the sermon; and, more difficult question than that, what has become of Me, as I was when I sat by your side?

What! Did that Christmas never really come when I and the priceless pearl who was my young choice were received, after the happiest of totally impossible marriages, by the two united families previously at daggers-drawn on our account? When brothers- and sisters-in-law who had always been rather cool to me before our relationship was effected, perfectly doted on me, and when fathers and mothers overwhelmed me with unlimited incomes? Was that Christmas dinner never really eaten, after which I arose, and generously and eloquently rendered honour to my late rival, present in the company, then and there exchanging friendship and forgiveness, not to be surpassed in Greek or Roman story, which subsisted until death? Has that same rival long ceased to care for that same priceless pearl, and married for money, and become usurious? Above all, do I really know, now, that I should probably have been miserable if I had won and worn the pearl, and that I am better without her?

Birthday followed birthday. Seventeen and eighteen are gone, then come nineteen and twenty; and then with the waning months comes an ever augmenting sense of the dignity of twenty-one. Heaven knows I had nothing to 'come into', save the bare birthday, and yet I esteemed it as a great possession. I now and then paved the way to my state of dignity, by beginning a proposition with the casual words 'say that a man of twenty-one', or by the incidental assumption of a fact that could not sanely be disputed, as, 'for when a fellow comes to be a man of twenty-one'.

I gave a party on the occasion. She was there. It is unnecessary to name Her more particularly; She was older than I, and had pervaded every chink and crevice of my mind for three or four years. I had held volumes of *Imaginary Conversations* with her mother on the subject of our union, and I had written letters more in number than Horace Walpole's, to that discreet woman, soliciting her daughter's hand in marriage. I had never had the remotest intention of sending any of those letters; but to write them, and after a few days tear them up, had been a sublime occupation. Sometimes, I had begun 'Honoured Madam. I think that a lady gifted with those powers of observation which I know you to possess, and endowed with those womanly sympathies with the young and ardent which it were more than heresy to doubt, can scarcely have failed to discover that I love your adorable daughter, deeply, devotedly.' In less buoyant states of mind I had begun, 'Honoured Madam, bear with a daring wretch who is about to make a surprising confession to you, wholly unanticipated by yourself, and which he beseeches you to commit to the flames as soon as you have become aware to what a towering height his mad ambition soars.' At other times – periods of profound mental depression, when She had gone out to balls where I was not – the draft took the affecting form of a paper to be left on my table after my departure to the confines of the globe. As thus: 'For Mrs Onowenever, these lines when the hand that traces them shall be far away. I could not bear the daily torture of hopelessly loving the dear one whom I will not name. Broiling on the coast of Africa, or congealing on the shores of Greenland, I am far better there than here.' (In this sentiment my cooler judgment perceives that the family of the beloved object would have most completely concurred.) 'If I ever emerge from obscurity, and my name is ever heralded by fame, it will be for her dear sake. If I ever amass Gold, it will be to pour it at her feet. Should I on the other hand become the prey of Ravens – 'I doubt if I ever quite made up my mind what was to be done in that affecting case; I tried 'then it is better so'; but not feeling convinced that it would be better so, I vacillated between leaving all else blank, which looked expressive and deep, or winding up with 'Farewell!'

This fictitious correspondence of mine is to blame for the foregoing digression. I was about to pursue the statement that on my twenty-first birthday I gave a party, and She was there. It was a beautiful party. There was not a single animate or inanimate object connected with it (except the company and myself) that I had ever seen before. Everything was hired, and the mercenaries in attendance were profound strangers to me. Behind a door, in the crumby part of the night when wine-glasses were to be found in unexpected spots, I spoke to Her – spoke out to Her. What passed, I cannot as a man of honour reveal. She was all angelic kindness, but a word was mentioned – a short and dreadful word of three letters, beginning with a B – which, as I remarked at the moment, 'scorched my brain'. She went away soon afterwards, and when the hollow throng (though to be sure it was no fault of theirs) dispersed, I issued forth, with a dissipated scorner, and, as I mentioned expressly to him, 'sought oblivion'. It was found, with a dreadful headache in it, but it didn't last; for, in the shaming light of next day's moon, I raised a heavy head in bed, looking back to the birthdays behind me, and tracking the circle by which I had got round, after all, to the bitter power and the wretchedness again.

My existence was entirely uprooted, moreover, and my whole Being blighted, by the Angel of my soul being sent to Paris to finish her education! But I subsequently encountered her in Cornhill, with her sister (betrothed) and her mother, going to St Mary Axe to order mysterious dresses – which afterwards turned out to be wedding garments. That was in a period when they all wore green cloaks, cut (in my remembrance) very round, and which I am resolved to believe were made of Merino. I escorted them with native gallantry to the dress-maker's door, and her mother, seized with an apprehension – groundless, upon my honour – that I might come in, said emphatically: 'And now, Mr Dickin' – which she always used to call me – 'we'll wish you good morning.'

I remember well that long after I came of age – I say long; well! it seemed long then – I wrote to her for the first time of all, with a dawn upon me of some sensible idea that we were changing into man and woman, saying would she forget our little differences and separations and let us begin again? She answered me very coldly and reproachfully – and so I went my way. But nobody can ever know with what a sad heart I resigned her, or after what struggles and what conflict. My entire devotion to her, and the wasted tenderness of those hard years which I have ever since half loved, half dreaded to recall, made so deep an impression on me that I refer to it a habit of suppression which now belongs to me, which I know is no part of my original nature, but which makes me chary of showing my affections, even to my children, except when they are very young.

I loved that girl with the most extraordinary earnestness. I have always believed since, and always shall to the last, that there never was such a faithful and devoted poor fellow as I was. Whatever of fancy, romance, energy, passion, aspiration and position belong to me, I never have separated and never shall separate from the hard-hearted little woman whom it is nothing to say I would have died for, with the greatest alacrity! I never can think, and I never seem to observe, that other people are in such desperate earnest or set so much, so long, upon one absorbing hope. It is a matter of perfect certainty to me that I began to find my way out of poverty and obscurity with one perpetual idea of her. This is so fixed in my knowledge that to this hour I never hear anybody addressed by her name, or spoken of by her name, without a start. The sound of it has always filled me with a kind of pity and respect for the deep truth that I had, in my silly hobbledehoyhood, to bestow upon one creature who represented the whole world to me.

It is impossible to over-rate the strength of my feeling at that time. It excluded every other idea from my mind for four years, at a time of life when four years are equal to four times four; and with the desperate intensity of my nature I went at it with a determination to overcome all the difficulties, which fairly lifted me up into that newspaper life, and floated me away over a hundred men's heads; I have positively stood amazed at myself ever since!

And so I suffered, and so worked, and so beat and hammered away at the maddest romances that ever got into a boy's head and stayed there, that to see the mere cause of it all, now, loosens my hold upon myself. Without for a moment sincerely believing that it would have been better if we had never got separated, I cannot see the occasion of so much emotion as I should see anyone else. She is always the same in my remembrance. I see her in a sort of raspberry coloured dress with a little black trimming at the top – black velvet it seems to be made of – cut into vandykes – an immense number of vandykes – with my boyish heart pinned like a captured butterfly on every one of them. I have never seen a girl play the harp, from that day to this, but my attention has been instantly arrested, and a drawing room in a house in Lombard Street (which is pulled down, as if it were necessary that the very bricks and mortar should go the way of my airy castles) has stood before me so plainly that I could write a most accurate description of it. When we were falling off from each other, I came from the House of Commons many a night at two or three o'clock in the morning, only to wander past the place that she was asleep in. And I have gone over that ground within these twelve months hoping it was not ungrateful to consider whether any reputation the world can bestow is repayment to a man for the loss of such a vision of his youth as mine.

I forget nothing of those times. They are just as still and plain and clear as if I had never been in a crowd since, and had never seen or heard my own name out of my own house. What should I be worth, or what would labour and success be worth, if it were otherwise!

A faithful reflection of the passion I had for her can be found in *David Copperfield* and it is possible to see in little bits of 'Dora' touches of her old self and a grace here and there that may be revived in her little girls, years hence, for the bewilderment of some other young lover – though he will never be as terribly in earnestness as I and David Copperfield were. People used to say to me how pretty all that was, and how fanciful it was, and how elevated it was above the little foolish hopes of very young men and women. But they little thought what reason I had to know it was true and nothing more nor less. No one can imagine in the most distant degree what pain the recollection gave me in *Copperfield*. And, just as I can never open that book as I open any other book, I cannot see the face (even at four and forty), or hear the voice, without going wandering away over the ashes of all that youth and hope in the wildest manner.

But, here have I been running over these early attachments, and forgetting the first time I was ever treated as a man! O memorable occasion! It was after dinner somewhere (I had gone there with my sister; only a year older than myself, but universally admitted to be a woman, while I unjustly laboured under the tremendous reproach of boyhood) and was left alone, with an aged Being – fifty, perhaps – who was my host, and another patriarch of forty or so. I was simpering behind the decanters, extremely doubtful of my having any business there, when the host uttered these remarkable expressions:

'Mr Dickens, will you help yourself, and pass the wine?'

I did it, and felt that I had passed the Rubicon too. I helped myself feebly, awkwardly, consciously. I felt that they were thinking: 'Will he take more than is good for him? Will his eyes roll in his head? Will he disappear beneath the table?' But I did it, and bashfully sipped my wine, and even made impotent attempts to close my left eye critically, and look at it against the light. I have been promoted twice or thrice since, and have even sat in high places, and received honour; but my host has never said, with the same deep significance –

'Mr Dickens, will you help yourself, and pass the wine?'

Pressing engagements

Novelty, pleasant to most people, is particularly delightful, I think, to me. I am not easily dispirited when I have the means of pursuing my own fancies and occupations; and I believe I have some natural aptitude for accommodating myself to circumstances. But it is to the wholesome training of newspaper work when I was a very young man that I constantly refer my first success.

I was in high repute for my accomplishment in all pertaining to the art of shorthand and went into the gallery of the House of Commons as a parliamentary reporter when I was still a boy, joining with eleven others in reporting the debates in Parliament for the *Morning Chronicle*. Night after night, I recorded predictions that never came to pass, professions that were never fulfilled, explanations that were only meant to mystify. I wallowed in words. Britannia, that unfortunate female, is always before me, like a trussed fowl: skewered through and through with office-pens, and bound hand and foot with red tape. I am quite an Infidel about it, and shall never be converted.

I pursued the calling of a reporter under circumstances of which subsequent generations can form no adequate conception. I often transcribed for the printer, from my shorthand notes, important public speeches in which the strictest accuracy was required, and a mistake in which would have been, to a young man, severely compromising, writing on the palm of my hand, by the light of a dark lantern, in a post-chaise and four, galloping through a wild country, and through the dead of night, at the then surprising rate of fifteen miles an hour. The very last time I was at Exeter, I strolled into the castle-yard there to identify, for the amusement of a friend, the spot on which I once 'took', as we used to call it, an election speech of Lord John Russell at the Devon bonds in that division of the country, and under such a pelting rain, that I remember two good-natured colleagues, who chanced to be at leisure, held a pocket-handkerchief over my note-book, after the manner of a state canopy in an ecclesiastical procession.

I have worn my knees by writing on them on the old back row of the old gallery of the old House of Commons; and I have worn my feet by standing to write in a preposterous pen in the old House of Lords, where we used to be huddled together like so

Dickens posting his first literary contribution in the editor's box.

many sheep – kept in waiting, say, until the Woolsack might need re-stuffing. Returning home from exciting political meetings in the country to the waiting press in London, I do verily believe I have been upset in almost every description of a vehicle known in this country. I have been, in my time, belated on miry by-roads, towards the small hours, forty or fifty miles from London, in a wheelless carriage, with exhausted horses and drunken post-boys, and have got back in time for publication, to be received with never-forgotten compliments by the late Mr Black, coming in the broadest Scotch from the broadest of hearts I ever knew. These trivial things I mention as an assurance that I never have forgotten the fascination of that old pursuit. The pleasure that I used to feel in the rapidity and dexterity of its exercise has never faded out of my breast. Whatever little cunning of hand or head I took to it, or acquired in it, I have so retained that I fully believe I could resume it tomorrow, very little the worse from long disuse. To this present year of my life, when I sit in a hall, or where not, hearing a dull speech (the phenomenon does occur), I sometimes beguile the tedium of the moment by mentally following the speaker in the old, old way; and sometimes I even find my hand going on the table-cloth, taking an imaginary note of it all.

I recollect that one of my earliest assignments was the reporting of a banquet held at Edinburgh in honour of Lord Grey. It had been announced that the dinner would take place at five o'clock precisely; but earl Grey, and the other principal visitors, as might have been expected, did not arrive until shortly after six. Previous to their arrival, some slight confusion, and much merriment, was excited by the following circumstance. A gentleman who, I presume, had entered with one of the first sections, having sat with exemplary patience for some time in the immediate vicinity of cold fowls, roast beef, lobsters, and other tempting delicacies (for the dinner was a cold one), appeared to think that the best thing he could possibly do would be to eat his dinner while there was anything to eat. He accordingly laid about him with right goodwill, the example was contagious, and the clatter of knives and forks became general. Hereupon, several gentlemen, who were not hungry, cried out 'Shame!' and looked very indignant; and several gentlemen who were hungry cried 'Shame!' too, eating, nevertheless, all the while, as fast as they possibly could. In this dilemma, one of the stewards mounted a bench, and feelingly represented to the delinquents the enormity of their conduct, imploring them, for decency's sake, to defer the process of mastication until the arrival of earl Grey. This address was loudly cheered, but totally unheeded; and this is, perhaps, one of the few instances on record of a dinner having been virtually concluded before it began.

It may be from some imperfect development of my organ of veneration, but I do not remember having ever fainted away, or having even been moved to tears of joyful pride, at the sight of either our own or any other legislative body. I have borne the House of Commons like a man, and have yielded to no weakness, but slumber, in the House of Lords. I have even seen elections for borough and county, and have never been impelled (no matter which party won) to damage my hat by throwing it up into the air in triumph, or to crack my voice by shouting forth any reference to our Glorious Constitution, to the noble purity of our independent voters, or, the unimpeachable integrity of our independent masters. Having withstood such strong attacks upon my fortitude, it is possible that I may be of a cold and insensible temperament, amounting to iciness, in such matters.

I remained with the *Morning Chronicle* until I had begun to publish *Pickwick*, when I found myself in a position to relinquish that part of my labours. I left the reputation behind me of being the best and most rapid reporter ever known, it being generally acknowledged that I could do anything in that way under any sort of circumstances, and often did. (I daresay I am at this present writing the best shorthand writer in the world.)

A traveller's tales

There never was anybody connected with newspapers who in the same space of time had so much express and post-chaise experience as I. And what gentlemen they were to serve in such things at the old *Morning Chronicle*! Great or small, it did not matter. I have had to charge for the damage of a great-coat from the drippings of a blazing wax candle, in writing through the smallest hours of the night in a swift-flying carriage and pair. I have had to charge for all sorts of breakages fifty times in a journey without question, such being the ordinary results of the pace which we went at. I have charged for broken hats, broken luggage, broken chaises, broken harnesses – everything but a broken head, which is the only thing they would have grumbled to pay for.

Charles Dickens.

Most of my contemporaries in the reporting fraternity will have had experience of the extinct 'fast coaches' – the 'Wonders', 'Taglionis' and 'Tallyhoes' – of other days. Most of us remember certain modest post-chaises dragging us down interminable roads through slush and mud, to little country towns with no visible populations except half-a-dozen men in smock frocks smoking pipes under the lee of the town hall; half-a-dozen women with umbrellas and patterns, and a washed-out dog or so shivering under the gables to complete the desolate picture. We can all discourse, if so minded, upon our recollections, of the 'Talbot', the 'King's Head' or the 'Lion' of those days. We have all been to that room on the ground floor on one side of the old inn yard, not quite free from a fragrant smell of tobacco, where the crusts on the sideboard were usually absorbed by the skirts of the box coats that hung from the wall, where driving seats were laid out at every turn like so many human mantraps, where county members framed and glassed were eternally presenting that petition which somehow or other made their glory in the county, though nothing else had ever come of it. Where the *Book of the Roads*, the first and last thing always required, was always missing, and generally wanted the first and last dozen leaves, and where one man was always arriving at some unusual hour in the middle of the night, and requiring his breakfast at a similarly unusual hour in the middle of the day. I have no doubt we could all be very eloquent on the comforts of our favourite hotel, wherever it was – its beds, its stables, its vast amount of posting, its excellent cheese, its head waiter, its capital dishes, its pigeon pie, or its 1820 port, or possibly we could recall our chaste and innocent admiration of the landlady, or our fraternal regard for its handsome chambermaid.

With the travelling characteristics of later times we are all, no doubt, equally familiar. We know all about that station of which we have a clear idea although we were never there; we know that if we arrive after dark we are certain to find it half-a-mile from the town, where the old road is sure to have been abolished, and the new road is going to be made, where the old neighbourhood has been tumbled down, and the new one is not half built up. We know all about that porter on the platform who with the best intentions in the world cannot do anything particularly efficacious with the luggage by looking at it with that bell in his hand. We know all about that particularly short omnibus, in which one is to be doubled up to the imminent danger of the crown of one's hat, and about that fly, whose leading peculiarity is never to be there when it is wanted. We know, too, how instantaneously the lights of the station disappear the moment the train slips away, and about that grope to the new Railway Hotel, which will be an excellent home when the customers come, but which at present has nothing to offer but a liberal allowance of deep mortar and new lime.

There was a good inn down in Wiltshire where I put up once, in the days of the hard Wiltshire ale, and before all beer was bitterness. It was on the skirts of Salisbury Plain, and the midnight wind that rattled my lattice window came moaning at me from Stonehenge. There was a hanger-on at that establishment (a supernaturally preserved Druid I believe him to have been, and to be still), with long white hair, and a flinty blue eye always looking afar off; who claimed to have been a shepherd, and who seemed to be ever watching for the reappearance, on the verge of the horizon, of some ghostly flock of sheep that had been mutton for many ages. He was a man with a weird belief in him that no one could count the stones of Stonehenge twice, and make the same number of them; likewise, that any who counted them three times nine times, and then stood in the centre and said, 'I dare!' would behold a tremendous apparition, and be stricken dead. He pretended to have seen a bustard (I suspect him to have been familiar with the dodo), in manner following: He was out upon the plain at the close of a late autumn day, when he dimly discerned, going on before him at a curious fitfully bounding pace, what he at first supposed to be a gig-umbrella that had been blown from some conveyance, but what he presently believed to be a lean man upon a little pony. Having followed this object for some distance without gaining on it, and having called to it many times without receiving any answer, he pursued it for miles and miles, when, at length coming up with it, he discovered it to be the last bustard in Great Britain, degenerated into a wingless state, and running along the ground. Resolved to capture him or perish in the attempt, he closed with the bustard; but the bustard, who had formed a counter-resolution that he should do neither, threw him, stunned him, and was last seen making off due west. This weird man, at that stage of metempsychosis, may have been a sleep-walker or an enthusiast or a robber; but I awoke one night to find him in the dark at my bedside, repeating the Athanasian Creed in a terrific voice. I paid my bill next day, and retired from the county with all possible precipitation.

Once I passed a fortnight at an inn in the north of England, where I was haunted by the ghost of a tremendous pie. It was a Yorkshire pie, like a fort – an abandoned fort with nothing in it; but the waiter had a fixed idea that it was a point of ceremony at every meal to put the pie on the table. After some days I tried to hint, in several delicate ways, that I considered the pie done with; as, for example, by emptying fag-ends of glasses of wine into it; putting cheese-plates and spoons into it, as into a basket; putting wine-bottles into it, as into a cooler; but always in vain, the pie being inevitably cleaned out again and brought up as before. At last, beginning to be doubtful whether I was not the victim of a spectral illusion, and whether my health and spirits might not sink under the horrors of an imaginary pie, I cut a triangle out of it, fully as large as the musical instrument of that name in a powerful orchestra. Human prevision could not have foreseen the result – but the waiter mended the pie. With some effectual species of cement, he adroitly fitted the triangle in again, and I paid my reckoning and fled.

I recall another inn, in the remotest part of Cornwall. A great annual Miners' Feast was being holden at the inn, when I and my travelling companions presented ourselves at night among the wild crowd that were dancing before it by torchlight. We had had a breakdown in the dark, on a stony morass some miles away; and I had the honour of leading one of the unharnessed post-horses. If any lady or gentleman, on perusal of the present lines, will take any very tall post-horse with his traces hanging about his legs, and will conduct him by the bearing-rein into the heart of a country dance of a hundred and fifty couples, that lady or gentleman will then, and only then, form an adequate idea of the extent to which that post-horse will tread on his conductor's toes. Over and above which, the post-horse, finding three hundred people whirling about him, will probably rear, and also lash out with his hind legs, in a manner incompatible with dignity or self-respect on his conductor's part. With such little drawbacks on my usually impressive aspect, I appeared at this Cornish inn, to the unutterable wonder of the Cornish miners. It was full, and twenty times full, and nobody could be received but the pack-horse – though to get rid of that noble animal was something. While my fellow-travellers and I were discussing how to pass the night and so much of the next day as must intervene before the jovial blacksmith and the jovial wheelwright would be in a condition to go out of the morass and mend the coach, an honest man stepped forth from the crowd and proposed his unlet floor of two rooms, with supper of eggs and bacon, ale and punch. We joyfully accompanied him home to the strangest of clean houses, where we were well entertained to the satisfaction of all parties. But the novel feature of the entertainment was, that our host was a chairmaker, and that the chairs assigned to us were mere frames, altogether without bottoms of any sort; so that we passed the evening on perches. Nor was this the absurdest consequence; for when we unbent at supper, and any one of us gave way to laughter, he forgot the peculiarity of his position, and instantly disappeared. I myself, doubled up into an attitude from which self-extrication was impossible, was taken out of my frame like a clown in a comic pantomime who has tumbled into a tub, five times by the taper's light during the eggs and bacon.

There was a story with a singular idea in it, connected with an inn I once passed a night at in a picturesque old town on the Welsh border. In a large double-bedded room of this inn there had been a suicide committed by poison, in one bed, while a traveller slept unconscious in the other. After that time, the suicide bed was never used, but the other constantly was; the disused bedstead remaining in the room empty, though as to all other respects in its old state. The story ran, that whosoever slept in this room, though never so entire a stranger, from never so far off, was invariably observed to come down in the morning with an impression that he smelt laudanum, and that his mind always turned upon the subject of suicide; to which, whatever kind of man he might be, he was certain to make some reference, if he conversed with anyone. This went on for years, until at length it induced the landlord to take the disused bedstead down, and bodily burn it – bed, hangings, and all. The strange influence (this was the story) now changed to a fainter one, but never changed afterwards. The occupant of that room, with occasional but very rare exceptions, would come down in the morning, trying to recall a forgotten dream he had had in the night. The landlord, on his mentioning his perplexity, would suggest various commonplace subjects, not one of which, as he very well knew, was the true subject. But the moment the landlord suggested 'Poison', the traveller started, and cried 'Yes!' He never failed to accept that suggestion, and he never recalled any more of the dream.

This reminiscence brings the Welsh inns in general before me; with the women in their round hats, and the harpers with their white beards (venerable, but humbugs, I am afraid), playing outside the door while I take my supper. I also recall Highland inns, with the oatmeal bannocks, the honey, the venison steaks, the trout from the loch, the whisky, and perhaps (having the materials so temptingly at hand) the Athol breeze. Once was I coming south from the Scottish Highlands in hot haste, hoping to change quickly at the station at the bottom of a certain wild historical glen, when these eyes did with mortification see the landlord come out with a telescope and sweep the whole prospect for the horses; which horses were away picking up their own living, and did not heave in sight under four hours.

Every traveller has a home of his own, and he learns to appreciate it the more from his wandering. If he has no home, he learns the same lesson unselfishly by turning to the homes of other men. He may have his experiences of cheerful and exciting pleasures abroad; but home is best, after all, and its pleasures are the most heartily and enduringly prized.

Dreams

Yet dreams, forgotten or otherwise, are a matter worth lingering upon, for I have read something on the subject and have long observed it with the greatest attention and interest.

In the first place I would suggest that the influence on them of the day's occurrences, and of recent events, is by no means so great (generally speaking) as is usually supposed. I rather think there is a kind of conventional philosophy and belief on this head. My own dreams are usually of twenty years ago. I often blend my present position with them; but very confusedly; whereas my life of twenty years ago is very distinctly represented. I have been married fourteen years, and have nine children, but I do not remember that I ever, on any occasion, dreamed of myself as being invested with those responsibilities, or surrounded by those relations. This would be so remarkable if it were an idiosyncrasy that I have asked many intelligent and observant men, whether they found their dreams usually of the same retrospective character. Many have thought not, at first; but on consideration have strongly confirmed my own experience. Ladies, affectionately and happily married, have often recalled, when I have made

Charles Dickens is the young man paying his booking fee in this etching by Cruikshank from Sketches by Boz.

the same remark in conversation, that while they were engaged – though their thoughts were naturally much set on their engagement – they never dreamed of their lovers. I should say the chances were a thousand to one against anybody's dreaming of the subject that closely occupies the waking mind except in a sort of allegorical manner.

For example. If I have been perplexed during the day, in bringing out the incidents of a story as I wish, I find that I dream at night – never by any chance, of the story itself – but perhaps of trying to shut a door that *will* fly open – or to screw something tight that *will* be loose – or to drive a horse on some very important journey, who unaccountably becomes a dog, and can't be urged along – or to find my way out of a series of chambers that appears to have no end. I sometimes think that the origin of all fables and Allegory – the very first conception of such fictions – may be referable to this class of dreams.

Did you ever hear of any person who, by trying and resolving to fix the mind on any subject, could dream of it – or who did not, under such circumstances, dream preposterously wide of the mark? When dreams *can* be directly traced to any incidents of recent occurrence, it appears to me that the incidents are usually of the most insignificant character – such as made no impression, of which we were conscious, at the time – such as present themselves again, in the wildest eccentricity. The obvious convenience and effect of making the dreams of heroes and heroines bear on the great themes of a story as illustrated by their late experiences, seem to have led the Poets away from the truth, on this head – and to have established the conventional belief from which I differ.

The assistance supposed to be sometimes furnished, in sleep, towards the solution of Problems, or invention of things that had baffled the waking mind, I take to be the result of a sudden vigorous effect of the refreshed intellect in waking. But language has a great part in dreams. I think, on waking, the head is usually full of words.

Are our dreams so very various and different, as is commonly supposed? Or is there, taking into consideration our vast differences in point of mental and physical constitution, a remarkable sameness in them? Surely, it is an extremely unusual circumstance to hear any narration of a dream that does violence to our dreaming experience or enlarges it very much. And how many dreams are common to us all, from the Queen to the Costermonger! We all fall off that Tower – we all skim above the ground at a great pace and can't keep on it – we all say 'This *must* be a dream, because I was in this strange, low-roofed, beam-obstructed place once before, and it turned out to be a dream' – we all take unheard-of trouble to go to the Theatre and never get in – or go to a Feast, which can't be eaten or drunk – or to read letters, placards, or books, that no study will render legible – or to break some Thraldom or other, from which we can't escape – or we all confound the living with the dead, and all frequently have a knowledge or suspicion that we are doing it – we all astonish ourselves by telling ourselves, in a dialogue with ourselves, the most astonishing and terrific secrets – we all go to public places in our night dresses and are horribly disconcerted, lest the company should observe it.

And this appears, to me, to suggest another curious point – the occasional endeavour to correct our delusions, made by some wakening and reasoning faculty of the brain. For, it is to be observed that we *are*, actually, in our night dress at the time. I suspect that a man who lay down in his clothes under a hedge, or on a ship's deck, would not have, and could not have, this very common kind of dream. It has no connexion with our being cold, for it constantly presents itself to people warm in bed. I cannot help thinking that this observant and corrective speck of the brain suggests to you, 'My good fellow how *can* you be in this crowd, when you *know* you are in your shirt?' It is not strong enough to dispel the vision, but is just strong enough to present this inconsistency.

Recurring dreams which come back almost as certainly as the night – an unhealthy and morbid species of these visions – should be particularly noticed. Secrecy on the part of the dreamer, as to these illusions, has a remarkable tendency to perpetuate them. But more of this anon.

A few conventionalities

After having attended the debates in the house of Commons and other public gatherings for some little time, I began to ask myself a few questions – and, indeed, I am asking them still. I do not ask them with any expectation of getting an answer, but in the comforting hope that I shall find some thousands of sympathetic readers, whose minds are constantly asking similar questions.

Why must an honourable gentleman always 'come down' to this House? Why can't he sometimes 'come up' – like a horse – or 'come in' like a man? What does he mean by invariably coming down? Is it indispensable that he should 'come down' to get into the House of Commons – say, for instance, from St Albans? Or is that house on a much lower level than most other houses? Why is he always 'free to confess'? It is well known that Britons never never never will be slaves; then why can't he say what he has to say, without this superfluous assertion of his freedom? Why must an Irish member always 'taunt' the noble Lord with this, that or the other? Can't he tell him of it civilly, or accuse him of it plainly? *Must* he so ruthlessly taunt him? Why does the Honourable Member for Groginhole call upon the Secretary of State for the Home Department to 'lay his hand on his heart', and proclaim to the country such and such a thing? The Home Secretary is not in the habit of laying his hand upon his heart. When he has anything to proclaim to the country, he generally puts his hands under his coat-tails. Why is he thus personally and solemnly adjured to lay one of them on the left side of his waistcoat for any Honourable Member's gratification? What makes my honourable friend, the Member for Gammonrife, feel so acutely that he is required to 'pin his faith' upon the measures of Her Majesty's Government? Is he always required to attach it in that particular manner only; and are needles and thread, hooks and eyes, buttons, wafers, sealing-wax, paste, bird-lime, gum, and glue, utterly prohibited to him?

Who invested the unfortunate Speaker with all the wealth and poverty of the Empire, that he should be told – 'Sir, when you look around you, and behold your seas swarming with ships of every variety of tonnage and construction – when you behold your flag waving over the forts of a territory so vast that the Sun never sets upon it – when you consider that your storehouses are teeming with the valuable products of the earth – and when you reflect that millions of your poor are held in the bonds of pauperism and ignorance – can you, I ask, reconcile it to yourself; can you, I demand, justify it to your conscience; can you, I inquire, Sir, stifle within you, by these selfish, these time-serving, these shallow, hollow, mockeries of legislation?' It is

Charles Dickens aged nineteen.

really dreadful to have an innocent and worthy gentleman bullied in this manner. Again, why do I 'hold in my hand' all sorts of things? Can I never lay them down, or carry them under my arm? There was a Fairy in the *Arabian Nights* who could hold in her hand a pavilion large enough to shelter the Sultan's army, but she could never have held half the petitions, blue books, bills, reports, volumes of Hansard, and other miscellaneous papers, that a very ordinary Member for a very ordinary place will hold in his hands anyway.

Then again, how did it come to be necessary to the Constitution that I should be such a very circuitous and prolix peer as to 'take leave to remind you, my Lords, of what fell from the noble and learned lord on the opposite side of your Lordships' House, who preceded my noble and learned friend on the cross-benches when he addressed himself with so much ability to the observations of the Right Reverend Prelate near me, in reference to the measures now brought forward by the Noble Baron' – when, all this time, I mean, and only want to say, Lord Brougham? Is it impossible for my honourable friend the Member for Drowsyshire to wander through his few dreary sentences immediately before the division, without premising that 'at this late hour of the night and in this stage of the debate', etc? Because if it be not impossible why does he never do it?

And why, why, above all, in either House of Parliament, must the English language be set to music – bad and conventional beyond any parallel on earth – and delivered, in a manner barely expressible to the eye, as follows:

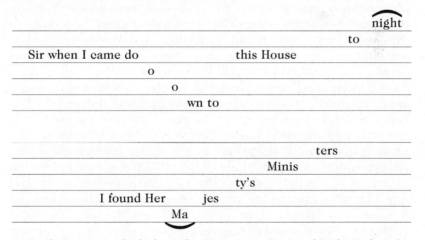

Is Parliament included in the Common Prayer-book under the denomination of 'quires and places where they sing'? And if so, wouldn't it be worth a small grant to make some national arrangement for instruction in the art by Mr Hullah?

Why have six hundred men been trying through several generations to fold their arms? The last twenty Parliaments have directed their entire attention to this graceful art. I have heard it frequently declared by individual senators that a certain ex-senator still producible, 'folded his arms better than any man in the House'. I have seen aspirants inflamed with a lofty ambition, studying through whole sessions the folded arms on the Treasury Bench, and trying to fold their arms according to the patterns there presented. I have known neophytes far more distracted about the folding of their arms than about the enunciation of their political views, or the turning of their periods. The injury inflicted on the nation by Mr Canning, when he folded his arms and got his portrait taken, is not to be calculated. Every member of Parliament from that hour to the present has been trying to fold his arms. It is a graceful, a refined, a decorative art; but, I doubt if its results will bear comparison with the infinite pains and charges bestowed upon its cultivation.

Then, at public dinners and meetings, why must Mr Wilson refer to Mr Jackson as 'my honourable friend, if he will permit me to call him so'? Has Wilson any doubt about it? Why does Mr Smithers say that he is sensible that he has already detained you too long, and why do *you* say, 'No, no; go on!' when you already know you are sorry for it directly afterwards? You are not taken by surprise when the Toastmaster cries, in giving the Army and Navy, 'Upstanding, gentlemen, *and* good fires' – then what do you laugh for? No man could ever say why he was greatly refreshed and fortified by forms of words, as 'Resolved. That this meeting respectfully but firmly views with sorrow and apprehension, not unmixed with abhorrence and dismay' – but they *do* invigorate the patient, in most cases, like a cordial. It is a strange thing that the chairman is obliged to refer to 'the present occasion' – that there is a horrible fascination in the phrase which he can't elude. Also, that there should be an unctuous smack and relish in the enunciation of titles, as 'And may I be permitted to inform this company that when I had the honour of waiting on His Royal Highness, to ask His Royal Highness to be pleased to bestow his gracious patronage on our excellent Institution, His Royal Highness did me the honour to reply, with that condescension which is ever His Royal

Highness's most distinguishing characteristic' – and so forth. As to the singular circumstance that such and such a duty should not have been entrusted to abler hands than mine, everybody is familiar with that phenomenon, but it's strange that it *must* be so!

When the old stage-coaches ran, and overturns took place in which all the passengers were killed or crippled, why was it invariably understood that no blame whatever was attributable to the coachman? In railway accidents of the present day, why is the coroner always convinced that a searching inquiry must be made, and that the railway authorities are affording every possible facility in aid of the elucidation of this unhappy disaster? When a new building tumbles into a heap of ruins, why are architect, contractor, and materials always the best that could be got for money, with additional precautions – as if that splendid termination were the triumph of construction, and all the buildings that don't tumble down were failures? When a boiler bursts, why was it the very best of boilers; and why, when somebody thinks that if the accident were not the boiler's fault it is likely to have been the engineer's, is the engineer then morally certain to have been the steadiest and skilfullest of men? If a public servant be impeached, how does it happen that there never was such an excellent public servant as he will be shown to be by Red-Tape-osophy? If an abuse be brought to light, how does it come to pass that it is sure to be, in fact (if rightly viewed) a blessing? How can it be, that we have gone on, for so many years, surrounding the grave with ghastly, ruinous, incongruous and inexplicable mummeries, and curtaining the cradle with a thousand ridiculous and prejudicial customs?

All these things are conventionalities. It would be well for us if there were no more and no worse in common use. But, having run the gauntlet of so many, in a breath, I must yield to the unconventional necessity of taking a breath, and stop here.

'Sketches by Boz'

I was considered very remarkable on the *Chronicle* for an extraordinary facility in writing and so forth and was very liberally paid during my whole connection with the paper. Having attained the dignity of twenty-one, and come legally to man's estate, I took lodgings in Cecil Street, off the Strand, but they did not prove satisfactory. The Cecil Street people put too much water in the hash, lost a nutmeg grater, attended on me most miserably, dirtied the table-cloth, and so (detesting petty miseries) I gave them warning and moved elsewhere, eventually finding a satisfactory base at Furnival's Inn, High Holborn, where I remained until 1837. I was joined there by my brother Fred. (He had been my favourite when he was a child, and I was his tutor when he was a boy.)

I came out as a drama critic during this period, although (with interests developing in other directions) speedily concluded that nothing is more wretched than to sit one's body in the theatre when every thought and idea have fled to another and very different object.

I had also come out in another way. I had taken, with fear and trembling, to authorship. I wrote a little story in secret, entitled 'A Sunday out of Town', which I dropped stealthily one evening at twilight into a dark letter box, in a dark office, up a dark court in Fleet Street. It appeared in all the glory of print in the December 1833 issue of *The Monthly Magazine*, its name transmogrified to 'A Dinner at Poplar Walk', on which occasion – how well I remember it! – I walked down to Westminster Hall, and turned into it for half-an-hour, because my eyes were so dimmed with joy and pride, that they could not bear the street, and were not fit to be seen there.

Thereafter, albeit for next to nothing, I took heart to write a good many trifling pieces. Some appeared in *The Monthly Magazine*, some in the *Morning Chronicle*, and early in 1836 a series of these were collected and published in two volumes, illustrated by my esteemed friend Mr George Cruickshank. It must be emphasised that these sketches were written and published, one by one, when I was still a very young man. They were collected and republished while I was still a very young man, and sent into the world with all their imperfections (a good many) on their heads. They comprised my first attempts at authorship – with the exception of those tragedies, already referred to, achieved at the mature age of eight or ten, and represented with great applause to overflowing nurseries. I am conscious now of their often being extremely crude and ill-considered, and bearing obvious marks of haste and inexperience, but they were very leniently and favourably received on their first appearance.

The title-page from Sketches by Boz.

'Boz', my signature in the *Morning Chronicle*, and in *The Monthly Magazine*, and retained long afterwards, was the nickname of a pet child, a younger brother, whom I had dubbed Moses, in honour of the Vicar of Wakefield; which being facetiously pronounced through the nose, became Boses, and being shortened, became Boz. Boz was a very familiar household word to me, long before I was an author, and so I came to adopt it.

'The Pickwick Papers'

I have seen various accounts of the origins of *The Pickwick Papers* which have, at all events, possessed – for me – the charm of perfect novelty. As I may infer, from the occasional appearance of such histories, that my readers have an interest in the matter, I will relate how they came into existence.

I was a young man of two or three-and-twenty, when Messrs. Chapman and Hall, attracted by the aforementioned *Sketches*, waited upon me to propose a something that should be published in shilling numbers – then only known to me, or, I believe, to anybody else, by a dim recollection of certain interminable novels in that form, which used to be carried about the country by pedlars, and over some of which I remember to have shed innumerable tears before I had served my apprenticeship to Life.

When I opened my door in Furnival's Inn to the partner who represented the firm, Mr William Hall, I recognised in him the person from whose hands I had bought, two or three years previously, and whom I had never seen before or since, that copy of *The Monthly Magazine* in which my first effusion had appeared. I told my visitor of the coincidence, which we both hailed as a good omen; and so fell to business.

The idea propounded to me, was, that the monthly something should be a vehicle for certain plates to be executed by Robert Seymour; and there was a notion, either on the part of that admirable humorous artist, or of my visitor, that a 'Nimrod Club', the members of which were to go out shooting, fishing, and so forth, and getting themselves into difficulties through their want of dexterity, would be the best means of introducing these. I objected, on consideration, that although born and partly bred in the country I was no great sportsman, except in

'Public Dinners' from Sketches by Boz. Dickens is portrayed as the young usher second from the left, Cruikshank as his bewhiskered partner on the right. The leading stewards are probably Chapman and Holl.

regard of all kinds of locomotion; that the idea was not novel, and had been already much used; that it would be infinitely better for the plates to arise naturally out of the text; and that I would like to take my own way, with a freer range of English scenes and people, and was afraid I should ultimately do so in any case, whatever course I might prescribe to myself at starting. My views being deferred to, I thought of Mr Pickwick, and wrote the first number; from the proof sheets of which, Mr Seymour made his drawing of the Club, and that happy portrait of its founder by which he is always recognised, and which may be said to have made him a reality. I connected Mr Pickwick with a club, because of the original suggestion, and I put in Mr Winkle expressly for the use of Mr Seymour. We started with a number of twenty-four pages instead of thirty-two, and four illustrations in lieu of a couple. My Seymour's sudden and lamented death, before the second number was published, brought about a quick decision upon a point already in agitation; the number became one of thirty-two pages with only two illustrations, and remained so to the end. My friends said it was a low, cheap form of publication; by which I should ruin my rising hopes; and how right my friends turned out to be, everybody now knows.

It is with great unwillingness that I notice some incoherent assertions which have been made, professedly on behalf of Mr Seymour, to the effect that he had some share in the invention of the book, or of anything in it, not faithfully described in the foregoing paragraph. The facts are as follows:

Mr Seymour never originated, suggested, or in any way had to do with, save as illustrator of what I devised, an incident, a character (except the sporting tastes of Mr Winkle), a name, a phrase, or a word, to be found in *The Pickwick Papers*. I never saw Mr Seymour's handwriting, I believe, in my life. I never even saw Mr Seymour but once in my life, and that was within eight-and-forty hours of his untimely death. Two persons were present on that short occasion, my brother Frederick and my wife. Mr Seymour died when only the first twenty-six pages of *The Pickwick Papers* were published; I think before the next three or four pages were completely written; I am sure before one subsequent line of the book was invented. I recall Frederick afterwards knocking at our door before we were up, to tell us that it was in the papers that Seymour had shot himself, and of his perfect knowledge that the poor little man and I looked upon each other for the first and last time that night at Furnival's Inn.

In July 1849 some assertions made by the widow of Mr Seymour, in the course of certain endeavours of hers to raise money, induced me to address a letter to Mr Edward Chapman, then the only surviving business partner in the original firm of Chapman & Hall, who first published *The Pickwick Papers*, requesting him to inform me in writing whether the foregoing statements were correct. In Mr Chapman's confirmatory answer, immediately written, he reminded me that I had given Mr Seymour more credit than was his due. 'As this letter is to be historical,' he wrote, 'I may as well claim what little belongs to me in the matter, and that is, the figure of Pickwick. Seymour's first sketch', made from the proof of my first chapter, 'was of a long, thin man. The present immortal one he made from my description of a friend of mine at Richmond.'

My object in writing *The Pickwick Papers* was to place before the reader a constant succession of characters and incidents; to paint them in as vivid colours as I could command; and to render them, at the same time. life-like and amusing. Finding that the machinery of the club tended rather to my embarrassment than otherwise, I gradually abandoned it, considering it a matter of very little importance to the work whether strictly epic justice were awarded to the club, or not. The publication of the book in monthly numbers, containing only thirty-two pages in each, rendered it an object of paramount importance that, while the different incidents were linked together by a chain of interest strong enough to prevent their appearing unconnected or impossible, the general design should be so simple as to sustain no injury from this detached and desultory form of publication, extending over no fewer than twenty months. In short, it was necessary – or it appeared so to me then – that every number should be, to a certain extent, complete in itself, and yet that the whole twenty numbers, when collected, should form one tolerably harmonious whole, each leading to the other by a gentle and not unnatural progress of adventure. It seemed obvious that in a work published with a view to such considerations, no artfully interwoven or ingeniously complicated plot could with reason be expected. Experience and study afterwards taught me something, and I could perhaps wish now that these chapters were strung together on a stronger thread of general interest. Still, what they are they were designed to be.

*The first meeting of the Pickwick Club and 'that happy portrait
of the founder by which he is always recognised'.*

It has been observed of Mr Pickwick, that there is a decided
change in his character, as the pages proceed, and that he

becomes more good and more sensible. I do not think this change will appear forced or unnatural to my readers, if they will reflect that in real life the peculiarities and oddities of a man who has anything whimsical about him, generally impress us first, and that it is not until we are better acquainted with him that we usually begin to look below these superficial traits, and to know the better part of him.

Lest there should be any well-intentioned persons who do not perceive the difference (as some such could not, when *Old Mortality* was newly published), between religion and the cant of religion, piety and the pretence of piety, a humble reverence for the great truths of Scripture and an audacious and offensive obtrusion of its letter and not its spirit in the commonest dissensions and meanest affairs of life, to the extraordinary confusions of ignorant minds, let them understand that it is always the latter, and never the former, which is satirised here. Further, that the latter is here satirised as being, according to all experience, inconsistent with the former, impossible of union with it, and one of the most evil and mischievous false-hoods existent in society – whether it establish its headquarters, for the time being, in Exeter Hall, or Ebenezer Chapel, or both. It may appear unnecessary to offer a word of observation on so plain a head. But it is never out of season to protest against that coarse familiarity with sacred things which is busy on the lip, and idle in the heart; or against the confounding of Christianity with any class of persons who, in the words of Swift, have just enough religion to make them hate, and not enough to make them love, one another.

The most serious and pathetic point I tried with all indigna-tion and intensity to make, in this my first book, was the slow torture and death of a Chancery prisoner. From that hour to this, if I have been set on anything, it has been on exhibiting the abuses of the Law. I have therefore found it curious and interesting, looking over the pages of *Pickwick*, to mark what important social improvements have taken place about us, almost imperceptibly, since they were originally written.

The licence of Counsel, and the degree to which Juries are ingeniously bewildered, are yet susceptible of moderation; while an improvement in the mode of conducting parliamen-tary elections (and even parliaments too, perhaps) is still within the bounds of possibility. But legal reforms have pared the claws of Messrs. Dodson and Fogg; a spirit of self-respect, mutual forbearance, education, and co-operation for such good ends, has diffused itself among their clerks; places far apart are brought together, to the present inconvenience and advantage of the Public, and to the certain destruction, in time, of a host of petty jealousies, blindnesses, and prejudices, by which the Public alone have always been the sufferers; the laws relating to imprisonment for debt are altered; and the Fleet Prison is pulled down!

Who knows, but that one day not too far distant it may be discovered that there are even magistrates in town and country, who should be taught to shake hands every day with Common-sense and Justice; that even Poor Laws may have mercy on the weak, the aged, and unfortunate; that Schools, on the broad principles of Christianity, are the best adornment for the length and breadth of this civilised land; that Prison-doors should be barred on the outside, no less heavily and carefully than they are barred within; that the universal diffusion of common means of decency and health is as much the right of the poorest of the poor, as it is indispensable to the safety of the rich, and of the State; that a few petty boards and bodies – less than drops in the great ocean of humanity, which roars around them – are not for ever to let loose Fever and Consumption on God's creatures at their will, or always to keep their jobbing little fiddles going, for a Dance of Death.

If I were to live a hundred years, and write three novels in each, I should never be so proud of any of them as I am of *Pickwick*, feeling as I do, that it has made its own way, and hoping, as I must own I do hope, that long after my hand is withered as the pens it holds, *Pickwick* will be found on many a dusty shelf with many a better work.

Triumph

The great success of the *Sketches*, and the name it had established for me among the publishers, had meanwhile enabled me to settle at an earlier period than I had at first supposed possible. On 2 April 1836 I married Miss Catherine Hogarth, the daughter of a gentleman who had recently distinguished himself by a celebrated work on music, who was the most intimate companion of Sir Walter Scott, and one of the most eminent among the literati of Edinburgh.

We lived, to begin with, at a larger set of chambers at Furnival's Inn. From the day of our marriage my wife's sixteen-year-old sister Mary was the grace and life of our home, our constant companion, and the sharer of all our little pleasures. The love and affection which existed between her and her sister, no one can imagine the extent of. We might have known that we were too happy together to be long without a change. I shall never be so happy again as in those chambers three storeys high – never, if I roll in wealth and fame.

By the summer of 1836 the pressure of my different occupations rendered it impossible for me to exceed the distance of twelve miles from St Paul's Cathedral. I was engaged in revising the proof sheets of the second edition of the *Sketches*, which were to appear shortly; I was preparing another series which needed to be published before Christmas, I had just finished an opera (*Village Coquettes*) which would be produced at Braham's theatre in October, I had to get Mr Pickwick's lucubrations ready, every month; and I had, in addition, to perform the duties (neither slight nor few) which my engagement with the *Morning Chronicle* imposed upon me. I had found, moreover, that I never could write with effect – especially in the serious way – until I had got my steam up, or in other words until I had become so excited with my subject that I could not leave off.

With regard to *The Village Coquettes*, 'Either the Honourable Gentleman is in the right, or he is not', is a phrase in very common use within the walls of Parliament. This drama may have a plot, or it may not; and the songs may be poetry, or they may not; and the whole affair, from beginning to end, may be great nonsense, or it may not, just as the honourable gentleman or lady who reads it may happen to think. So, retaining my own private and particular opinion upon the subject, I leave every such gentleman or lady to form his or hers, as he or she may think proper, without saying one word to influence or conciliate them. All I wish to say is this: That I hope Mr Braham, and all the performers who assisted in the representation of this opera, will accept my warmest thanks for the interest they evinced in it, from its very first rehearsal, and for their zealous efforts in my behalf – efforts which have crowned

Catherine Dickens.

it with a degree of success far exceeding my most sanguine anticipations; and of which no form of words could speak my acknowledgment. It is needless to add that the *libretto* of an opera must be, to a certain extent, a mere vehicle for the music, and that it is scarcely fair or reasonable to judge it by those strict rules of criticism which would be justly applicable to a five-act tragedy, or a finished comedy.

I remained with the *Chronicle* until the first seven or eight numbers of *The Pickwick Papers* had appeared and then quitted it, by which time *Pickwick* was rapidly approaching the zenith of its fame and popularity. I became editor of *Bentley's Miscellany* a little while later and it was in the pages of this journal that Oliver Twist made his first appearance. I learnt, about this time, that one should never make a fair copy of a much corrected manuscript. A manuscript with few or no corrections is always given to the boy beginner to set up and the author receives a full proof full of errors. The manuscript which is difficult to decipher is put into the hands of a first-rate compositor whose proof will give very little trouble.

At quarter past six o'clock pm on Friday, 6 January 1837, Mrs Dickens presented me with a son and heir. Our living accommodation being now somewhat restricted, we moved from Furnival's Inn to 48 Doughty Street, situated in a distinguished metropolitan parish, two months later. Having newly taken the lease of a house which then appeared to me a frightfully first-class Family Mansion, involving awful responsibilities, I became the prey of a Beadle.

I think the Beadle must have seen me going in or coming out, and must have observed that I tottered under the weight of my grandeur. Or he may have been in hiding under the straw when I bought my first horse (in the desirable stable-yard attached to the first-class Family Mansion) and when the vendor remarked to me, in an original manner, on bringing him for approval, taking his cloth off and smacking him, 'There, Sir! *There's* a Orse!' And I said gallantly, 'How much do you want for him?' and when the vendor said, 'No more than sixty guineas from you', and when I said smartly, 'Why no more than sixty from me?' And when he said crushingly, 'Because upon my soul and body he'd be considered cheap at seventy, by one who understood the subject – but you don't!' – I say, the Beadle may have been in hiding under the straw, when this disgrace befell me, or he may have noted that I was too raw and young an Atlas

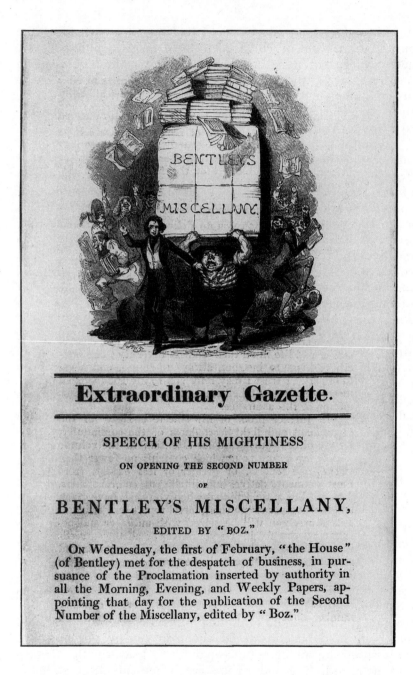

The front page of a circular composed by Dickens for the second number of Bentley's Miscellany.

to carry the first-class Family Mansion in a knowing manner. Be this as it may, the Beadle did what Melancholy did to the Youth in Gray's *Elegy* – he marked me for his own. And the way in which the Beadle did it, was this: he summoned me as a Juryman on his Coroner's Inquests.

In my first feverish alarm I repaired 'for safety and succour' – like those sagacious Northern shepherds, who, having had no previous reason whatever to believe in young Norval, very prudently did not originate the hazardous idea of believing in him – to a deep householder. This profound man informed me that the Beadle counted on my buying him off; on my bribing him not to summon me; and that if I would attend an Inquest with a cheerful countenance, and profess alacrity in that branch of my country's service, the Beadle would be disheartened and would give up the game.

I roused my energies and the next time the wily Beadle summoned me, I went. The Beadle was the blankest Beadle I have ever looked on when I answered to my name; and his discomfiture gave me courage to go through with it.

'Oliver Twist'

While *Pickwick* was yet in course of publication, *Oliver Twist* was begun in monthly portions in *Bentley's Miscellany*. The first chapter of *Oliver Twist* appeared concurrently either with the tenth or eleventh number of *Pickwick*. They then went on together until *Pickwick* was finished.

Once upon a time it was held to be a coarse and shocking circumstance, that some of the characters in *Oliver Twist* were chosen from the most criminal and degraded of London's population, that Sikes is a thief, and Fagin a receiver of stolen goods; that the boys are pickpockets, and Nancy is a prostitute.

As I saw no reason, when I wrote this book, why the dregs of life (so long as their speech did not offend the ear) should not serve the purpose of a moral, as well as its froth and cream, I made bold to believe that this same Once upon a time would not prove to be All-time or even a long time. In this spirit, when I wished to show, in little Oliver, the principle of Good surviving through every adverse circumstance, and triumphing at last; and when I considered among what companions I could show him best, having regard to that kind of men into whose hands he would most naturally fall, I bethought myself of those who figure in this volume. When I came to discuss the subject more maturely with myself, I saw many strong reasons for pursuing my course. I had read of thieves by scores; seductive fellows (amiable for the most part), faultless in dress, plump in pocket, choice in horse-flesh, bold in bearing, fortunate in gallantry, great at a song, a bottle, pack of cards or dice-box, and fit companions for the bravest. But I had never met (except in Hogarth) with the miserable reality. It appeared to me that to draw a knot of such associates in crime as really did exist; to paint them in all their deformity, in all their wretchedness, in all the squalid misery of their lives; to show them as they really were, for ever skulking uneasily through the dirtiest paths of life, with the great black ghastly gallows closing up their prospect, turn them where they might; it appeared to me that to do this, would be to attempt a something which was needed, and which would be a service to society. And I did it as best I could.

In every book I know, where such characters are treated of, allurements and fascinations are thrown around them. Even in *The Beggar's Opera*, the thieves are represented as leading a life which is rather to be envied than otherwise: while Macheath, with all the captivations of command, and the devotion of the most beautiful girl and only pure character in the piece, is as much to be admired and emulated by weak beholders, as any fine gentleman in a red coat who has purchased, as Voltaire says, the right to command a couple of thousand men, or so, and to affront death at their head. Johnson's question, whether any man will turn thief because Macheath is reprieved, seems to me beside the matter. I ask myself, whether any man will be deterred from turning thief, because of Macheath's being sentenced to death, and because of the existence of Peachum and Lockit; and remembering the captain's roaring life, great appearance, vast success, and strong advantages, I feel assured that nobody having a bent that way will take any warning from him, or will see anything in the play but a flowery and pleasant road, conducting an honourable ambition – in course of time – to Tyburn Tree.

In fact, Gay's witty satire on society had a general object, which made him quite regardless of example in this respect, and gave him other and wider aims. The same may be said of Sir Edward Bulwer's admirable and powerful novel of *Paul Clifford*, which cannot be fairly considered as having, or as being intended to have, any bearing on this part of the subject, one way or other.

I incline as little to the sickly feeling which makes every canting lie or maudlin speech of a notorious criminal a subject of newspaper report and general sympathy, as I do to those good old customs of the good old times which made England even so recently as the reign of the Third King George, in respect of her criminal code and her barbarous regulations, one of the most bloody-minded and barbarous countries on the earth. If I thought it would do any good to the rising generation, I would cheerfully give my consent to the disinterment of the bones of any genteel highwayman (the more genteel, the more cheerfully), and to their exposure, piecemeal, on any signpost, gate, or gibbet, that might be deemed a good elevation for the purpose. My reason is as well convinced that these gentry were as utterly worthless and debauched villains, as it is that the laws and jails hardened them in their evil courses, or that their wonderful escapes were effected by the prison-turnkeys who, in those admirable days, had always been felons themselves, and were, to the last, their bosom-friends and pot-companions.

(I am, on the other hand, by no means a wholesale admirer of our legal solemnities, many of which impress me as being exceedingly ludicrous. Strange as it may seem too, there is undoubtedly a degree of protection in the wig and gown – a dismissal of individual responsibility in dressing for the part – which encourages that insolent bearing and language, and that gross perversion of the office of a pleader for The Truth, so frequent in our courts of law.)

What manner of life is that which is described in *Oliver Twist* as the everyday existence of a Thief? What charms has it for the young and ill-disposed, what allurements for the most jolter-headed of juveniles? Here are no canterings on moonlit heaths, no merry-makings in the snuggest of all possible taverns, none of the attractions of dress, no embroidery, no lace, no jack-boots, no crimson coats and ruffles, none of the dash and freedom with which 'the road' has been out of time invested. The cold wet shelterless midnight streets of London; and the foul and frowzy dens, where vice is closely packed and lacks the room to turn; the haunts of hunger and disease; the shabby rags that scarcely hold together; where are the attractions of these things?

There are people, however, of so refined and delicate a nature, that they cannot bear the contemplation of such horrors. Not that they turn instinctively from crime; but that criminal characters, to suit them, must be, like their meat, in delicate disguise. A Massaroni in green velvet is an enchanting creature; but a Sikes in fustian is insupportable. A Mrs Massaroni, being a lady in short petticoats and a fancy dress, is a thing to imitate in tableaux and have in lithographs on pretty songs; but a Nancy, being a creature in a cotton gown and cheap shawls, is not to be thought of. It is wonderful how Virtue turns from dirty stockings; and how Vice, married to ribbons and a little gay attire, changes her name, as wedded ladies do, and becomes Romance.

Cant as we may, and as we shall to the end of all things, it is very much harder for the poor to be virtuous than it is for the rich; and the good that is in them, shines the brighter for it.

But as the stern truth, even in the dress of this (in novels) much exalted race, was a part of the purpose of this book, I did not, for these readers, abate one hole in the Dodger's coat, or one scrap of curl-paper in Nancy's dishevelled hair. I had no faith in the delicacy which could not bear to look upon them. I had no desire to make proselytes among such people. I had no respect for their opinion, good or bad; did not covet their approval; and did not write for their amusement. I venture to say this without reserve, for I am not aware of any writer in our language having a respect for himself, or held in any respect by his posterity, who ever has descended to the taste of this fastidious class.

On the other hand, if I look for example, and for precedents, I find them in the noblest range of English literature. Fielding, Defoe, Goldsmith, Smollett, Richardson, Mackenzie – all these for wise purposes, and especially the two first, brought upon the scene the very scum and refuse of the land. Hogarth, the moralist and censor of his age – in whose great works the times in which he lived, and the characters of every time, will never cease to be reflected – did the like, without the compromise of a hair's breadth; with a power and depth of thought which belonged to few men before him, and will probably appertain to fewer still in time to come. Where does this giant stand now in the estimation of his countrymen? And yet, if I turn back to the days in which he or any of these men flourished, I find the same reproach levelled against them by every one, each in his turn, by the insects of the hour, who raised their little hum, and died, and were forgotten.

Cervantes laughed Spain's chivalry away, by showing Spain its impossible and wild absurdity. It was my attempt, in my humble and far-distant sphere, to dim the glitter surrounding something which really did exist, by showing it in its unattractive and repulsive truth. No less consulting my own taste, than the manners of the age, I endeavoured, while I painted it in all its follies and degraded aspect, to banish from the lips of the lowest character I introduced, any expression that could by possibility offend: and rather to lead to the unavoidable inference that its existence was of the most debased and vicious kind, than to prove it elaborately by words and deeds. In the case of Nancy, in particular, I kept this intention constantly in view. Whether it is apparent in the narrative, and how it is executed, I leave my readers to determine.

It has been observed of Nancy that her devotion to the brutal house-breaker does not seem natural. And it has been objected to Sikes in the same breath – with some inconsistency, as I venture to think – that he is surely overdrawn, because in him there would appear to be none of those redeeming traits which are objected to as unnatural in his mistress. Of the latter objection I will merely remark, that I fear there are in the world some insensible and callous natures, that do become utterly and incurably bad. Whether this be so or not, of one thing I am certain: that there are such men as Sikes, who, being closely followed through the same space of time and through the same current of circumstances, would not give, by the action of a moment, the faintest indication of a better nature. Whether every gentler human feeling is dead within such bosoms, or the proper chord to strike has rusted and is hard to find, I do not pretend to know; but the fact is as I state it, I am sure.

It is useless to discuss whether the conduct and character of the girl seems natural or unnatural, probable or improbable, right or wrong. *It is true.* Every man who has watched these melancholy shades of life, must know it to be so. From the first introduction of the poor wretch, to her laying her blood-stained head upon the robber's breast, there is not a word exaggerated or over-wrought. It is emphatically God's truth, for it is the hope He leaves in such depraved and miserable breasts; the hope yet lingering there; the last fair drop of water at the bottom of the weed-choked well. It involves the best and worst shades of our nature; much of its ugliest hues, and something of its most beautiful; it is a contradiction, an anomaly, an apparent impossibility; but it is a truth. I am glad to have had it doubted, for in that circumstance I should find a sufficient assurance (if I wanted any) that it needed to be told.

A church at Cooling is where I witnessed the pauper's funeral, exactly as it is written in the fourth chapter of *Oliver Twist*. A few weeks afterwards I received a letter from the clergyman who behaved in an unseemly way on that occasion, asking me whether I conceived it possible that such a thing could ever occur. I wrote back to him and said, 'Thou art the man.'

Tragedy

On the evening of Saturday, 6 May 1837, Mary Hogarth accompanied Catherine and myself to St James Theatre, apparently in the best of health. She went upstairs to bed at about one o'clock in her usual delightful spirits but was taken ill before she had undressed. We lost no time in procuring medical assistance, or on applying every remedy that skill and anxiety could suggest. The dear girl however sank beneath the attack. She died in my arms next afternoon at three o'clock and the very last words she whispered were of me. The medical men were of the opinion that her heart had been diseased for a great length of time. Her general state of health, and above all the awful suddenness of her death, induce me to think they were right.

She died in such a calm and gentle sleep, that although I had held her in my arms for some little time before, when she was certainly living (for she swallowed a little brandy from my hand), I continued to support her lifeless form, long after her soul had fled to Heaven.

Of our sufferings at the time, and all through the dreary week that followed, I will say nothing – no one can imagine what they were. I solemnly believe that so perfect a creature never breathed. I knew her inmost heart, and her real worth and value. She had not a fault. I could have better spared a much nearer relation or an older friend, for she had been to us what we could never replace and left a blank which no one who ever knew her could have the faintest hope of seeing supplied.

Mary Hogarth.

My wife had a trying task, for in the midst of her own affliction she had to soothe the sufferings of her bereaved mother,
who was called to Doughty Street in time to see her child
expire. Mrs Dickens bore up through her severe trial like what
she was – a fine-hearted noble-minded girl. She made such

strong efforts to console her mother, that she unconsciously summoned up all her fortitude at the same time, and brought it to her own assistance. From their earliest infancy to this moment she could call to mind no single recollection of an unkind word between herself and Mary, and she knew that if ever a mortal went up to Heaven, her sister was there; she had nothing to remember but a long course of affection and attachment, perhaps never exceeded.

I was so shaken and unnerved by the loss of the dear girl whom I loved, after my wife, more deeply and fervently than anyone on earth, that I was compelled for once to give up all idea of my monthly work, and to try a fortnight's rest and quiet. We hired a small cottage in Hampstead and repaired thither for a little change of air and scene.

It was made clear that the publication of *Pickwick* had been interrupted by a severe domestic affliction of no ordinary kind, but its non-appearance gave rise to various idle speculations and absurdities which were industriously propagated during the month of June. By one set of intimate acquaintances, especially well informed, the author had been killed outright; by another, driven mad; by a third, imprisoned for debt; by a fourth, sent per steamer to the United States; by a fifth, rendered incapable of any mental exertion for evermore – by all, in short, represented as doing anything but seeking in a few weeks' retirement the restoration of that cheerfulness and peace of which a sad bereavement had temporarily deprived him.

I dreamed of Mary every night for many months, at home or away from home, sometimes as a spirit, sometimes as a kind of living creature, never with any of the bitterness of my real sorrow, but always with a kind of quiet happiness, which became so pleasant to me that I never lay down at night without a hope of the vision coming back in one shape or other. And so it did. I went down to Yorkshire, researching for *Nicholas Nickleby*, and stayed at a lonely inn in a wide moorland place. Finding the vision still present to me in a strange scene and a strange bed, I could not help mentioning the circumstances in a note I wrote home to Catherine. I had always, until that hour, kept it within my own breast that I dreamed every night of the dear lost one. But in the letter that I wrote I recorded the circumstances, and added that I felt much interested in proving whether the subject of my dream would still be faithful to me, travel-tired, and in that remote place. No. I lost the beloved figure of my vision in parting with the secret. From that moment I ceased to dream of her, though she is so much in my thoughts at all times (especially when I am successful and have prospered in anything) that the recollection of her is an essential part of my being, and is as inseparable from my being as the beating of my heart is.

My sleep has never looked upon the figure since, in sixteen years, but once. I was in Italy, and awoke (or seemed to awake), the well-remembered voice distinctly in my ears, conversing with it. I entreated it, as it rose above my head and soared up to the vaulted roof of the old room, to answer me a question I had asked touching the Future Life. My hands were still outstretched towards it as it vanished, when I heard a bell ringing by the garden wall, and a voice in the deep stillness of the night calling on all good Christians to pray for the souls of the dead; it being All Souls' Eve.

If she were with us now, the same winning, happy, amiable companion, sympathising with all my thoughts and feelings more than anyone I knew ever did or will, I think I should have nothing to wish for but a continuance of such happiness.

'The Life and Adventures of Nicholas Nickleby'

This story was begun, within a few months after the publication of the completed *Pickwick Papers*. There were, then, a good many cheap Yorkshire schools in existence. There are very few now.

Of the monstrous neglect of education in England, and the disregard of it by the State as a means of forming good or bad citizens, and miserable or happy men, private schools long afforded a notable example. Although any man who had proved his unfitness for any other occupation in life, was free, without examination or qualification, to open a school anywhere; although preparation for the functions he undertook, was required in the surgeon who assisted to bring a boy into the world, or might one day assist, perhaps, to send him out of it; in the chemist, the attorney, the butcher, the baker, the candlestick maker; the whole round of crafts and trades, the schoolmaster excepted; and although schoolmasters, as a race, were the blockheads and impostors who might naturally be expected to spring from such a state of things, and to flourish in it; these Yorkshire schoolmasters were the lowest and most rotten round in the whole ladder. Traders in the avarice, indifference, or imbecility of parents, and the helplessness of children; ignorant, sordid, brutal men, to whom few considerate persons would have entrusted the board and lodging of a horse or dog; they formed the worthy cornerstone of a structure, which, for absurdity and a magnificent high-minded *laissez-aller* neglect, has rarely been exceeded in the world.

We hear sometimes of an action for damages against the unqualified medical practitioner, who has deformed a broken limb in pretending to heal it. But, what of the hundreds of thousands of minds that have been deformed for ever by the incapable pettifoggers who have pretended to form them!

I make mention of the race, as of the Yorkshire schoolmasters, in the past tense. Though it has not yet finally disappeared, it is dwindling daily. A long day's work remains to be done about us in the way of education, Heaven knows; but great improvements and facilities towards the attainment of a good one have been furnished, of late years.

I cannot call to mind, now, how I came to hear about Yorkshire schools when I was a not very robust child, sitting in by-places near Rochester Castle, with a head full of Partridge, Strap, Tom Pipes, and Sancho Panza; but I know that my first impressions of them were picked up at that time, and that they were somehow or other connected with a suppurated abscess that some boy had come home with, in consequence of his Yorkshire guide, philosopher, and friend, having ripped it open with an inky pen-knife. The impression made upon me, however made, never left me. I was always curious about Yorkshire schools – fell, long afterwards and at sundry times, into the way of hearing more about them – at last, having an audience, resolved to write about them.

With that intent I went down into Yorkshire before I began this book, in very severe winter time which is pretty faithfully described therein. As I wanted to see a schoolmaster or two, and was forewarned that those gentlemen might, in their modesty, be shy of receiving a visit from the author of *The Pickwick Papers*, I consulted with a professional friend who had a Yorkshire connexion, and with whom I concerted a pious fraud. He gave me some letters of introduction, in the name, I think, of my travelling companion (Hablot K. Browne, otherwise known as 'Phiz'); they bore reference to a supposititious little boy who had been left with a widowed mother who didn't know what to do with him; the poor lady had thought, as a means of thawing the tardy compassion of her relations in his behalf, of sending him to a Yorkshire school; I was the poor lady's friend, travelling that way; and if the recipient of the letter could inform me of a school in his neighbourhood, the writer would be very much obliged. We encountered, on our journey northwards, an old lady who turned out to be the mistress of a Yorkshire school returning from a holiday-stay in London. She was a very queer old lady and showed us a long letter she was carrying to one of the boys from his father, containing a severe lecture (enforced and aided by many texts from Scripture) *on his refusing to eat boiled meat.* She was very communicative, drank a great deal of brandy and water, and towards evening became insensible, in which state we left her.

I went to several places in that part of the country where I understood the schools to be most plentifully sprinkled, and had no occasion to deliver a letter until I came to a certain town which shall be nameless. The person to whom it was addressed was not at home; but he came down at night, through the snow, to the inn where I was staying. It was after dinner; and he needed little persuasion to sit down by the fire in a warm corner, and take his share of the wine that was on the table. I am afraid he is dead now. I recollect he was a jovial, ruddy, broad-faced man; that we got acquainted directly; and that we talked on all kinds of subjects, except the school, which he showed a great anxiety to avoid. 'Is there any large school near?' I asked him, in reference to the letter. 'Oh yes,' he said; 'there is a pratty big 'un.' 'Is it a good one?' I asked. 'Ey!' he said, 'it's as good as anoother; that's a' matter of opinion'; and he fell to looking at the fire, staring round the room, and whistling a little. On my reverting to some other topic that we had been discussing, he recovered immediately; but, though I tried him again and again, I never approached the question of the school, even if he were in the middle of a laugh, without observing that his countenance fell, and that he became uncomfortable. At last, when we had passed a couple of hours or so, very agreeably, he suddenly took up his hat, and looking me full in the face, said, in a low voice, 'Weel, Misther, we've been vara pleasant toogather, and ar'll spak' my moind tiv'ee.

Phiz's drawing of the Yorkshire Schoolmaster at the Saracen's Head, made after his tour with Dickens of Yorkshire schools.

Dinnot let the weedur send her lattle boy to yan o' our school-measthers, while ther's a harse to hoold in a' Lunnun, or a goother to lie asleep in. Ar wouldn't mak' ill words among my neeburs, and are speak tiv'ee quiet loike. But I'm dom'd if ar can gang to bed and not tellee, for weedur's sak', to keep the lattle boy from a'sike scoondrels while there's a harse to hoold in a' Lunnun, or a goother to lie asleep in!' Repeating these words with great heartiness, and with a solemnity on his jolly face that made it look twice as large as before, he shook hands and went away. I never saw afterwards, but I sometimes imagine that I descry a faint reflection of him in John Browdie.

In reference to these gentry, I may here quote a few works from the original preface to *Nicholas Nickleby*.

It has afforded the Author great amusement and satisfaction, during the progress of this work, to learn, from country friends and from a variety of ludicrous statements concerning himself in provincial newspapers, that more than one Yorkshire schoolmaster lays claim to being the original of Mr Squeers. One worthy, he has reason to believe, has actually consulted authorities learned in the law, as to his having good grounds on which to rest an action for libel; another, has meditated a journey to London, for the express purpose of committing an assault and battery on his traducer; a third, perfectly remembers being waited on, last January twelvemonth, by two gentlemen, one of whom held him in conversation while the other took his likeness; and, although Mr Squeers has but one eye, and he has two, and the published sketch does not resemble him (whoever he may be) in any other respect, still he and all his friends and neighbours know at once for whom it is meant, because – the character is *so* like him.

While the Author cannot but feel the full force of the compliment thus conveyed to him, he ventures to suggest that these contentions may arise from the fact, that Mr Squeers is the representative of a class, and not of an individual. Where imposture, ignorance, and brutal cupidity, are the stock in trade of a small body of men, and one is described by these characteristics, all his fellows will recognise something belonging to themselves, and each will have a misgiving that the portrait is his own.

The Author's object in calling public attention to the system would be very imperfectly fulfilled, if he did not state now, in his own person, emphatically and earnestly, that Mr Squeers and his school are faint and feeble pictures of an existing reality, purposely subdued and kept down lest they should be deemed impossible. That there are, upon record, trials at law in which damages have been sought as a poor recompense for lasting agonies and disfigurements inflicted upon children by the treatment of the master in these places, involving such offensive and foul details of neglect, cruelty and disease, as no writer of fiction would have the boldness to imagine. And that, since he has been engaged upon these *Adventures*, he has received, from private quarters far beyond the reach of suspicion or distrust, accounts of atrocities, in the perpetration of which upon neglected or repudiated children, these schools have been the main instruments, very far exceeding any that appear in these pages.

This comprises all I need say on the subject; except that if I had seen occasion, I had resolved to reprint a few of these details of legal proceedings, from certain old newspapers.

EDUCATION, by Mr. SHAW, at BOWES
ACADEMY, Greta-bridge, Yorkshire.—YOUTH are carefully INSTRUCTED in the English, Latin, and Greek languages, writing, common and decimal arithmetic, bookkeeping, mensuration, surveying, geometry, and navigation, with the most useful branches of the mathematics, and are provided with board, clothes, and every necessary, at 20 guineas per annum each. No extra charges whatever, doctors' bills excepted. No vacations except by the parents' desire. The French language 2 guineas per annum extra. Further particulars may be known on application to Mrs. Young, Plough-yard, Crown-street, Soho; or Mr. Walker, 37, Drury-lane. Also for further particulars see a card of Mr. Shaw, who attends daily at the George and Blue Boar, High Holborn, from 12 to 2 o'clock. Mr. Seaton, agent, 10, Frederick-place, Goswell-street-road.

An advertisement for the original Dotheboys Hall.

One other quotation from the same preface may serve to introduce a fact that my readers may think curious.

To turn to a more pleasant subject, it may be right to say, that there *are* two characters in this book which are drawn from life. It is remarkable that what we call the world, which is so very credulous in what professes to be true, is most incredulous in what professes to be imaginary; and that, while, every day in real life, it will allow in one man no blemishes, and in another no virtues, it will seldom admit a very strongly-marked character, either good or bad, in a fictitious narrative, to be within the limits of probability. But those who take an interest in this tale, will be glad to learn that the Brothers Cheeryble live; that their liberal charity, their singleness of heart, their noble nature, and their unbounded benevolence, are no creations of an Author's brain; but are prompting every day (and oftenest by stealth) some munificent and generous deed in that town of which they are the pride and honour.

If I were to attempt to sum up the thousands of letters, from all sorts of people in all sorts of latitudes and climates, which this unlucky paragraph brought down upon me, I should get into an arithmetical difficulty from which I could not easily extricate myself. Suffice it to say, that I believe the applications for loans, gifts, and offices of profit that I have been requested to forward to the originals of the Brothers Cheeryble (with whom I never interchanged any communication in my life) would have exhausted the combined patronage of all the Lord Chancellors since the House of Brunswick, and would have broken the rest of the Bank of England.

The brothers are now dead.

There is only other point, on which I would desire to offer a remark. If Nicholas be not always found to be blameless or agreeable, he is not always intended to appear so. He is a young man of an impetuous temper and of little or no experience; and I saw no reason why such a hero should be lifted out of nature.

Valedictory

It is not easy for a man to speak of his own books. I dare say that few persons have been more interested in mine than I; and if it be a general principle in nature that a lover's love is blind, and that a mother's love is blind, I believe it may be said of an author's attachment to the creatures of his own imagination, that it is a perfect model of constancy and devotion, and is the blindest of all. But the objects and purposes I have in view are very plain and simple, and may easily be told.

I have always had, and always shall have, an earnest and true desire to contribute, as far as in me lies, to the common stock of healthful cheerfulness and enjoyment. I have always had, and always shall have, an invincible repugnance to that mole-eyed philosophy which loves the darkness and winks and scowls in the light. I believe that Virtue shows quite as well in rags and patches as she does in purple and fine linen. I believe that she, and every beautiful object in external nature, claim some sympathy in the breast of the poorest man who breaks his scanty loaf of daily bread. I believe that she goes barefoot as well as shod. I believe that she dwells rather oftener in alleys and by-ways than she does in courts and palaces, and that it is good, and pleasant, and profitable to track her out and follow her. I believe that to lay one's hand upon some of those rejected ones whom the world has too long forgotten, and too often misused, and to say to the proudest and most thoughtless, 'These creatures have the same elements and capacities of goodness as yourselves, they are moulded in the same form, and made of the same clay; and though ten times worse than you, may, in having retained anything of their original nature amidst the trials and distresses of their condition, be really ten times better' – I believe that to do this is to pursue a worthy and not useless avocation.

Dickens in 1837, when he was beginning to be known as an elegant young man about town.

To change the customs even of civilised and educated men, and impress them with new ideas, is – I have good need to know it – a most difficult and slow proceeding. I must say, above all things – especially to young people writing: For the love of God, don't condescend! Don't assume the attitude of saying, 'See how clever I am, and what fun everybody else is!' Take any shape but that. I have systematically tried to turn Fiction to the good account of showing the preventable wretchedness and misery in which the mass of the people dwell, and of expressing again the conviction, founded upon observation, that the reform of their habitations must precede all other reforms; and that without it, all other reforms must fail. Neither Religion nor Education will make any way, in this nineteenth century of Christianity, until a Christian government shall have discharged its first obligation, and secured to the people Homes, instead of polluted dens. I have no sympathy with Demagogues, but am a grievous Radical, and think the political signs of the times to be just about as bad as the spirit of the people will admit of their being.

My moral creed, which is a very wide and comprehensive one, and includes all sects and parties, is very easily summed up. I take it that we are born and that we hold our sympathies, hopes and energies in trust for the many, and not for the few. That we cannot hold in too strong a light of disgust and contempt, before the view of others, all meanness, falsehood, cruelty, and oppression, of every grade and kind. Above all, that nothing is high, because it is in a high place; and that nothing is low, because it is in a low one. This is a lesson taught us in the great book of nature. This is the lesson which may be read, alike in the bright track of the stars, and in the dusty course of the poorest thing that drags its tiny length upon the ground.

I hold my inventive capacity on the stern condition that it must master my whole life, often have complete possession of me, make its own demands upon me, and sometimes for months together put everything else away from me. Whoever is devoted to an Art must be content to deliver himself wholly up to it, and to find his recompense in it. I shall never rest much while my faculties last, and (if I know myself) have a certain something in me that would still be active in rusting and corroding me, if I flattered myself that I was in repose. On the other hand, I think that my habit of easy self-abstraction and withdrawal into fancies has always refreshed and strengthened

Charles Dickens.

me in short intervals wonderfully. I always seem to myself to have rested far more than I have worked; and I do really believe that I have some exceptional faculty of accumulating young feelings in short pauses, which obliterates a quantity of wear and tear.

THE LONG VOYAGE: A NEW YEAR'S EVE REFLECTION

'I have outgrown no story of voyage and travel,
no love of adventure, no ardent interest in voyagers
and travellers.'
– 'Where We Stopped Growing', January 1853

WHEN the wind is blowing and the sleet or rain is driving against the dark windows, I love to sit by the fire, thinking of what I have read in books of voyages and travel. Such books have had a strong fascination for my mind from my earliest childhood; and I wonder it should have come to pass that I have never been round the world, never have been shipwrecked, ice-environed, tomahawked, or eaten.

Sitting on my ruddy hearth in the twilight of New Year's Eve, I find incidents of travel rise around me from all the latitudes and longitudes of the globe. They observe no order or sequence, but appear and vanish as they will – 'come like shadows, so depart'. Columbus, alone upon the seas with his disaffected crew, looks over the waste of waters from his high station on the poop of his ship, and sees the first uncertain glimmer of the light, 'rising and falling with the waves, like a torch in the bark of some fisherman', which is the shining star of a new world. Bruce is caged in Abyssinia, surrounded by the gory horrors which shall often startle him out of his sleep at home when years have passed away. Franklin, come to the end of his

175

unhappy overland journey – would that it had been his last! – lies perishing of hunger with his brave companions: each emaciated figure stretched upon its miserable bed without the power to rise: all, dividing the weary days between their prayers, their remembrances of the dear ones at home, and conversations on the pleasures of eating; the last-named topic being ever present to them, likewise, in their dreams. All the African travellers, wayworn, solitary and sad, submit themselves again to drunken, murderous, man-selling despots, of the lower order of humanity; and Mungo Park, fainting under a tree and succoured by a woman, gratefully remembers how his Good Samaritan has always come to him in woman's shape, the wide world over.

Captain Bligh (a worse man to be entrusted with arbitrary power there could scarcely be) is handed over the side of the *Bounty*, and turned adrift on the wide ocean in an open boat, by orders of Fletcher Christian, one of his officers, at this very minute. Another flash of my fire, and 'Thursday October Christian', five-and-twenty years of age, son of the dead and gone Fletcher by a savage mother, leaps aboard His Majesty's ship *Briton*, hove-to off Pitcairn's Island; says his simple grace before eating, in good English; and knows that a pretty little animal on board is called a dog, because in his childhood he had heard of such strange creatures from his father and the other mutineers, grown grey under the shade of the bread-fruit trees, speaking of their lost country far away.

See the *Halsewell*, East Indiaman outward bound, driving madly on a January night towards the rocks near Seacombe, on the island of Purbeck! The captain's two dear daughters are aboard, and five other ladies. The ship has been driving many hours, has seven feet of water in her hold, and her mainmast has been blown away. The description of her loss, familiar to me from my early boyhood, seems to be read aloud as she rushes to her destiny.

An universal shriek, in which the voice of female distress was lamentably distinguished, announced the dreadful catastrophe. In a few moments all was hushed, except the roaring of the winds, and the dashing of the waves; the wreck was buried in the deep, and not an atom of it was ever afterwards seen.

The most beautiful and affecting incident I know, associated with a shipwreck, succeeds this dismal story for a winter night. The *Grosvenor*, East Indiaman, homeward bound, goes ashore on the coast of Caffraria. It is resolved that the officers, passengers, and crew, in number one hundred and thirty-five souls, shall endeavour to penetrate on foot, across trackless deserts, infested by wild beasts and cruel savages, to the Dutch settlements at the Cape of Good Hope. With this forlorn object before them, they finally separate into two parties – never more to meet on earth.

As I recall the dispersal and disappearance of nearly all the participants in this once famous shipwreck (a mere handful being recovered at last), and the legends that were long afterwards revived from time to time among the English officers at the Cape, of a white woman with an infant, said to have been seen weeping outside a savage hut far in the interior, who was whisperingly associated with the remembrance of the missing ladies saved from the wrecked vessel, and who was often sought but never found, thoughts of another kind of travel come into my mind.

Thoughts of a voyager unexpectedly summoned from home, who travelled a vast distance, and could never return. Thoughts of this unhappy wayfarer in the depths of his sorrow, in the bitterness of his anguish, in the helplessness of his self-reproach, in the desperation of his desire to set right what he had left wrong, and to do what he had left undone.

For there were many things he had neglected. Little matters while he was at home and surrounded by them, but things of mighty moment when he was at an immeasurable distance. There were many blessings that he had inadequately felt, there were many trivial injuries that he had not forgiven, there was love that he had but poorly returned, there was friendship that he had too lightly prized: there were a million kind words that he might have spoken, a million kind looks that he might have given, uncountable slight easy deeds in which he might have been most truly great and good. O for a day (he would exclaim), for but one day to make amends! But the sun never shone upon that happy day, and out of his remote captivity he never came.

Why does this traveller's fate obscure, on New Year's Eve, the other histories of travellers with which my mind was filled but now, and cast a solemn shadow over me? Must I one day make his journey? Even so. Who shall say, that I may not then be tortured by such late regrets: that I may not then look from my exile on my empty place and undone work? I stand upon a seashore, where the waves are years. They break and fall, and I may little heed them; but with every wave the sea is rising, and I know that it will float me on this traveller's voyage at last.

SOURCE NOTES AND
SUPPLEMENTARY INFORMATION

Most of the material in this volume (in addition to the actual remnants of Dickens's aborted autobiography, as preserved by Forster) is taken from three distinct sources – essays, speeches and letters. The essays, in the main, appeared originally in 'Household Words' and 'All the Year Round' and were subsequently collected in *The Uncommercial Traveller*, *Reprinted Pieces*, *Christmas Stories* and *Miscellaneous Papers*. Additional material is identified in *The Uncollected Writings of Charles Dickens: Household Words, 1850–59*, edited by Harry Stone and published (in two volumes) by Allen Lane, the Penguin Press, in 1969. The first collection of speeches was originally published in 1870. A second collection appeared in 1938 but the one which must surely be definitive is *The Speeches of Charles Dickens*, edited by K.J. Fielding (1960). There have been, similarly, three editions of the letters. The first, published in two volumes in 1880, with a supplementary volume in 1882, was 'edited by his sister-in-law and his eldest daughter', i.e. Georgina Hogarth and Mamie Dickens: references to it in the notes which follow are to the one-volume edition of 1893. The second (and very elusive) edition, edited by Walter Dexter, was the three-volume Nonesuch collection published in 1938. The magnificent Pilgrim edition (eight volumes to date, 1965–95) is, however, the one which supersedes all others and will itself be unsurpassed. The earlier chapters of W.T. Ley's annotated edition of *The Life of Charles Dickens* by John Forster, published by Cecil Palmer in 1928, provided invaluable guidance as did Nina Burgis's Introduction to the Clarendon edition of *David Copperfield* (1981). And there is, finally, an immeasurable debt to be paid to 'The Dickensian' (published from 1904 onwards), a veritable treasure-trove of material.

The following abbreviations have been used:

AYR	'All the Year Round'
Dkn	'The Dickensian'
Forster	*The Life of Charles Dickens* by John Forster, edited by W.T. Ley
HW	'Household Words'
LCD	*The Letters of Charles Dickens*, edited by his sister-in-law and his eldest daughter

PROLOGUE: CHATHAM REVISITED

Most of this comes from *Dullborough Town* (*AYR* 30.6.60, listed in the 'Contents' as the first part of *Associations of Childhood*, reprinted in *The Uncommercial Traveller*) with 'Chatham' substituted for 'Dullborough' and 'Simpson' for 'Timpson'. Incorporated within it, however, are substantial portions from two quite separate essays (both included in *Uncollected Writings*). The first of these, *One Man in a Dockyard* (*HW* 6.9.51), was written in partnership with R.B. Horne, but the sections written by CD himself have been identified for us by Horne (and the style, in any case, is unmistakable). Two passages from this essay are utilised (the first being the two paragraphs commencing with the sentence 'Of what use on earth is a single man?' and the second being the three paragraphs commencing with the words 'As I sauntered along the old High Street...'), these passages being linked by a description of Rochester Cathedral taken from *The Doom of English Wills* (*HW* 28.9.50) which CD wrote in association with W.H. Wills. The sentence in parenthesis, exclaiming upon the impossibility of telling where Rochester ends and Chatham begins, is taken from *The Seven Poor Travellers* (*HW* Christmas number 1854, reprinted in *Christmas Stories*).

Simpson's Blue-Eyed Maid was a well-known Kentish coach service: it is mentioned at the beginning of the third chapter of *Little Dorrit*, when Arthur Clennam travels from Dover to London; the S.E.R., which superseded it, was the South Eastern Railway. The battle of Seringapatam (1799) resulted in the death and defeat of Tipu Sultan, the rebellious Sultan of Mysore. More details concerning the house founded by Richard Watts will be found in *The Seven Poor Travellers*. It is generally accepted that 'Lucy Green' was Lucy Stroughill, a little girl whose family lived next door to the Dickens family in Ordnance Terrace, Chatham, and it has been surmised that 'Dr Joe Specks' was Dr John Dan Brown. *The Adventures of Roderick Random* (1748) by Tobias Smollett was one of the young CD's favourite books – see *My father's library* (below).

For a curious similarity between the closing words of this section and some sentiments expressed by Charles Lamb forty years earlier see *Plays and players*, below.

PART ONE: CHILDHOOD

My birth and early life

The first paragraph comes from a letter which CD wrote to Miss Angela Burdett-Coutts on 5 September 1857 (Charles C. Osborne (ed.), *Letters of Charles Dickens to the Baroness Burdett-Coutts* (1931), p. 30).*

CD wrote two brief accounts of his early childhood and manhood, the first in a letter to J.H. Kuenzel in July (?) 1838, from which the second paragraph (excluding the final sentence) is taken (*Letters*, Pilgrim edition, Volume One [1820–1839] (1965), edited by Madeline House and Graham Storey, pp. 423–4), and the second in a letter to Wilkie Collins on 6 June 1856 (*LCD*, pp. 398–9). 'I have never seen anything about myself in print', he told Collins, 'which has much correctness in it – any

---

*It may well be that the second and third sentences of *David Copperfield* constituted the original opening of CD's autobiography. Robert Langton, in *The Childhood and Youth of Charles Dickens* (1883), states that CD was indeed born at midnight on a Friday, although subsequent biographers have been less sure about this.

biographical account I mean. I do not supply such particulars when I am asked for them by editors and compilers, simply because I am asked for them every day. If you want to prime Forgues [editor of *Revue des Deux Mondes*], you may tell him without fear of anything wrong, that I was born at Portsmouth on the Seventh of February 1812; that my father was in the Navy Pay Office; that I was taken by him to Chatham when I was very young, and lived there and was educated there till I was twelve or thirteen, I suppose.' He had evidently forgotten, by 1856, that he had written a similar letter eighteen years earlier. 'This is the first time', he told Collins, 'I ever set down even these particulars, and, glancing them over, I feel like a wild beast in a caravan describing himself in the keeper's absence.' (The 'keeper' would presumably have been Forster.) The final sentence in this paragraph is taken from a letter to G.H. Adams written on 18 January 1840 (*LCD*, p. 33).

The third paragraph restores to direct speech some remarks which CD made in May 1866 to Dolby, his readings manager, during a visit to Southsea (*Charles Dickens as I Knew Him* by George Dolby (1885), p. 38) and the fourth paragraph is taken from the letter to Kuenzel.

The Dickens family were living at 387 Mile End Terrace, Landport, Portsea at the time of CD's birth in February 1812. The tenancy expiring in June they moved to 16 Hawke Street, where they lodged for eighteen months, and thence to 39 Wish Street, Southsea, where they remained throughout 1814. Early in 1815 John Dickens was recalled to London, where the family stayed for two years (seemingly at 10 Norfolk Street, St Marylebone, near the Middlesex Hospital), and in April 1817, after a brief spell at Sheerness, he was transferred to Chatham, moving his ever-expanding family into a newly-built house at 2 Ordnance Terrace. They would remain there until the spring of 1821, when they moved to 18 St Mary's Place, The Brook, Chatham. (See *Charles Dickens' Childhood* by Michael Allen (1988), pp. 16–30, 36 and 41.)

Earliest recollections

The first three paragraphs of this section are taken from the second chapter of *Copperfield*. The fourth paragraph comes from a letter (1857?) quoted in *Forster*, p. 2. Robert Langton (*op. cit.*, 1892 edn., pp. 26–9) surmised that 'Somebody' was Mary Weller, a servant girl destined, in the event, to out-live CD, but it is nowadays thought to have been Mary Allen, a widowed maternal aunt who lived with the family until her marriage to James Lamert in 1821 and died in 1822 (see *Letters*, Pilgrim edition, Volume Eight [1856–1858] (1995), edited by Graham Storey and Kathleen Tillotson, p. 452*n*). The surname 'Weller' was, at all events, one with which CD was familiar from his very youngest days and it seems probable that it was also the name of the phlegmatic greengrocer whom he re-encountered on his stroll around 'Dullborough' (see page 10). Marcus Stone, accompanying CD on a walk in 1869, called his companion's attention to a tilt-cart with the name 'Weller' on it: 'Yes,' came the response, 'and he is more or less the immortal man; he is a fruiterer who keeps a shop in Chatham market' (*Dkn*, vol. 6 (1910), p. 63).

The first part of the fifth paragraph (down to 'used to do,') comes from the fourth chapter of *Copperfield* and the remainder from *A Christmas Tree* (*HW* 21.12.50, reprinted in *Christmas Stories*). CD's recollection of waving to the Prince Regent is also taken from some remarks he made to Marcus Stone (*Dkn*, vol. 6 (1910), p. 63 and Michael Slater (ed.), *Catalogue of the Suzannet Charles Dickens Collection* (1975), p. 157): the event probably took place on 2 November 1821 (see Allen, *op. cit.*, p. 128). The rest of this section (with the exception of the final sentence, taken from the fourth chapter of *Copperfield*) comes from *New Year's Day* (*HW* 1.1.59, reprinted in *Miscellaneous Papers*).

'A was an archer, and shot at a frog' will be found in *The Hobby-Horse, or the High Road to Learning* published in 1820 by J. Harris & Son (reproduced by Iona and Peter Opie in *A Nursery Companion* (1980), together with, among other delights, *The History of an Apple Pie*, also published by J. Harris & Son in 1820).

Toys

The whole of this section is taken from *A Christmas Tree*. 'Barmecide justice' is a reference to a tale in *The Arabian Nights* in which a number of empty dishes are spread before a beggar and he is assured that they constitute a sumptuous feast. *The Miller and His Men*, written by Isaac Pocock (1782–1835) in 1813, was a melodrama of which CD long remained fond: see Percy Fitzgerald's article in *Dkn*, vol. 4 (1908), pp. 313–15. *Elizabeth, or the Exiles of Siberia* (1806) was a story by the French novelist 'Sophie' Cottin (1770–1807), translated into English in 1809 and evidently adapted for the stage.

Books

The first sentence comes from *The Child's Story* (*HW* Christmas number 1852, reprinted in *Christmas Stories*), the second from *A Christmas Tree*. The section that follows (down to '... taken to Great Camomile Street.') comes from *First Fruits* (*HW* 15.5.52, included in *Uncollected Writings*) which CD wrote in collaboration with G.A. Sala. *The Dandies' Ball; or, High Life in the City*, containing the verses recalled by CD, was published by John Marshall in 1819.

The reference to the old spelling book is taken from *Some Particulars Concerning a Lion*, an essay (subsequently appended to *Sketches by Boz*) which was originally published in May 1837 in 'Bentley's Miscellany'. Professor Kathleen Tillotson has identified the publication in question (also referred to, obliquely, in the twenty-second chapter of *Copperfield*, when Steerforth compares himself to 'the bad boy who "didn't care", and became food for lions') as Daniel Fenning's *Universal Spelling Book*, first published in 1756 (*Steerforth's Old Nursery Tale*, *Dkn*, vol, 79 (1983), pp. 31–4).

The next section of this paragraph (down to '... became somewhat mitigated.') is from a speech which CD delivered to the Printers' Pension

Society on 6 April 1864 (*Speeches*, pp. 323–4). Almost thirty years before, in *Astley's* (*Evening Chronicle* 9.5.35, reprinted in *Sketches by Boz*) he had written: 'We never see any very large, staring, black Roman capitals, in a book, or shop-window, or placarded on a wall, without their immediately recalling to our mind an indistinct and confused recollection of the time when we were first initiated in the mysteries of the alphabet. We almost fancy we see the pin's point following the letter, to impress its form more strongly on our bewildered imagination; and wince involuntarily, as we remember the hard knuckles with which the reverend old lady who instilled into our mind the first principles of education for ninepence a week, or ten and sixpence per quarter, was wont to poke our juvenile heads occasionally, by way of adjusting the confusion of ideas in which we were generally involved.' The old lady was presumably the Mrs Pipchin prototype whose establishment CD attended circa 1820 (see Introduction, page xvii). In his speech to the printers CD again reflected (see *Earliest recollections*, above) on the pleasing quality of letters. 'I now feel gratified', he declared, 'at looking at the jolly letter O, the crooked S, with its full benevolent turns, and the Q with its comical tail, that first awoke in me a sense of the humorous.' The second half of this paragraph comes from *A Christmas Tree*.

The short paragraph about giants comes from *Where We Stopped Growing* (*HW* 1.1.53, included in *Reprinted Pieces*) and the long paragraph on the same subject from *American Notes* (Chapter XII) (1842). The paragraph on Little Red Riding hood is taken from *A Christmas Tree*, the paragraph on fairy stories from *Frauds on the Fairies* (*HW* 1.10.53, reprinted in *Miscellaneous Papers*) and the Robinson Crusoe paragraph from *Where We Stopped Growing*. In later years, however, CD had strong reservations about Defoe's masterpiece. 'You remember my saying to you some time ago', he wrote to Forster in 1856, 'how curious I thought it that *Robinson Crusoe* should be the only instance of a universally popular book that could make no one laugh and could make no one cry. I have been reading it again just now, in the course of my numerous refreshings at these English wells, and I will venture to say that there is not in literature a more surprising instance of an utter want of tenderness and sentiment, than the death of Friday. It is as heartless as *Gil Blas*, in a very different and far more serious way. But the second part ... is perfectly contemptible, in the glaring defect that it exhibits a man who was thirty years on that desert island with no visible effect made on his character by that experience' (*Forster*, p. 611n).

Most of what follows, concerned primarily with *The Arabian Nights* (CD's favourite childhood reading), is taken from *A Christmas Tree*. A short passage at the end of the first paragraph (from 'all about scimitars' to 'all new and all true.') comes from *The Child's Story*. The extract from *A Christmas Tree* ends with the words 'we all three breathe again' and the passages which follow are taken from *The Haunted Man* (1848). The final sentence comes from *Lying Awake* (*HW* 30.10.52, included in *Reprinted Pieces*).

Valentine, glancingly referred to here, was the noble lord of medieval French literature responsible for the capture and taming of his unfortunate brother Orson (brought up by wild animals, like the future Lord

Greystoke) from whom he had been separated since infancy. (In the fifteenth chapter of *Barnaby Rudge* John Chester, languid and suave, describes his recent encounter with the bluntly-spoken Geoffrey Haredale as 'quite a Valentine and Orson business'.)

The Yellow Dwarf was the creation, in 1698, of the Comtesse d'Aulnoy (c.1650–1705), a famous French writer of fairy stories: see Iona and Peter Opie, *The Classic Fairy Stories* (1974), p. 25 and pp. 66–80. Many of Mme d'Aulnoy's stories were published in an English translation by Francis Newberry in 1773 under the title *Mother Bunch's Fairy Tales, published for the amusement of ... Little Masters and Misses* (a rival, in effect, to the *Mother Goose* collection) with reprints of which CD was doubtless familiar. He refers, in *The Haunted House* (*AYR* Christmas number 1859, reprinted in *Christmas Stories*), to 'an illustrious lady who brightened my own childhood ... the brilliant Mother Bunch'. A pantomime, *Mother Bunch and the Yellow Dwarf*, was staged at Astley's in 1807 and would presumably have been performed in the provinces in later years. (The original Mother Bunch, referred to in works by Nash and Dekker, was a sixteenth-century ale-house wife; in the seventeenth century her name was attached to various compilations and *Mother Bunch's Closet Newly Broke Open*, a compendium of dubious tips and remedies, enjoyed a certain popularity.)

We are on familiar ground, after perusing this section, when we encounter Tom Pinch, in the fifth chapter of *Martin Chuzzlewit*, gazing into the window of a shop 'where children's books were sold, and where poor Robinson Crusoe stood alone in his might, with dog and hatchet, goat-skin cap and fowling-pieces; calmly surveying Philip Quarll and the host of imitators round him, and calling Mr Pinch to witness that he, of all the crowd, impressed one solitary foot-print on the shore of boyish memory, whereof the tread of generations should not stir the lightest grain of sand. And there too were the Persian tales, with flying chests and students of enchanted books shut up for years in caverns: and there too was Abdullah, the merchant, with the terrible little old woman hobbling out of the box in his bedroom: and there the mighty talisman, the rare *Arabian Nights*, with Cassim Baba, divided by four, like the ghost of a dreadful sum, hanging up, all gory, in the robbers' cave.'

Mr Barlow

Taken from *Mr Barlow* (*AYR* 16.1.69, reprinted in *The Uncommercial Traveller*). Mr Barlow did indeed loom large in the three-volume *History of Sandford and Merton* (1783–89) by Thomas Day (1748–89). Day's original sub-title, *Intended for the Use of Children*, was considered somewhat too modest by subsequent editors and by CD's time it had become *Moral and Instructive Entertainment for Young People* – obligatory reading, in short, for the nation's future citizens.

Mr Merton, having made his fortune in Jamaica, where he was the 'master of many servants, who cultivated sugar and other valuable things for his advantage', returns to England and seeks a tutor for his shockingly spoilt and snobbish six-year-old son, bad Master Tommy. A short distance away lives 'a plain honest farmer', Mr Sandford, whose son – the same age as Tommy – is good Master Harry. Harry is a pupil of the local vicar, Mr Barlow, and so impressed is Mr Merton by Harry's erudition that he arranges for Mr Barlow to undertake the education of both boys on a regular basis. Mr Barlow reluctantly accepts the task and the reader observes how, under his firm tuition, and with the example of Harry always before him, Tommy gradually mends his ways and develops into a potentially useful member of the local community. In the second volume he suffers, admittedly, something of a relapse, for the genteel guests at his father's house-party, to which he has invited Harry, include the obnoxious Master Mash, who 'had acquired the idea that to bet successfully was the summit of all human ambition'. Under Master Mash's evil influence, and with Mr Barlow absent from the scene, Tommy reverts to his former bad ways, much to Harry's distress. Only when Harry has rescued Tommy from a mad bull (goaded beyond endurance by a pack of dogs, encouraged by Master Mash), and Mr Barlow has reappeared, does Tommy truly repent of his sins. 'To your example', he tells Harry at the end of the book, 'I owe most of the little good that I can boast: you have taught me how much better it is to be useful than rich or fine: how much more amiable to be good than to be great.' Geography, natural history, mathematics, science and even rudimentary economics are woven into the narrative, as well as a host of classical stories.

In fairness to Mr Barlow, it should be stressed that he is not quite the killjoy that CD would have us believe, although his somewhat ponderous sense of humour is effectively concealed beneath great layers of earnestness. 'Every body that eats,' says Mr Barlow, 'ought to assist in procuring food', but since Tommy is not prepared to soil his hands by working in his tutor's garden – unlike Harry and Mr Barlow himself – he is denied a share in the dish of cherries that the other two subsequently devour. (But next day, of his own accord, he takes a hoe and gets busy.) 'The contemplation of a starry night' paves the way for some useful reflections, occasioned primarily by the fact that the two boys are found by Mr Barlow after having been lost in a wood for several hours. As they walk home Tommy remarks upon the 'innumerable number' of stars in the sky. Mr Barlow smilingly encourages Harry, as 'a little farmer', to pick out Charlie's Wain and then draws Tommy's attention to the Pole Star, always in the north, as a means of finding his bearings in the future.

The really important thing about Mr Barlow is his Radicalism, which must surely have played a part in fashioning CD's own, for we are left in no doubt that, in Mr Barlow's opinion, the rich (by and large) are idle parasites while the poor (by and large) are virtuous and industrious – nor, for that matter, that slavery and blood sports are wrong. Norman Collins, describing *Sandford and Merton* as 'the infants' Bible', declares that Day, 'in the ingratiating form of the parable, preached the exact spirit, if not the text, of Mr Lloyd George's Limehouse speech' (*The Facts of Fiction* (1932), p. 127). 'How hard,' exclaims Mr Barlow, 'is the lot of the poor, when they are afflicted with sickness! How intolerable do we find the least bodily disorder, even though we possess every convenience which can mitigate its violence! Not all the dainties which can be collected from all the elements, the warmth of downy beds and silken couches, the attendance of obsequious dependants, are capable of making us bear with common patience the commonest disease. How pitiable then must be the state of a fellow creature, who is at once tortured by bodily suffering and destitute of every circumstance which can alleviate it! who sees around him a family that are not only incapable of assisting their parent, but destined to want the common necessaries of life, the moment he intermits his daily labours! How indispensable then is the obligation, which should continually impel the rich to exert themselves in assisting their fellow creatures, and rendering that condition of life which we all avoid, less dreadful to those who must support it always!' The creator of Jo the crossing-sweeper must surely have owed something to Mr Barlow. CD did, in effect, acknowledge his indebtedness to *Sandford and Merton* in a letter to R.H. Horne dated 13 July 1848. 'I should say', he remarked, '[that] that story had had great influence on many boys' (and subsequently men's) minds' (*Letters*, Pilgrim edition, Volume Five [1847–1849] (1981), edited by Graham Storey and K.J. Fielding, pp. 372–3).

Frightening encounters

The first and second paragraphs are taken from *A Christmas Tree*, the third from *Lying Awake*. *The Adventures of Philip Quarll*, supposedly written by Edward Dorrington, but usually attributed to Peter Longueville, were published in 'The Hermit' in 1727 and reprinted in simplified form many times thereafter. They were, in effect, another version of the *Robinson Crusoe* story (see the Philip Quarll reference in the extract from *Martin Chuzzlewit* quoted in *Books*, above).

Plays and players

The first and second paragraphs are taken from *First Fruits*, the third from *A Christmas Tree* and the fourth from *Dullborough Town*.

Sir Michael Costa (1804–84) was a celebrated conductor; Camillo Sivori (1815–94) an Italian violinist and composer; Joseph Richardson (1814–62) a well-known flautist and Giovanni Bottesini (1821–89) an Italian double-bass player, conductor and composer who had made a sensational London début in 1849.

La Chien de Montargis (1814) by Guilbert de Pixerecourt (1773–1844) was a popular French melodrama, translated into English without delay by William Barrymore, which told how Aubrey de Mondidies was murdered by Richard de Macaure in 1371 near the castle of Montargis. The victim's faithful dog, Dragon, witnessed the crime and his subsequent ferocious attack on Macaure at the French court resulted in the murderer confessing all. Jane Shore (c.1445–1527), the mistress of Edward IV, imprisoned by Richard III on a charge of witchcraft, was the subject of two tragedies: one (1563) by Thomas Churchyard and another (1714) by Nicholas Rowe.

The History of George Barnwell, or The London Merchant (1731) was a famous melodrama by George Lillo (1693–1734). It told how a guileless young apprentice was seduced by the scheming Millwood and inveigled by her into robbing his employer and murdering his uncle. Barnwell and his mistress were both hanged, Barnwell being full of remorse but Millwood unrepentant. Sam Weller, in Chapter X of *Pickwick Papers*, remarks that it had always been his opinion 'that the young 'ooman deserved scragging a precious sight more than he did'. Sim Tappertit, the potential leader of an army of rebellious apprentices, is reportedly of the opinion (in the fourth chapter of *Barnaby Rudge*) 'that in former times a stigma had been cast upon by the body by the execution of George Barnwell, to which they should not have basely submitted'. In Chapter IX of *Martin Chuzzlewit* we are introduced to a young gentleman once known by the nickname of Uncle 'that, by an easy transition, had again passed into Barnwell, in memory of the celebrated relative in that degree who was shot by his nephew George, while meditating in his garden at Camberwell'. A confused Pip, having had the story of George Barnwell imparted to him by Mr Wopsle, is 'at first disposed to believe' – at the beginning of the sixteenth chapter of *Great Expectations* – 'that *I* must have had some hand in the attack upon my sister'.*

There is an intriguing parallel between CD's recollections and those of Charles Lamb, as set out in *My First Play* (written in 1821). The following brief extracts from the latter are certainly not without interest:

> The afternoon had been wet, and the condition of our going (the elder folks and myself) was, that the rain should cease... I seem to remember the last spurt, and the glee with which I ran to announce it... But when we got in, and I beheld the green curtain that veiled a heaven to my imagination, which was soon to be disclosed – the breathless anticipation I endured! ... The orchestra lights at length arose, those 'fair Auroras'! Once the bell sounded... It rang the second time. The curtain drew up – I was not past six years old – and the play was *Artaxerxes*! ... It was all enchantment and a dream... The transformation of the magistrates into reverend beldams seemed to me a piece of grave historic justice, and the tailor carrying his own head seemed to be as sober a verity as the legend of St Denys.

But when he revisited that theatre six years later, Lamb tells us (in a passage strangely suggestive of *Dullborough Town*), the magic had disappeared:

> I had left the temple a devotee, and was returned a rationalist. The same things were there materially; but the emblem, the reference, was gone! The green curtain was no longer a veil, drawn between two worlds ... but a certain quantity of green baize... The lights – the orchestra lights – came up a clumsy machinery. The first ring, and the second ring, was now but a trick of the prompter's bell... The actors were men and women painted. I thought the fault was in them; but it was in myself, and the alterations which those many centuries – of six short twelve months – had wrought in me.

---

* But insofar as the weapon used to strike down Mrs Joe is the leg-iron from which Pip had freed Magwitch, ten years before, there was some degree of justification for this apprehension. Old Orlick is perhaps Pip Pirrip writ dark.

Many of Lamb's essays – *New Year's Eve, Witches, and Other Night Fears, The Praise of Chimney-Sweepers, Poor Relations* and *The Superannuated Man*, to name but a few – could almost have passed muster as the work of the illustrious editor had they featured in 'Household Words' or 'All the Year Round'. Percy Fitzgerald, one of CD's protégés, published a study of Lamb in 1866 and drew a comparison, in its closing pages, between the essays of Elia and the musings of *The Uncommercial Traveller*. They had, he daringly concluded, many points in common but he hastened to add that CD was unrivalled when it came to recreating the magic of childhood. There was an ominous silence from Gad's Hill and he feared that his comparison might have caused annoyance in high places. Some tentative enquiries produced, however, the following reassuring response on 2 February 1866:

> I ought to have written to you days and days ago, to thank you for your charming book on Charles Lamb, to tell you with what interest and pleasure I read it ... and to add that I was honestly affected (far more so than your modesty will readily believe) by your intimate knowledge of those touches of mine concerning childhood... It has become a matter of real feeling with me, and I postponed its expression because I couldn't satisfactorily get it out of myself, and at last I came to the conclusion that it must be left in (*LCD*, pp. 597–8).

Pantomimes and clowns

The first paragraph is taken from *A Christmas Tree* and the four that follow from CD's Introduction to *Memoirs of Joseph Grimaldi* (1838). Then come two paragraphs from *Mr Barlow*, a short paragraph concerning CD's own faint recollections of Grimaldi adapted from a letter which he drafted in 1838 (see *Forster*, pp. 104–5) and a final paragraph from *A Curious Dance Round a Curious Tree* (*HW* 17.1.52, included in *Uncollected Writings*) which CD wrote in collaboration with W.H. Wills.

The Harlequin's Wand

Taken from *New Year's Day*. The Soho Bazar, established in 1816, was a venue through which the widows and dependants of British soldiers could sell their home-made goods to the public. For 'the lions', see *Books* above. On this occasion 'Mrs Pipchin' was probably CD's paternal grandmother, who died in 1824, as distinct from the 'Mrs Pipchin' whose school he attended at the age of eight (see Introduction, page xvii).

My nurses's stories

The first paragraph comes from *Travelling Abroad* (*AYR* 7.4.60) and the second from *Chatham Dockyard* (*AYR* 29.8.63), both of which feature in

The Uncommercial Traveller. So too does *Nurse's Stories* (*AYR* 6.9.60, listed in the 'Contents' as the second part of *Associations of Childhood*) from which the subsequent five paragraphs are taken – although the description of the story-teller as 'a sallow woman with a fishy eye' is from *The Holly Tree* (*HW* Christmas number 1855, reprinted in *Christmas Stories*), as is the penultimate paragraph. The final paragraph is from *Nurse's Stories*. *The Bleeding Nun, or Raymond and Agnes* was a Gothic novel (author unknown) published in 1820.

Birthdays

Taken from *Birthday Celebrations* (*AYR* 6.6.63, reprinted in *The Uncommercial Traveller*). An Orrery was a clockwork model of the planetary system, the very first one being invented for Charles Boyle, the 4th Earl of Orrery, c.1700 by George Graham and manufactured by J. Rowley.

My preparatory school

Taken from *Our School* (*HW* 11.10.51, included in *Reprinted Pieces*). CD here claims to have no recollection of the 'mistress of the Establishment', but unless he went to *two* such establishments it was surely the Mrs Pipchin prototype referred to in *Books* (above) and in his letter to Forster of 4 November 1846 (see Introduction, page xvii). According to Forster, it was located in Rome Lane, Chatham.

Pulpit passions

The first paragraph is taken from the third chapter of *American Notes* (1842) and the second from a letter to Frank Stone written on 13 December 1858 (*LCD*, pp. 472–3). The three remaining paragraphs come from *City of London Churches* (*AYR* 5.5.60, reprinted in *The Uncommercial Traveller*).

Other recollections

The first paragraph is taken (again) from the fourth chapter of *Copperfield* and the second comes from the seventeenth chapter of *American Notes*.

The third paragraph comes from a variety of sources. The first sentence is adapted from CD's letter to Kuenzel (see *My birth and early life*, above), the epithet 'a little pale' being taken from a letter written by CD to John Scott on 22 March 1841 (*Letters*, Pilgrim edition, Volume Two [1840–1841] (1969), edited by Madeline House and Graham Storey, p. 241). The second and third sentences come from *Forster*, p. 9. The schoolmaster in question was the Rev. William Giles (1798–1856), who took a close interest in CD's development and made contact with him on several occasions in later years. 'When I read your handwriting,' CD wrote to him on 31 October 1848, 'I half believe I am a very small boy again; and you magnify, in my bewildered spirit, into something awful, though not at all severe. I call to mind how you gave me Goldsmith's *Bee* when I left Chatham (that was my first knowledge of it) and can't believe that I have been fledging any little Bees myself, whose buzzing has been heard abroad' (*Letters*, Pilgrim edition, Volume Five, p. 432). The second half of the third paragraph is taken from the seventh chapter of *Great Expectations*. For confirmation that it was indeed a genuine childhood recollection see *The Parents of Charles Dickens* by Mrs E. Davey, 'Lippincott's Magazine', vol. XIII (June 1874), pp. 772–4 (largely reprinted by Philip Collins (ed.) in *Dickens: Interviews and Recollections* (1981), pp. 130–1).

The fourth paragraph is taken from *The Holly Tree*. The narrator ('Charley') informs us that 'The Mitre' inn was situated 'in the cathedral town where I went to school'. Its location was actually Chatham High Street. The landlord was John Tribe and the Tribe family were close friends of the Dickens family. CD and his sister Fanny were often, it seems, the star performers of comic songs at 'The Mitre', being hoisted on to the dining-room table for this purpose, although CD feared, looking back, that he must have been a 'horrible little nuisance ... to many unoffending grown-up people' called upon to admire him (see *Forster*, pp. 6 and 19).

The fifth paragraph comes from *First Fruits* and the sixth from *Smuggled Relations* (*HW* 23.6.55, included in *Miscellaneous Papers*). The remaining paragraphs are taken from *Medicine Men of Civilisation* (*AYR* 26.9.63, reprinted in *The Uncommercial Traveller*).

The scenes of my childhood

The first paragraph is taken from *A Little Talk about Spring, and the Sweeps* (published in the 'Library of Fiction' in June 1836 and reprinted in *Sketches by Boz* as *The First of May*).

Three references to Rochester are combined in the opening sentence of the second paragraph: the first from a letter to Percy Fitzgerald dated 6 November 1866, the second from a letter to H.G. Adams dated 6 October 1861 (*LCD*, pp. 608 and 527) and the third from *The Great Winglebury Duel* (written in 1836 and first published in *Sketches by Boz*). The second sentence is taken from a letter to W.B. Rye dated 3 November 1865 (*LCD*, p. 589). The remainder of this paragraph comes from *Seven Poor Travellers*.

The third paragraph is adapted from the opening section of the fifth chapter of *Pickwick*. The fourth paragraph is very much a concocted one, being woven from material taken from eight separate sources. The four main sources are a famous passage from *Travelling Abroad* and letters which CD wrote to Miss Burdett-Coutts on 9 February 1856 (Osborne, *op. cit.*, pp. 162–3) and to M. de Cerjat on 17 January 1857 and 7 July 1858 (*LCD*, pp. 420 and 450–1). Supplementary phrases are taken from letters to W.H. Wills (9 February 1855), Edmund Yates (29 March 1859), the Earl of Carlisle (8 August 1860) and Percy Fitzgerald (4 July 1863) (*Ibid.*, pp.

356, 479, 500 and 562). 'I think I told you', wrote CD to another correspondent on 15 December 1858, 'that I live, in the summer, on the top of the veritable Gad's Hill where Falstaff committed that little indiscretion. Our highwaymen in that country have degenerated into tramps, and our Carriers are Pickford & Co. But Rochester is still a queer old place with a savage old castle in it' (*Letters*, Pilgrim edition, Volume Eight, p. 721).

The final paragraph comes from *Chatham Dockyard*.

Satisfaction is demanded

Taken from *New Year's Day*. Bamfylde Moore Carew (1693–c.1770), the disreputable son of a Devon rector, was a famous 'King of the Gipsies'; Mother Shipton, custodian of the limestone Dropping Well at Knaresborough, was a sixteenth-century prophetess who foretold, amongst other things, the invention of the motor car.

My father's library

The first paragraph is taken from the fourth chapter of *Copperfield*, with an inserted reference to *Cooke's Pocket Library* (identified on page 3 of the elaborate Victoria and Albert Museum catalogue *Charles Dickens: An exhibition to commemorate the centenary of his death, June–September 1970* (1970)). (There is a curious parallel between the well-known *Copperfield* paragraphs and Coleridge's recollections, penned half a century earlier: 'My father's sister kept an *everything* shop at Crediton – and there I read through all the ... tales of Tom Hickathrift, Jack the Giant-killer, etc... I was accustomed to race up and down the churchyard, and act over all I had been reading... At six years old I remember to have read *Belisarius, Robinson Crusoe* and *Philip Quarles*; and then I found *The Arabian Nights' Entertainments* ... [which made a] deep impression on me' (*Letters of Samuel Taylor Coleridge* (1895), vol. I, pp. 11–12).

The second paragraph is taken from *Where We Stopped Growing*. A passage in similar vein forms part of the prologue to *Nurse's Stories*. It will be appreciated that the works of Tobias Smollett (1721–71) loom very large in this list, for Smollett was the author of *The Adventures of Roderick Random* (1748), *The Adventures of Peregrine Pickle* (1751) and *The Expedition of Humphrey Clinker* (1771). 'Humphrey Clinker', CD told Frank Stone on 2 November 1854, 'is certainly Smollett's best. I am rather divided between *Peregrine Pickle* and *Roderick Random* – both extraordinarily good in their way, which is a way without tenderness – but you will have to read them both, and I send the first Volume of *Peregrine* as the richer of the two' (*Letters*, Pilgrim edition, Volume Seven [1853–1855], edited by Graham Storey, Kathleen Tillotson and Angus Easson, p. 458). *Gil Blas* (1715–35) was written by the French author Alaine René Lesage (1665–1747). *Tales of the Genii; or, The Delightful Lessons of Hasam, the Son of Asmar* (1764), drawing much of its inspiration from *The Arabian Nights*, was written by James Ridley (1736–65).

Some literature of a lighter kind was also devoured by the young CD, for in the spring of 1856 he was delighted to find a seaside bookshop which included some of his earliest childhood favourites, not seen for many a year, among its remnants. 'Here,' he writes, 'Dr Faustus was still going down to very red and yellow perdition... Here, were *Little Warblers* and Fairburn's *Comic Songsters*. Here, too, were ballads on the old ballad paper and in the old confusion of types... All these as of yore, when they were infinite delights to me!' (*Out of the Season*, HW 28.6.56, included in *Reprinted Pieces*.)

The third and fourth paragraphs both come from the fourth chapter of *Copperfield*. The fifth paragraph is, basically, a 'merger' of relevant extracts from the letters which CD wrote to Kuenzel and Collins (see *My birth and early life*, above). The Kuenzel extract runs: '... that I was a great reader as a child, being well versed in most of our English Novelists before I was ['twelve' deleted] ten years old – that I wrote tragedies and got other children to act them.' (One of these 'tragedies', *Misnar, the Sultan of India*, was adapted from a Ridley story.) The Collins extract runs: '... that I had been a writer when I was a mere baby, and always an actor from the same age.' Also to be taken into account is an extract from a letter he wrote to Mary Howitt on 7 September 1859: 'Do you care to know that I was a great writer at eight years old or so – was an actor and a speaker from a baby – and worked many young struggles into *Copperfield*?' (*Letters*, Nonesuch edition, vol. III, 1858–1870, p. 122.)

CD's fondness for *Tom Jones* proved short-lived. 'Unlike Thackeray', so George Russell subsequently recalled, 'Dickens was not a great admirer of Fielding. 'Tom Jones is always in tears, and rates my contempt,' he said, 'and excepting Blifil, there is not an original character in the book' (Philip Collins, *George Russell's Recollections of Dickens*, Dkn, vol. 78 (1982), p. 154).

My departure for London

Taken from *Dullborough Town*. The opening paragraphs of the twentieth chapter of *Great Expectations* should be borne in mind:

> The journey from our home to the metropolis was a journey of about five hours. It was a little past mid-day when the four-horse stage-coach by which I was a passenger, got into the ravel of traffic frayed out about the Cross Keys, Cheapside, London.
>
> We Britons had at that time particularly settled that it was treasonable to doubt our having and our being the best of everything; otherwise, while I was scared by the immensity of London, I think I might have had some faint doubts whether it was not rather ugly, narrow and dirty.

The Dickens family apparently left Chatham in the spring of 1822, John Dickens taking up an Admiralty appointment at Somerset House in the June of that year, but CD remained in Chatham for a little while longer and boarded with Mr Giles. The schoolmaster's sister, Mrs Godfrey, interviewed by Robert Langton in 1882 in her eighty-ninth year, believed that

'Charles was (almost at the last moment) left with her brother' (Langton, *op.cit.* (1891 edition), p. 63). This is confirmed, in effect, by CD himself, for he makes it clear in the *Dullborough Town* paragraph that he travelled alone to London while telling us earlier, in *Other recollections*, that 'on the night before we came away' Mr Giles 'came flitting in among the packing cases to give me ... a keepsake'. CD is unlikely to have used the 'royal we' on this occasion nor is a small boy likely to have been burdened with many packing cases. It must surely have been on the night when he came 'flitting in', therefore, that Mr Giles persuaded CD's parents to let his favourite pupil stay on in Chatham until the term came to an end. Mrs Godfrey, almost twenty years older than CD, remembered him as 'a very handsome boy, with long curly hair of a light colour ... [and an] amiable, agreeable disposition'.

Some writers have suggested that CD rejoined his family in December 1822, in time for Christmas. 'And I *do* come home at Christmas,' he exclaims in *A Christmas Tree*. 'We all do, or we all should.' Fanny Scrooge hastens to the school to fetch her brother home, so that they can 'be together all the Christmas long, and have the merriest time in the world', but CD's account of his departure from Chatham is anything but merry. Michael Allen suggests that he was summoned to London in September 1822 to attend the funeral of Mary Lamert, his Aunt Fanny (Allen, *op. cit.*, p. 68), but according to Michael and Mollie Harwick 'he travelled up to rejoin his family early in 1823, recalled dismally enough to attend the funeral of his baby sister' (*As They Saw Him ... Charles Dickens* (1970), p. 17). The doleful manner in which Master B's happiness is shattered in *The Haunted House* is, perhaps, an echo of this experience – 'I was taken home, and there was Debt at home as well as death' – for 'Master B', CD later admitted, was simply 'Master Boz'.

PART TWO: BOYHOOD

I go astray

This is basically the complete text of *Gone Astray* (*HW* 13.8.53, included in *Miscellaneous Papers*). The reference to Bayham Street has been editorially inserted, however, and CD's recollection of tending a sick uncle has been adapted from a letter which he wrote to that uncle, Thomas Barrow, on 31 March 1836 (*Letters*, Pilgrim edition, Volume One, p. 144). Forster tells us that Barrow had 'broken his leg in a fall; and, while laid up with this illness, his lodging was in Gerrard Street, Soho, in the upper part [of a bookseller's house]... Attracted by the look of the lad as he went upstairs, these good people lent him books to amuse him; among them, Miss Porter's *Scottish Chiefs*, Holbein's *Dance of Death*, and Colman's *Broad Grins*. The latter seized his fancy ... and he was so impressed by its description of Covent Garden ... that he stole down to the market by himself to compare it with the book. He [snuffed] up the flavour of the faded cabbage leaves as if it were the very breath of comic fiction' (*Forster*, p. 12).

George Hudson (1800–71) was a ruthless tycoon, chairman at one time of five railway companies and popularly known as 'the Railway King', whose dubious business methods eventually resulted in his horrendous downfall in 1849. Sir James Hogg (1790–1876) was a director of the East India Company.

Our neighbourhood

Taken from *An Unsettled Neighbourhood* (*HW* 11.11.54, included in *Miscellaneous Papers*), the opening eight words being editorially inserted. The reference to Stabber's Band explains some remarks which appear in a letter of 3 November 1852: 'I know a bassoon by sight pretty well, and have some reason to, having had part of my childhood haunted by musical instruments of every description' (*Letters*, Nonesuch edition, vol. II, p. 426).

The Dickens family moved into 16 Bayham Street, Camden Town in June 1822 and CD joined them there a little later. (See *Dickens in Bayham Street* by Willoughby Matchett, *Dkn*, vol. 5 (1909), pp. 147–52 and 180–84, *Mr Micawber and the Redefinition of Experience* by William Oddie, *Dkn*, vol. 63 (1967), pp. 100–10 and Allen, *op. cit.*, pp. 71–2.)

Chimney sweeps

Taken from *A Little Talk about Spring, and the Sweeps.*

The Field of the Forty Footsteps

Taken from a speech delivered on 12 April 1864 to mark the foundation of University College Hospital (*Speeches*, pp. 326–7). (See *Dkn*, vol. 9 (1913), pp.210–11 and 274–6.) CD revisited the Spanish Main in *Holiday Romance* (1868). 'I am ... particularly glad you like the pirate,' he told Percy Fitzgerald. 'I remember very well when I had a general idea of occupying that place in history at the same age. But I loved more desperately than Boldheart' (*LCD*, vol. II (1880), p. 294; omitted from 1893 edition).

Unforgettable scenes and unshakeable convictions

Most of this is taken from *Where We Stopped Growing* (hereinafter referred to as *WWSG*) with supplementation from two other sources.

The first sentence of the first paragraph comes from *WWSG* but the rest of it is taken from *Red Tape* (*HW* 15.2.51, included in *Miscellaneous Papers*). The second paragraph comes from *WWSG* but the third and most of the fourth are taken from *The Old Bailey* (*Morning Chronicle* 23.10.35, reprinted as *Criminal Courts* in *Sketches by Boz*). The final twenty-five words of the fourth paragraph (from 'and have never outgrown its rugged walls' onwards) come from *WWSG* as do the four remaining paragraphs.

'Colman's *Broad Grins*' is a reference to a collection of comic poems written by George Colman the younger (1762–1836) first published in 1802. (See *I go astray*, above.) The White Woman must surely have provided the creator of Miss Havisham with his initial inspiration, although other 'originals' have been claimed for that good lady.

My education is neglected

The first and third paragraphs, which are obviously biographical in character, are both taken from *Great Expectations* (Chapters VIII and XIX respectively). The second is taken from *Forster*, p. 10 (an extract, presumably, from CD's autobiography) and so too is the fourth, although the statement was made 'very bitterly' by CD in conversation rather than writing. (But why, one wonders, had he longed to be 'sent back to any other school'? Was there some specific reason why he could not resume his studies with Mr Giles?)

The first half of the fifth paragraph (down to 'ESTABLISHMENT.') merges the account given in *Forster*, p. 13 with the corresponding account in *Copperfield* of Mrs Micawber's forlorn attempt to set up a school. The second half comes from CD's autobiography (*Forster*, p. 13).

I am employed at a blacking warehouse

Taken from CD's autobiography (*Forster*, pp. 24–6) but with the sequence of the two opening paragraphs reversed. The warehouse sojourn commenced on 9 February 1824.

My father's imprisonment

The first and second paragraphs have, in effect, been 'clawed back' from *Copperfield* (Chapter XI). The third and fourth paragraphs are taken from *Forster*, pp. 13–14 and the fifth from *Copperfield* ('Captain Hopkins' being de-fictionalised into Captain Porter). The two paragraphs which follow are taken, again, from *Copperfield*, with 'City Road' being changed to 'Hampstead Road', but we have Forster's assurance that they originally featured in the autobiography. The opening sentence of the eighth paragraph comes from *Copperfield* but the rest of this paragraph is adapted from *The Haunted Man* – for Forster has confirmed that this too is a fragment of autobiography (*Forster*, p. 674). The first two sentences of the final paragraph 'merge' a passage from *Copperfield* with passages in *Forster* (pp. 15 and 26): the rest come from CD's autobiography (*Forster*, pp. 26–7). John Dickens's imprisonment commenced on 20 February 1824.

My solitary life

The first eleven paragraphs (down to 'a bow of acknowledgment as I went out.') are taken from CD's autobiography (*Forster*, pp. 27–31) with the exception of the first sentence of the first paragraph, which has been editorially inserted. ('Results', in the penultimate sentence of the seventh paragraph, has been changed to 'remnants'.) Then follow two paragraphs 'clawed back' from *Copperfield*. The next three paragraphs both come from CD's autobiography (*Forster*, pp. 32–3) – with the exception of the first two sentences of the second paragraph, which have been editorially inserted.

The two final paragraphs, written in 1857, are taken from CD's Preface to *Little Dorrit*. 'There is a room there', CD excitedly informed Forster on 7 May 1857, the day after his visit, ' – still standing, to my amazement – that I think of taking! It is the room through which the ever-memorable signers of Captain Porter's petition filed off in my boyhood' (*Forster*, p. 626).

It will be noted from the first paragraph that a *third* Mrs Pipchin original, namely the 'reduced old lady' (whose name was Mrs Roylance), has appeared on the scene.

The Dickens family had moved to 4 Gower Street North in December 1823. Mrs Dickens and her children remained there until the spring of 1824 and she then joined her husband in the Marshalsea, accompanied by her three youngest children. CD stayed in Little College Street for about a month and then moved into lodgings in Lant Street.

My father is released – and so am I

The first three sentences have been editorially inserted. What follows is taken from CD's autobiography (*Forster*, pp. 34–5). John Dickens, having been incarcerated for three months, was released from the Marshalsea on 28 May 1824 (but as the result of being declared insolvent and *not* – as was once thought – because of a legacy from his mother, who had died on 26 April: see '*I, Elizabeth Dickens': Light on John Dickens's Legacy* by Angus Easson, *Dkn*, vol. 67 (1971), pp. 35–40). It has usually been surmised, from this, that CD's employment at the blacking warehouse lasted for no more than four to six months, but Michael Allen has suggested that it may have been as long as thirteen – i.e., until March or April 1825 (Allen, *op. cit.*, p. 103). This is because the re-united Dickens family, after staying in Little College Street and lodgings in Hampstead, were not installed in 29 Johnson Street, Somers Town, until the end of 1824, whereas CD recalls 'coming across Russell Square from Somers Town' on his way to the blacking factory (p. 94). John Dickens retired from the Navy Pay Office with a small pension on 9 March 1825 and it may have been soon after this that he quarrelled with Lamert.

CD declares that, until writing these recollections, he had never mentioned 'that part of my childhood' to anyone, 'my own wife not excepted'. This obviously does not rule out the possibility that he revealed it to Catherine *after* he had written the recollections. In 1892, indeed, Charles Dickens the Younger announced that Catherine (much distressed by Forster's claim to be CD's sole confidant) had authorised him to state, after her death, that CD had read her the memoirs 'in strict confidence' and that she had dissuaded him from publishing them 'on the ground that he had spoken with undue harshness of his father, and especially of his mother' (Preface to Macmillan edition of *David Copperfield* (1892), reprinted by Leo Mason in *Dkn*, vol. 45 (1949), p. 221). At least one commentator (Stanley Dick, *Dickens's Past: Some Facts and Surmises*, *Dkn*, vol. 78 (1982), p. 41) has doubted the accuracy of this story, but Catherine is unlikely to have invented it.

My education is resumed

The first paragraph comes from CD's autobiography (*Forster*, pp. 39–40). The second is adapted from the corresponding passage in *Copperfield*, with 'Mick Walker' and 'Mealy Potatoes' being de-fictionalised into 'Bob Fagin' and 'Poll Green'. The third is taken from *Our School* and so, in essence, is the fourth – but inserted into it are some extracts from a speech which CD delivered on 5 November 1857, the third and final sentences being the most substantial of those extracts. The fifth and sixth paragraphs are both taken from that speech (*Speeches*, pp. 240–1).

The nine paragraphs which follow (down to 'was like a mother to them.') come from *Our School*, the names of the masters being editorially inserted. The first and second of the six remaining paragraphs (and rather doubtful ones so far as veracity is concerned) are taken from *Birthday Celebrations*, the third from *The Short-Timers* (*AYR* 20.6.63, reprinted in *The Uncommercial Traveller*), the fourth from a letter which CD wrote to Forster 'in his later years' (*Forster*, pp. 43–4), the fifth from *A Christmas Tree* and the sixth from *Our School*.

For *The Dog of Montargis* see *Plays and players*, above.

'Professor Owen' was Sir Richard Owen (1804–92), Europe's leading authority on anatomy. The editors of *LCD* tell us that 'there was a firm friendship and mutual admiration' between CD and the professor and quote, as confirmation, the following letter from CD to Owen, written on 12 July 1865:

> Studying the gorilla last night for the twentieth time it suddenly came into my head that I had never thanked you for that admirable treatise. This is to bear witness to my blushes and repentance. If you knew how much interest it has awakened in me, and how often it has set me a-thinking, you would consider me a more thankless beast than any gorilla that ever lived. But happily you do *not* know, and I am not going to tell you (*LCD*, p. 585).

The Terrific Register; or, Record of Crimes, Judgments, Providences and Calamities was obviously splendid value at one penny a week.

The two lines of poetry are taken from Wordsworth's *The Excursion*. CD, encountering Sir David Wilkie at a dinner party in October 1839, spoke to him 'of Mr Wordsworth who he knew I had lately seen, and to express a very great admiration for his genius, of which he thought the little poem of *We are Seven* was one of the most striking examples' (Slater, *op. cit.*, p. 183).

Mr Jones and his school served as models for Mr Creakle and Salem House in *Copperfield*. CD was probably a pupil there for two years (from the spring of 1825 until March 1827). Opinions differed, among his surviving contemporaries, as to whether or not he really was awarded prizes for his scholastic abilities (see *Forster*, p. 42, *Dickens at Wellington House Academy* by Willoughby Matchett and *Recollections of Charles Dickens* by A School-Fellow and Friend, *Dkn*, vol. 7 (1911), pp. 145–9, 180–4 and 229–31 and *Dickens: Interviews and Recollections*, pp. 4 – 9). 'My recollection of Dickens', writes the former School-Fellow, 'is of a rather short, stout, jolly-looking youth, very fresh coloured and full of fun and given to laugh immoderately without any apparent sufficient reason... I remember being at a juvenile party in Johnson Street, and he, quite a boy, singing ... 'The Cat's Meat Man' ... with great energy and action.'

PART THREE: MANHOOD

I begin the world

The first paragraph 'merges' the relevant extracts from the letters which CD wrote to Kuenzel and Collins (see *My birth and early life*, above).

The opening lines of the second paragraph (down to 'Gray's Inn generally') have been editorially inserted, but the rest of it comes from *Chambers* (*AYR* 18.8.60, reprinted in *The Uncommercial Traveller*). The reference to the 'Russian jacket and a soldierly young cap' is taken from a letter which CD wrote to Louis D'Elboux on 24 November 1849 (see *Dkn*, vol. 31 (1935), p. 191 and vol. 66 (1970), p. 8). D'Elboux was a fellow clerk. George Lear, another fellow clerk, recalls that CD 'wore a frock-coat ... buttoned up, of dark blue cloth, trousers to match... His cap was like the undress coat of an officer in the army, of some shining material with a narrow shining leather strap running round the point of the chin. His appearance was decidedly military' (*Dickens: Interviews and Recollections*, p. 11).

CD was obliged to leave school 'tolerably early' because of another crisis in his father's affairs. The indefatigable John Dickens, after retiring from the Navy Pay Office, had taught himself shorthand and obtained a post with *The British Press*. CD proudly informed Lear that his father was 'a first-rate shorthand writer on Gurney's system, and a capital reporter' (*Ibid.*, p. 12) and John Dickens seems, indeed, to have been doing reasonably well in the world of journalism. By November 1826, however, *The British Press* had ceased publication and a useful source of additional income thus came to an end. The Dickens family were evicted from Johnson Street in March 1827 for non-payment of rates, finding alternative accommodation at The Polygon, Clarendon Square, and CD was evidently withdrawn from Wellington House Academy at Easter. In May he began his career as an office boy with Messrs. Ellis and Blackmore, a firm of attorneys based at 5 Holborn Court, Gray's Inn. (See two articles by William J. Carlton, *Mr Blackmore Engages an Office Boy* and *John Dickens, Journalist*, published in *Dkn*, vol. 48 (1952), pp. 162–7 and vol. 53 (1957), pp. 5 – 11).

I grow ambitious

The first paragraph, excluding the initial twenty-six words, is taken from *Discovery of a Treasure Near Cheapside*, written in collaboration with Henry Morley (*HW* 13.11.52, included in *Uncollected Writings*), and so too is the second. The first fourteen words of the first paragraph come from a letter which CD wrote to his sixth son, Henry, on 15 October 1868 (*LCD*, p. 699) and the subsequent eleven from a letter to Mrs Francis Dickinson dated 19 August 1860 (*Letters*, Nonesuch edition, vol. III, p. 172). 'Understandably' is an editorial insertion.

The first sentence of the third paragraph is taken from CD's letter to Collins (see *My birth and early life*, above); the rest of this paragraph, and the whole of the fourth and fifth paragraphs, come from *Copperfield* – the reference to Thomas Gurney's *Brachygraphy* being editorially inserted.

The reference to 'that savage stenographic mystery' at the beginning of the sixth paragraph is taken from *Copperfield* and the reference to Doctors' Commons from a letter written to Forster at the end of 1844 (*Forster*, p. 380), but the rest of this paragraph is adapted from letters which CD wrote to James Roney on 23 September 1856 and to the Hon. Mrs Richard Watson on 7 October 1856 – see William J. Carlton, *A Companion of the Copperfield Days* (*Dkn*, vol. 50 (1954), pp. 3–4).

The seventh and eighth paragraphs are taken from the letter to Forster (*Forster*, pp. 380 and 59–60). So too is the second sentence of the ninth and final paragraph: the preceding sentence of that paragraph merges extracts from the letters to Kuenzel and Collins (see *My birth and early life*, above). The last sentence of the ninth paragraph is taken from a letter to Mrs Richard Watson dated 9 December 1850 (*Letters*, Pilgrim edition, Volume Six [1850–1852] (1988), edited by Graham Storey, Kathleen Tillotson and Nina Burgis, p. 228).

'That celebrated purse of Fortunatus, which, whatever were its favoured owner's necessities, had one unvarying amount in it', as CD describes it in Chapter XXXI of *Barnaby Rudge*, first appeared in European literature in the fifteenth century and featured in a play (*Old Fortunatus*) written by Dekker in 1600. (It was once said of Mr Pecksniff 'by a homely admirer', so we learn from the second chapter of *Martin Chuzzlewit*, 'that he had a Fortunatus's purse of good sentiments in his inside').

CD was, in later life, extremely proud of his accomplishments as a very young man: he reported to Angela Burdett-Coutts on 14 January 1854 that he had been telling 'Charley' (his eldest son) 'that when I was a year older than he, I was in the gallery of the House of Commons; and that when I was his age, I was teaching myself a very difficult art, and walking miles every day to practise it all day long in the Courts of Law; he seemed to think I must have been one of the most unaccountable of youths' (*Letters from Charles Dickens to Angela Burdett-Coutts, 1841–1865* (1953), selected and edited by Edgar Johnson, pp. 254–5).

CD had followed in his father's footsteps in mastering the Gurney system (the achievement of John Dickens being, perhaps, the greater of the two) and he ensured that at least one of his own sons, Henry Fielding Dickens, would be familiar with it. 'He taught me to write shorthand,' that son recalled sixty years later, 'and in the course of his teaching his sense of fun was manifested in delightfully humorous fashion. The system he used was based upon Gurney's, but with many improvements and "arbitrary characters" created by himself. I made good progress under his tuition until the time came when I was sufficiently advanced to take down ... what he dictated to me. It was then that the trouble began. To take down anything correctly at that period of my training was quite difficult enough in itself. He would insist, however, on adding to my difficulties by the character of the speeches he delivered – speeches of an absurdly ridiculous and bombastic kind, mock travesties of those which in years gone by he had been in the habit of listening to in the gallery of the House of Commons... Whilst I was struggling with my laughter his denunciations of his imaginary opponent increased in volume and intensity. So much so, indeed, that between the two I was soon reduced to a state of helpless imbecility... I doubt whether any student of shorthand was ever exposed to such a trying test as this' (Sir Henry F. Dickens, K.C., *Memories of My Father* (1928), p. 27).

Sir Henry bears witness to the fact that the sentiments expressed so emphatically in the fifth paragraph are those which CD constantly endeavoured to instil in his own sons. "Do everything at your best,' he used to say. 'I can truly assure you that I have taken as great pains with the smallest thing I have undertaken as with the biggest" (*Ibid.*, p. 20).

Charles Matthews (1776–1835) was a well-known comic actor. 'A singular man,' noted Macaulay in his Journal on 11 January 1851; 'certainly the greatest actor I ever saw ... [and] far greater than Kean... I can hardly believe Garrick to have had more of the mimetic genius than Matthews. I often regret that I did not see him more frequently ... for I admired him, and laughed my sides when I saw him' (Sir G.O. Trevelyan, *The Life and Letters of Lord Macaulay*, vol. II (1876), p. 289).

The 'Hamiltonian system', devised by James Hamilton (1769–1831), was an allegedly foolproof method of learning foreign languages: its intricacies were unveiled in *The History, Principles, Practice and Result of the Hamiltonian System* which he published in 1829.

The Hunchback, a comedy by Sheridan Knowles, had its première at Covent Garden on 5 April 1832.

John Dickens resumed his career as a journalist in 1827 or 1828, obtaining a post with *The Morning Herald*. (He apparently specialised in items of news from the Borough police courts before going on to slightly higher things – see *Dkn*, vol. 62 (1966), p. 148). He then joined *The Mirror of Parliament*, a periodical started by his brother-in-law, John Henry Barrow, and CD once again followed in his father's footsteps, probably in 1831 (see *Doctors' Commons*, below).

A Reading Room encounter

Apart from the first twenty-six words (taken from the letter to Kuenzel) the whole of this section comes from *Shabby-Genteel People* (*Morning Chronicle* 5.11.34, reprinted in *Sketches by Boz*). CD applied for a Reading Room ticket the instant he became eligible for one, on his eighteenth birthday (7.2.30), and studied, *inter alia*, works by Addison, Goldsmith and Shakespeare.

Doctors' Commons

The first, second and fourth paragraphs are taken from *Doctors' Commons* (*Morning Chronicle* 11.10.36, reprinted in *Sketches by Boz*) and the third from *American Notes* (Chapter III). The fifth comes from *Copperfield* (Chapter XXIII). CD left Ellis and Blackmore in November 1828 and after being employed for a few weeks by another solicitor, Charles Molloy, became a freelance writer for the Consistory Court of Doctors' Commons, a calling which he apparently pursued, with increasing boredom, for at least two years (1829–31). He then joined his uncle's newspaper, *The Mirror of Parliament*, and also obtained employment with an evening newspaper, *The True Sun*. From March 1832 onwards the greater part of his working life was spent in the parliamentary gallery. He left *The True Sun* four months later and switched from *The Mirror of Parliament* to the *Morning Chronicle* in August 1834.

Early attachments

The first and third paragraphs are taken from *First Fruits* and the second from a letter which CD wrote to Thomas Powell on 2 August 1845 (Walter Dexter (ed.), *The Love Romance of Charles Dickens: Told in his letters to Maria Beadnell (Mrs Winter)* (1936), p. 21). The fourth comes from *City of London Churches* (with Maria Beadnell disguised as 'Angelica') and the fifth from *What Christmas is as we grow older* (*HW* Christmas number 1851, reprinted in *Christmas Stories*).

The three paragraphs which follow are all taken from *Birthday Celebrations* – 'She', once again, is Maria Beadnell and the word of three letters beginning with B is 'boy'. Maria, it will have been gathered from this, was slightly older than CD (by a whole thirteen months, in fact), and a partially-cancelled passage from Chapter XVIII of *Copperfield* (describing David's infatuation for the eldest Miss Larkins) is not without its relevance.

> I think continuously about my age. Say I am seventeen, and say that seventeen is young for the eldest Miss Larkins, what of that? ... Besides, I shall be one-and-twenty in no time almost. Two other points of reflection divide the empire of my mind with this. First, is the eldest Miss Larkins aware of my attachment? Secondly, what does she think of it, if she be aware of it? Sometimes I am persuaded she must be aware of it on account of my agitation and the expression of my face when I meet her; then I look in the glass, and getting up that expression as nearly as I can, doubt it, and suspect it may not reveal what I mean. The state of her mind torments me next. Whether she despises me, or laughs at me, or flirts with me, or is dying for me (she don't look like it, but she may be doing it secretly), and cannot tell

me so, because I cannot tell her what I feel myself' (*Dkn*, vol. 48 (1952), p. 159 and Clarendon edition of *David Copperfield* (1981), edited by Nina Burgis, p. 230).

The three paragraphs which follow (the first of them commencing with the words 'My existence was entirely uprooted') are taken from three fervent letters which CD wrote to Maria in February 1855, after she had made contact with him again. The first comes from one written on the 10th, the second from one written on the 22nd and the third from one written on the 15th (*The Love Romance of Charles Dickens*, pp. 83, 88–9 and 85–6).

The next paragraph is taken from a letter which CD wrote to Forster at about the same time (*Forster*, p. 49). So are the two opening sentences of the next paragraph (down to 'as I should see anyone else.'), the remainder coming from the letter of the 22nd (*The Love Romance of Charles Dickens*, pp. 90–1). The next short paragraph comes from the letter of the 10th (*Ibid.*, p. 81). Most of the subsequent paragraph (down to 'and nothing more nor less.') comes from the letter of the 15th (*Ibid.*, p. 86), the two final sentences being taken from the letter to Forster.

The rest of this section comes from *First Fruits*, 'Mr Bud' being converted into 'Mr Dickens'.

'Believe me,' CD told Maria in his letter of 10 February, 'you cannot more tenderly remember our old days and our old friends than I do. I hardly ever go into the City but I walk up an odd little court at the back of the Mansion House and come out by the corner of Lombard Street. Hundreds of times as I have passed the church there – on my way to and from the Sea, the Continent, and where not – I invariably associate it with somebody (God knows who) having told me that poor Anne* was buried there. If you would like to examine me in the name of a good-looking Cornish servant you used to have (I suppose she has twenty-nine great grandchildren now, and walks with a stick), you will find my knowledge on the point correct, though it was a monstrous name too' (*The Love Romance of Charles Dickens*, p. 81). He recalled, on the 15th, the keen interest with which he had 'once matched a little pair of gloves for you which I recollect were blue ones. (I wonder whether people generally wore blue gloves when I was nineteen or whether it was only you!)' 'I remember', he added on the 22nd, 'that there used to be a tendency in your eyebrows to join together; and sometimes in the most unlikely places – in Scotland, America, Italy – on the stateliest occasions and the most unceremonious – when I have been talking to a strange face and have observed ever such a slight association as this in it, I have been suddenly carried away at the rate of a thousand miles a second, and have thought 'Maria Beadnell'!' (*Ibid.*, pp. 85 and 91).

These three ardent letters to Maria Beadnell (now Mrs Winter) were followed, on 23 or 24 February, by his first meeting with the lady for several years, an event which proved a shattering disillusionment. The slim, flirtatious young girl of his recollections had warned him that she was now 'toothless, fat, old and ugly' and he had flatly refused to believe it. But

---

* Maria's sister.

confrontation revealed that she had indeed become fat – and garrulous too – and any thoughts of developing a different kind of relationship were banished in an instant. He would make use of the reunion in *Little Dorrit*, when Arthur Clennam comes face to face with Flora Finching after a long absence abroad, but his immediate reaction was to pen the following rueful paragraph in an essay entitled *Gone to the Dogs* published in *Household Words* on 10 March – a paragraph which foreshadows both the 'Angelica' reference in *City of London Churches* and *Birthday Celebrations*.

> What has become – to begin like Charity at home – what has become, I demand, of the inheritance I myself entered on, at nineteen years of age? A shining castle (in the air) with young Love looking out of window, perfect contentment and repose of spirit standing by with ethereal aspects in the porch, visions surrounding it by night and day with an atmosphere of pure gold. This was my only inheritance, and I never squandered it. I hoarded it like a miser. Say, bright-eyed Araminta (with the obdurate parents), thou who was sole lady of the castle, did I not? Down the flowing river by the walls, called Time, how blest we sailed together, treasuring our happiness unto death, and never knowing change, or weariness, or separation! Where is the castle now, with all its magic furniture? Gone to the Dogs. Canine possession was taken of the whole of that estate, my youthful Araminta, about a quarter of a century ago.

(The first five letters of the name 'Araminta' are an anagram of 'Maria' and 'inta' is, of course, an echo of 'Winter'. In much the same way, fifteen years later, would 'Charley D' be transformed into 'Dalchery'.)

Pressing engagements

The first two sentences of the first paragraph are taken from the fifth chapter ('Genoa and its Neighbourhood') of *Pictures from Italy* (1846); the third sentence comes from a speech delivered to New York newspaper editors on 18 April 1868 (*Forster*, p. 61).

The second paragraph is taken from *Copperfield* (Chapter XLIII) with a brief extract from a speech delivered on 20 May 1855 ('went into the gallery of the House of Commons as a parliamentary reporter when I was still a boy'), plus the *Morning Chronicle* reference, being inserted in the first sentence.

The third and fourth paragraphs come from the speech of 20 May 1855, delivered at the annual dinner of the Newspaper Press Fund (*Forster*, pp. 61–2 and *Speeches*, pp. 346–8).

The fifth paragraph, the first sentence of which has been editorially inserted, is taken from an account which appeared in the *Morning Chronicle* on 18 September 1834 (reprinted in *Dkn*, vol. 31 (1935), p. 9). CD did not have a high opinion of Grey: writing to Forster in August 1846 he recalled his dislike of his lordship's style of speaking and physical appearance: 'the shape of his head (I see it now) was misery to me, and weighed down my youth' (*Forster*, p. 414).

The sixth paragraph comes from *American Notes* (Chapter VIII) and the seventh from CD's letter of 6 June 1856 to Collins.

A traveller's tales

The first paragraph comes from a letter written to Forster in 1845 (*Forster*, p. 61), the second and third from a speech delivered on 30 December 1854 (*Speeches*, pp. 172–3). 'Taglionis' were so named after Maria Taglioni (1804–84), a famous Italian ballet dancer: CD, writing to Forster in 1842, declared that truth was occasionally 'so twisted and distorted [by American newspapers] that it has as much resemblance to the real fact as Quilp's leg to Taglioni's' (*Forster*, p. 218). All the paragraphs which follow (with the exception of the last, which again comes from the speech of 30 December 1854) are taken from *The Holly Tree*.

Dreams

This is taken from a letter written to Dr Thomas Stone on 2 February 1851 (*Letters*, Pilgrim edition, Volume Six, pp. 276–9).

A few conventionalities

Almost the whole of this section is taken from *A Few Conventionalities* (*HW* 28.6.51, included in *Miscellaneous Papers*). Most of the first sentence is editorially inserted (with the reference to 'a few questions' taken from *Conventionalities*); the second sentence is taken from *Why?* (*HW* 1.3.56, included in *Miscellaneous Papers*) and so too is the sixth paragraph (concerning the 'six hundred men').

'Sketches by Boz'

The first sentence of the first paragraph comes from CD's letter to Kuenzel. The second sentence has been editorially inserted. The first half of the third (down to 'gave them warning') is taken from a letter which CD wrote in 1833 (*Forster*, p. 72), the rest being editorially inserted. The next sentence is also editorially inserted but the one in parenthesis is adapted from a letter which CD wrote on 23 October 1868 to Dr Howison, who had tended Fred during the latter's final illness (*Letters*, Nonesuch edition, vol. III, p. 675).

The second paragraph is taken from a letter which CD wrote to Catherine in October 1835 (Walter Dexter, ed., *Mr & Mrs Charles Dickens* (1935), p. 19). The great majority of the productions which CD reviewed, during the mid-1830s, were performed at the Adelphi Theatre: see *Charles Dickens, Dramatic Critic* by William J. Carlton (*Dkn*, vol. 56 (1960), pp.

11–27). One of the first he saw, in October 1834, turned out to be a purloined version of his own *The Bloomsbury Christening*, which had appeared in *The Monthly Magazine* six months earlier. 'We hailed one or two of the characters with great satisfaction,' he grimly remarked in his review, '– they are old and very particular friends of ours.' An indignant letter from Boz, in which he registered his protest at this 'kidnapping process', featured in the next issue of *The Monthly Magazine* (see *Dkn*, vol. 30 (1934), pp. 223–5).

An actress whom he saw on many occasions at this time, and whose performances greatly impressed him, was Elizabeth Yates, thirteen years his senior. 'No one alive', he wrote to her on 15 May 1858, 'can have more delightful associations with the lightest sound of your voice than I have; and to give you a minute's interest and pleasure, in acknowledgement of the unaccountable hours of happiness you gave me when you were a mysterious angel to me, would honestly gratify my heart.' She died two years later and CD, recalling 'the old Adelphi days', sent a letter of commiseration to her son, Edmund (his favourite protégé) on 17 April 1860. 'I think of your mother', he wrote, 'as a beautiful part of my own youth, and this dream that we are all dreaming seems to darken' (*LCD*, pp. 450 and 506 and Slater, *op. cit.*, p. 260). The actor whose talents correspondingly impressed him, and whose greatest fan he certainly became, was William Charles Macready (1793–1873). 'I think I have told you sometimes,' CD wrote to him on 27 February 1851, 'my much-loved friend, how, when I was a mere boy, I was one of your faithful and devoted adherents in the pit; I believe as true a member of that true host of followers as it has ever boasted. As I improved myself and was improved by favouring circumstances in mind and fortune, I only became the more earnest (if it were possible) in my study of you' (*LCD*, p. 240).

The third paragraph combines the account in *Copperfield* (Chapter XLIII) with the one quoted in CD's 1847 Preface to *Pickwick*, the 'transmogrified' phraseology being taken from a letter to H.W. Kolle dated 3 December 1833 (*Letters*, Pilgrim edition, Volume One, p. 32). (*A Sunday out of Town* was the original title of his first story. It appeared in *The Monthly Magazine* in December 1833 as *A Dinner at Poplar Walk* and became *Mr Minns and His Cousin* when reprinted in *Sketches by Boz*.)

The fourth paragraph begins with another extract from *Copperfield* (although David's assurance that he was 'regularly paid' has been replaced by the 'for next to nothing' phraseology: see Robert L. Patten, *Charles Dickens and His Publishers* (1978), p. 21). The rest of this paragraph, after a brief extract from the 1847 *Pickwick* Preface, comes from CD's 1850 Preface to the *Sketches*.

The final paragraph is taken from the 1847 Preface to *Pickwick*.

Another account of the origins of the *Sketches* is given in CD's letter of 6 June 1856 to Collins. '[Tell Forgues]', he writes, 'that I began, without any interest or introduction of any kind, to write fugitive pieces for the old *Monthly Magazine*, when I was in the gallery for the *Mirror of Parliament*; that my faculty for descriptive writing was seized upon the moment I joined the *Morning Chronicle*, and that I was liberally paid there and handsomely acknowledged, and wrote the greater part of the short descriptive *Sketches by Boz* in that paper.'

'The Pickwick Papers'

CD wrote three Prefaces to *Pickwick* – in 1837, 1847 and 1867 – all of which appear in the Penguin English Library edition (1972), edited by Robert L. Patten. The 1867 Preface was basically a slightly revised version of the one written in 1847. Use has been made of all three of them in this section and also of an angry letter from CD which the *Athenaeum* published on 31 March 1866, the relevant portions of which will be found in Appendix C of the Penguin English Library edition.

The first five paragraphs are taken from the 1847/1867 Prefaces. Most of the sixth (down to 'of the book was invented.') comes from the *Athenaeum* letter, but the final sentence is taken from a letter which CD wrote to Charley on 4 April 1866, quoted on pp. 102–3 of *The Origin of Pickwick* (1936) by Walter Dexter and W.T. Ley. The seventh comes from the *Athenaeum* letter. The eighth is taken from the 1837 Preface except for the two final sentences, which come from the 1847/1867 Prefaces. The four paragraphs which follow also come from the latter, except for the two opening sentences of the third one (starting 'The most serious and pathetic point') which come from a letter to the Hon. Mrs Edward Cropper dated 20 December 1852 (*Letters*, Pilgrim edition, Volume Six, p. 827). The final sentence is taken from a letter which CD wrote to Messrs. Chapman and Hall on 1 November 1836 (*Ibid.*, Volume One, p. 189).

Triumph

The first paragraph is adapted from the letter which CD wrote to his uncle, Thomas Barrow, on 31 March 1836 (*Ibid.*, p. 144). To Collins, in his letter of 6 June 1856, CD boasted that he had 'married the daughter of a writer to the signet in Edinburgh, who was the great friend and assistant of Scott, and who first made Lockhart known to him'.

The first sentence of the second paragraph is editorially inserted. Most of what follows is taken from a letter to Richard Johns dated 31 May 1837 (*Ibid.*, pp. 263–4), the final sentence being taken from CD's diary (*Ibid.*, p. 630).

The third paragraph is based upon a letter to George Thomson dated 30 July 1836 (*Ibid.*, pp. 158–9), the final sentence being adapted from a letter to Catherine written in 1836 (*Mr & Mrs Charles Dickens*, p. 36).

The fourth paragraph is taken from the Preface (dated December 1836) to the published text of *The Village Coquettes*. In later years, CD endeavoured to draw a veil over his share in this production. 'I just put down for everybody what everybody at the St James's Theatre wanted to say and do,' he recalled on one occasion, 'and that they could say and do best, and I have been most sincerely repentant ever since' (quoted by Malcolm Morley, *Plays and Sketches by Boz*, *Dkn*, vol. 52 (1956), p. 86). Writing to his collaborator, John Hullah, on 8 May 1866 he permitted the songs to be republished but on the strict understanding that their author should be left 'to blush anonymously': 'I am not proud of my share in *The Village Coquettes*, and would rather let the songs (the words of the songs, I mean) die quietly, than revive them with the name of their respected parent attached' (*Dkn*, vol. 30 (1934), p. 22).

The first sentence of the fifth paragraph comes from the letter to Kuenzel (with 'seven or eight' being substituted for 'four or five'). The second sentence is editorially inserted. The rest are taken from some remarks which CD made to Marcus Stone (Slater, *op. cit.*, p. 156).

The first sentence of the sixth paragraph comes from a letter to George Cruikshank dated 9 January 1837 (*Letters*, Pilgrim edition, Volume One, p. 221). The second sentence is editorially inserted. The rest of this paragraph, and all that follows, is taken from *Some Recollections of Mortality* (*AYR* 16.5.63, reprinted in *The Uncommercial Traveller*).

Young Norval is a character in *Douglas* (1756), a romantic tragedy by John Home (1722–1808).

'Oliver Twist'

The opening paragraph is taken from a letter to Collins dated 8 January 1853 (*Letters*, Pilgrim edition, Volume Seven). The rest of this section is, basically, the Preface to *Oliver Twist* which CD wrote in 1841, as revised in 1867, but supplemented partly by some 1841 material deleted in 1867 (principally, the twelfth and thirteenth paragraphs) and partly by some relevant extracts from *American Notes*. The sixth and seventh paragraphs come from the *Notes* (Chapter III) and so does the tenth (Chapter XV). The last paragraph of all is taken from some remarks which CD made to Marcus Stone (*Dkn*, vol. 6 (1910), pp. 62–3).

Paul Clifford (1830) was the tale of a philanthropic highwayman. The Massaronis featured in *The Brigand, a Romantic Drama* by James Planché (1796–1880) staged at Covent Garden in 1829. Henry Mackenzie (1745–1831) was the author of *The Man of the World* (1773), which had a villain as its hero.

In carefully rejecting any language likely to offend, CD was, alas, defeating his own object of seeking to depict the lowest dregs of criminal society as they really were. His readers, despite his brave words, could scarcely be shocked if he insisted upon imposing rigorous self-censorship to ensure that nothing at all shockable appeared in his pages. Humphrey House pointed this out in 1941 (*The Dickens World*, pp. 215–19) but Thackeray had mockingly drawn attention to it a century earlier in *Catherine*. Fagin and his companions, Thackeray remarked, were 'agreeably low and delightfully disgusting characters' whereas the reader 'ought to be made cordially to detest, scorn, loathe, abhor, and abominate all people of this kidney'. Men of genius, he concluded, had 'no business to make these characters interesting or agreeable'.

Tragedy

CD wrote three detailed accounts of Mary's death in May 1837 – the first on the 8th to George Thomson, the second on the 17th to Thomas Beard and the third on the 31st to Richard Johns (*Letters*, Pilgrim edition, Volume

One, pp. 256–7, 259–60 and 263–4 respectively). Merging these accounts together produces the narrative set out in the first, third and fourth paragraphs of this section, the second being taken from a letter to an unknown correspondent dated 8 June 1837 (*Ibid.*, p. 268). The first nine words of the fifth paragraph come from the letter to Beard but the rest is taken from a letter to Harrison Ainsworth dated 17 May 1837 (*Ibid.*, p. 260).

The sixth paragraph is based upon an Address to the readers of *Pickwick*, drafted by CD and dated 30 June 1837, which prefaced the appearance of the fifteenth part.

The seventh paragraph merges a letter which CD wrote to Mrs George Hogarth on 8 May 1843 (*Letters*, Pilgrim edition, Volume Three [1842–1843] (1974), edited by Madeline House, Graham Storey and Kathleen Tillotson, pp. 483–4) with an account which appeared in *The Holly Tree*. (Basically, the first four sentences and the final sentence are taken from the letter.) The letter to Catherine is dated 1 February 1838 (*Mr & Mrs Charles Dickens*, p. 75).

The eighth paragraph comes from *The Holly Tree*. A detailed account of 'this dream, or an actual Vision' will be found in a letter which CD sent to Forster on 30 September 1844. 'I knew it was poor Mary's spirit,' he writes. 'I was not at all afraid, but in a great delight, so that I wept very much... 'What is the true religion?' [I asked]. As it paused a moment without replying, I said...'You think, as I do, that the Form of religion does not so greatly matter, if we try to do good? – or', I said, observing that it still hesitated, and was moved with the greatest compassion for me, 'perhaps the Roman Catholic is the best?' ... 'For you,' said the Spirit, full of such heavenly tenderness for me, that I felt as if my heart would break; 'for *you* it is the best!' Then I awoke, with the tears running down my face' (*Forster*, p. 349).

The final paragraph is taken from CD's diary for 1 January 1838 ((*Letters*, Pilgrim edition, Volume One, p. 629).

'The Life and Adventures of Nicholas Nickleby'

Most of this comes from a Preface which CD wrote in 1848. The 'original preface' from which he quotes was one published in 1839 (which included a substantial quotation from Henry Mackenzie – see *Oliver Twist*, above – on the special indulgence due to a periodical writer). The last three sentences of the sixth paragraph are taken from a letter sent to Catherine on 1 February 1838 (*Mr & Mrs Charles Dickens*, pp. 72–3). The parenthetical reference to Hablot K. Browne has been editorially inserted.

The 'original' of Squeers was William Shaw and two Manchester businessmen, William and David Grant, were the 'originals' of the Cheeryble brothers.

Valedictory

The first two paragraphs are taken from a speech which CD delivered in Boston on 1 February 1842 (*Speeches*, pp. 19–20). The first sentence of the third comes from *The Niger Expedition* (*The Examiner* 19.8.48, included in *Miscellaneous Papers*) and the second, third and fourth sentences from a letter to Frank Stone dated 1 June 1857 (*LCD*, p. 429). The fifth and sixth sentences are taken from [*An*] *Address to Working Men* (*HW* 7.10.54, included in *Miscellaneous Papers*) and the final sentence comes from a letter to the Earl of Carlisle dated 15 April 1857 (*Letters*, Volume Eight, p. 314).

The fourth paragraph comes from a speech delivered at Hartford on 7 February 1842 (*Speeches*, p. 24). Sentiments very similar to these will also be found in the account of an interview which CD gave to an enterprising American journalist, C. Edwards Lester, in July 1840 (reprinted by Philip Collins in *Dickens: Interviews and Recollections*, pp. 42–4).

The first and second sentences of the last paragraph are taken from a letter to Maria Winter written on 3 April 1855 (*The Love Romance of Charles Dickens*, pp. 100–1). The rest of it comes from a letter to W.H. Wills written on 6 June 1867 (*LCD*, p. 626). 'I have always felt of myself', CD told Forster in April 1856, 'that I must, if possible, die in harness... However strange it is to be never at rest, and never satisfied, and ever trying after something that is never reached, and to be always laden with plot and plan and care and worry, how clear it is that it must be, and that one is driven by an irresistible might until the journey is worked out! It is much better to go on and fret, than to stop and fret. As to repose – for some men there's no such thing in this life... Shall I ever, I wonder, get the frame of mind back as it used to be [in the old days]?' (*Forster*, p. 639.)

EPILOGUE: THE LONG VOYAGE

Taken from *The Long Voyage* (*HW* 31.12.53, included in *Reprinted Pieces*). Sir John Franklin, referred to halfway through the second paragraph, set out to discover the North West Passage in 1845 but his two ships became trapped in the ice. The 129 officers and crew then embarked on an overland trek to King William Island, but many of them died on the way and the rest, when they reached their destination, evidently succumbed to starvation and scurvy. Grim reports of cannibalism among the last survivors became current in 1854 (being reinforced, for that matter, by fresh discoveries in July 1983) but CD refused to believe such stories and devoted two *Household Words* articles (*The Lost Arctic Voyagers*, 2.12.54 and 9.12.54, included in *Miscellaneous Papers*) to their refutation.

LIST OF ILLUSTRATIONS

All illustrations were kindly provided by the Dickens House Museum with the exception of the view of Rochester from Star Hill, which was provided by the Guildhall Museum, Rochester.